Adolescence
and Adulthood

AIM HIGHER WITH *PALGRAVE INSIGHTS IN PSYCHOLOGY*

Also available in this series:

978-0-230-24986-8

978-0-230-27222-4

978-0-230-30150-4

978-0-230-24988-2

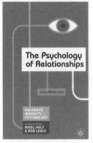
978-0-230-24941-7

978-0-230-25265-3

978-0-230-29537-7

978-0-230-24944-8

978-0-230-24987-5

978-0-230-24942-4

978-0-230-29640-4

978-0-230-24945-5

978-0-230-29536-0

978-0-230-30273-0

To find out more visit **www.palgrave.com/insights**

Adolescence and Adulthood

Transitions and Transformations

Leo B. Hendry and
Marion Kloep

PALGRAVE
INSIGHTS IN
PSYCHOLOGY

SERIES EDITORS:
NIGEL HOLT
& ROB LEWIS

palgrave
macmillan

First published 2012 by
PALGRAVE MACMILLAN

Palgrave Macmillan in the UK is an imprint of Macmillan Publishers Limited, registered in England, company number 785998, of Houndmills, Basingstoke, Hampshire RG21 6XS.

Palgrave Macmillan in the US is a division of St Martin's Press LLC, 175 Fifth Avenue, New York, NY 10010.

Palgrave Macmillan is the global academic imprint of the above companies and has companies and representatives throughout the world.

Palgrave® and Macmillan® are registered trademarks in the United States, the United Kingdom, Europe and other countries.

ISBN 978–0–230–29640–4

This book is printed on paper suitable for recycling and made from fully managed and sustained forest sources. Logging, pulping and manufacturing processes are expected to conform to the environmental regulations of the country of origin.

A catalogue record for this book is available from the British Library.

A catalog record for this book is available from the Library of Congress.

10   9   8   7   6   5   4   3   2   1
21 20 19 18 17 16 15 14 13 12

Printed in China

Contents

Acknowledgements

We would like to thank Zdenka Jankovska, MSc, and Lucia Homolova, MSc, for their invaluable help in tracking down the most recent research literature on adult development.

Note from series editors

Developmental psychology does not end at a particular age. We continue to develop and change right through adolescence to adulthood until we eventually stop. Adolescence might be described as the period during which a child develops into an adult, although of course you'll encounter different definitions. In this book we'll look at the psychology associated with this unique and often turbulent period of our lives, and the often just-as-turbulent adulthood that follows it.

Leo and Marion are masters of their subject and we were delighted that they agreed to write for us. They've spent a good deal of their lives studying psychology and their contribution to the topic has been considerable. Here they express their knowledge clearly and carefully. Their communication skills and passion for their subject are evident and we feel certain that those new to the topic, as well as those with an existing interest in the area, will benefit from the knowledge described so eloquently herein. Adolescence is one of those topics, like 'education' or 'the weather', that we all have experience of and about which we all have an opinion. Similarly, the majority of us reach adulthood and can express opinions about it and the pressures associated with it. This book provides a careful, detailed and effective narrative on these subjects that really will give us an insight into and understanding of these often very misunderstood times of our lives.

- *If you are reading this book in preparation for a university course,* you will be looking for coverage that will form a solid basis – a head start that you can build on when you begin. We are confident that this book will set you in the right direction. More than that, we feel certain that you will return to it as your studies progress.

- *If you are reading this book as part of your university course,* you'll be looking for relevant, focused knowledge of an appropriate level, range and depth. Leo and Marion, as well as being the editors, are experienced lecturers in psychology at the undergraduate level. We have all convened, taught and assessed courses and are aware of the exacting requirements a book of this type must meet. It may be that you are studying psychology, health, child development, education or any number of other relevant courses, and we feel sure that the authors have provided the information you will need to succeed.

- *If you are reading this book as part of a pre-university course, such as A-level psychology,* you'll have two things in mind. First, you need to be sure that you can find all the right information at the right level you need to develop your knowledge; second, you'll want to be sure that this book goes just that little bit further than the A-level texts you will be reading as part of your course. To help you navigate through the book, we've included a table in the Reading Guide, identifying where you can find the relevant information for your specification. The additional material is sure to stretch and challenge you, as you do all you can to achieve that A*.

Whatever your reason for reading this book, we hope that you'll enjoy it. We are very pleased to include it in the series.

NIGEL HOLT AND ROB LEWIS
Editors

Notes on contributors

Leo B. Hendry, MSc (Bradford), MEd with distinction (Leicester), PhD and DLitt (Aberdeen), FBPS, has been a school teacher; then a lecturer/senior lecturer at London and Leeds universities; Professor of Education, University of Aberdeen; Professor of Health Psychology, Norwegian University of Science and Technology, Trondheim; Research Professor, Norwegian Centre for Childhood Research, Trondheim; and Professor of Psychology, University of Glamorgan, 2004–2011. He is currently Emeritus Professor, University of Aberdeen.

He has been a visiting professor at many universities in Europe and North America; advisor to the Family and Youth Support Division, American Forces, Europe, 1983–1989; and keynote speaker at many national and international conferences.

Leo has published over 150 research articles, 27 book chapters, 20 books (translated into seven foreign languages), including three editions of *The Nature of Adolescence* with John C. Coleman, and he has been awarded grants and studentships by national and international funding bodies, including the Economic and Social Research Council; the Johann Jacobs Foundation, Zurich; the World Bank; the Scottish Office, Edinburgh; the Health Promotion Research Trust, Cambridge; and the Grampian Health Board. He has co-researched and co-written with Marion Kloep over the last 18 years.

In 2011 Leo was presented with a Lifetime Achievement Award by the European Association for Research on Adolescence for his research and publication contributions on European adolescence.

In 2011 he published (with Jeff Arnett, Marion Kloep and Jennifer Tanner) *Debating Emerging Adulthood: Stage of Process?* and he co-authored *Adolescence and Adulthood: Transitions and Transformations* (2012) with Marion Kloep.

Marion Kloep received her doctorate from the RWTH University in Aachen, Germany. She then worked as a school psychologist in Sweden, and became a lecturer of psychology at Mid Sweden University. She also worked as Senior Lecturer at the Norwegian University for Science and Technology in Trondheim, and she is now a professor at Glamorgan University in Wales.

Marion's research is concentrated on lifespan development. She conducted a longitudinal study with children during the political changes in Albania, a study on adolescent lifestyles in rural Sweden (as part of a cross-cultural comparison between Norway and Scotland), qualitative studies with older Norwegian and Welsh people on transitions to retirement and, recently, studies on pathways to adulthood with adolescents and young adults.

Introduction

Have you ever wondered what your grandmother looked like when she was a teenager and what she did in her leisure time? What mischief your father got up to as a schoolboy? How he courted your mother? Do you think you will ever marry? How you will be as a parent? What changes do you envisage as you move into old age? Will you enjoy your retirement? This book will not answer all these questions, but it will give you some insights into the life course from adolescence to retirement and beyond.

Hence, the book is about transitions and transformations. Transitions are the processes involved in the different kinds of 'shifts' and 'turning points' that happen in people's lives as they go from adolescence through early adulthood and mid-life towards old age – puberty, leaving school, work, romance, marriage, children, health, illnesses, mid-life reflections, biological changes, menopause, retirement, ageing, friendships, losses and recovery.

Transformations are the psychosocial outcomes of these transitions that occur as people progress across the lifespan. The social, cultural and physical environment together with the historical context also have influence on the changes and development in people's lives.

So, individual trajectories are unique and somewhat unpredictable. Nevertheless, since the beginning of the twentieth century, physical and social scientists, academics and researchers have made various attempts to illuminate the psychosocial aspects of the life course, and from these descriptions and interpretations have derived various theoretical approaches to understanding human development from a lifespan perspective.

Perhaps then, life's journey can be somewhat likened to magical mystery tour towards a particular destination. We all start at different places and at different times and are constantly in transit which is influenced by a variety of forces and factors including personal desires and preferences, the particular ways we attempt to progress – biological disposition, encounters with others – and the kind of journey we embark on – fast or slow, direct or meandering. Yet all we really know is our final destination but not when we will arrive, though we may receive hints and clues about our position and development as we travel onward. Cultural 'route-maps' of social norms can provide us with a general description and timing for our journey, but little is predictable: We truly do not know what tomorrow may bring.

In attempting to offer some psychological insights into the journey across the lifespan, this book considers human change and development from adolescence onward. Because modern life does not necessarily allow the individual to follow clear-cut pathways, nor bring life-events to the developing individual in a set sequence, certain topics in the book – 'work and unemployment' and 'dating' are obvious candidates for this – may appear in more detail in one chapter than in others, even though the topic may be equally relevant for adolescents, emerging adults, mid-lifers and senior citizens.

So, we begin our lifespan journey in the first two chapters of the book by outlining how a number of theorists have presented their ideas and descriptions of the stages people normally pass through across the lifespan; and then how other academics disagree with these descriptions and employ different ecological approaches to gain an understanding of the mechanisms and processes of change over the life course.

Thereafter, the book explores teenage life in two chapters: One, dealing with the effects of puberty and other physiological changes with their psychological manifestations in risk-taking; and one that considers the effects of relationships and social contexts in adolescent development – family, peers, school and romantic partners.

We then consider early adulthood, discussing a recent academic debate about whether or not a new life stage has been created by social and economic changes in Western societies, and looking at some of the life-events likely to happen at this age.

Next, mid-life is examined to demonstrate the vast array of pathways and trajectories into the later years of life. Though middle age appears superficially to be a quiet period of the lifespan, there are topics such as 'sandwich' parents and 'boomerang' children, divorce, bodily changes, the menopause and the 'mid-life crisis.'

The penultimate chapter deals with retirement and the transitions into old age, and provides an optimistic message about growing old in modern society.

The final chapter reflects on human development and argues for a positive, ecological approach to explaining and understanding lifespan change.

We trust you enjoy our psychosocial journey across the lifespan, and, in the process, learn more than you know now about your present and future life course and how to cope with it successfully.

Chapter 1

Stage Theories of Lifespan Development

Summary

In this chapter on stage theories we examine:
- Four influential stage theories looking at human development over the lifespan;
- Differences and similarities in these theories; and
- Criticisms of these theories.

Introduction

In this book, we are exploring and explaining the various psychological and psychosocial transitions from adolescence through adulthood into old age, and the transformations that accompany these changes and developments. The discipline of Developmental Psychology has for a long time been dealing only with the childhood years – and sometimes still does. Yet, there is no question that 'things do happen' across the whole of the life course and these events will make people change at any age. Actually, it might be a terrifying thought if there were no developments or changes beyond the teenage years! Fortunately, not all scientists and academics endorse the notion that development only occurs during childhood, or at best into adolescence. Already by the beginning of the last century there were pioneers who posited theories of human development from birth to death. In this chapter we will present a brief description of their views.

Most of us will remember our childhood embarrassment when some relative we met only from time-to-time greeted us with an exclamation such as 'Oh, how much you have grown!' Yet, now we have to bite our tongue whenever we occasionally meet our friends' children – because, yes, in the interim they have grown! Not only have they grown. Pimply, grumpy teenagers change into confident and friendly young adults, who change into successful career people, who again transform into respectable senior citizens, spoiling their grandchildren as they would never have done with their own children. While observing these changes, we are hardly aware of what is happening to ourselves, until we notice the reactions of others as they perceive us differently from a few years ago.

Of course, these obvious alterations have attracted the interests of psychologists, who try to explain why and how we change, not only in our appearance, but also in our behaviour, in our attitudes, our values and goals. Many have been interested only in child development, but there has been an increasing number of researchers who expanded this interest to exploring human development across the whole lifespan. Here is an outline of some of these theories.

⊙ The theory of Erik Erikson

One of the most influential scientists in this area was Erik Erikson. He was born in 1902 in Germany. First, he was a student of arts in Vienna, but then decided to become a psychoanalyst. As he was Jewish, he was forced to emigrate to the United States when the Nazis came to power. He worked at different universities, finally at Harvard, and he researched and published with his wife Joan until his mid-eighties. He died in 1994, when he was nearly 92 years old.

Like many of his contemporary colleagues, Erikson (1950, 1959) viewed development as occurring in stages. Though being influenced by Freud, he did not emphasize inner biological needs as the only driving force of development, but focused more on the person's interaction with the social environment. During the entire lifespan, individuals develop by meeting a sequence of personal and social tasks that need to be accomplished for further growth to take place. Each of them causes a 'crisis' in individuals until they have learned ways of coping with them. The aim is to achieve a balance between the two possible outcomes of each crisis; leaning too much towards any extreme can have psychologically negative consequences. These challenges appear at certain points in the life course. Hence development is discontinuous, occurring in stages, but lifelong. These psychosocial stages are as follows:

Infancy (up to one year of age). This is the time when babies are utterly dependent on care-givers for survival. The task during this period is therefore to develop a certain amount of *trust* towards others (in contrast to *mistrust*) and to develop a belief that the environment can be relied upon to provide for one's needs. This condition is fulfilled in a caring environment, where babies can develop a sense of relying on the people who look after them. If they are neglected or treated badly in this early period, mistrust will develop; children will view the world as unfriendly and might have difficulties forming relationships later on.

Early childhood (1–3 years). During this period, children learn to move and to talk, and to express their wishes. They are no longer completely reliant on their care-givers, and start to test their boundaries. If they are allowed to experiment, they have a chance to develop *self-control* and *autonomy*. However, if their attempts are restricted and their achievements not acknowledged, they might develop *shame* and *doubt in their abilities*.

Play age (3–6 years). In this stage, children can do many things on their own, and can be mischievous. Often they are aware of what they are allowed to do and what not. Thus, they develop a sense of personal *initiative* in mastering the environment. If guided well through this phase, they learn to keep a balance between their own and others' needs and develop the skill of judgement. However, if others discourage the pursuit of activities, and punish them too often, too harshly and inconsistently, they start to feel *guilty* about their wishes to explore and about conflicts of interest with others.

School age (6–12 years). When starting school, most children are for the first time confronted with standards of excellence. Their work will be marked, and compared with others. If they do well, they will develop *industry* and self-esteem. However, if they constantly feel they are failing and are 'not good at anything', they will develop feelings of *inferiority*.

Adolescence (12–20 years). This is a time of huge changes. First of all, the body is transformed. But this leads to other challenges, in relation to peers, parents and romantic partners. There are career decisions to be made, and an increasing number of other decisions are now presented to the young person. These decisions emerge from questions such as: 'Who am I?' And 'Who do I want to be?' During this time the adolescent tries to establish a social, sexual and occupational *identity*. If this process is interrupted by external factors, the outcome might be *role-confusion* (we will discuss this issue in more depth in Chapter 3).

Young adulthood (20–40 years). It has been fun to have lots of friends during the adolescent years, and there has been a great deal of romantic and sexual experimentation. But now is the time to settle down and to achieve real *intimacy*: That is a full commitment to others, and in particular to a partner with whom to share one's life and to have children. If young adults cannot make a sincere commitment to others, they risk *social isolation* (we will comment on this idea in Chapter 6).

Middle adulthood (40–65 years). For most people, life has now become fairly settled. They know who they are, and now see their main task in life as caring for others, either by raising children or by contributing to society in ways that will benefit the next generation. Erikson called this endeavour '*generativity*'. Failing to do so may lead to *stagnation* and self-indulgence.

Old age (65+ years). In this stage of life, one has either achieved one's goals and fulfilled one's dreams, or it is now too late to do so. People at this stage evaluate their lives, and they either come to the conclusion that it was meaningful or accept their impending death – Erikson calls this '*integrity*' – or they become bitter about lost opportunities and *despair* in the face of death.

During each of these stages, one is surrounded by, and interacts with, others, who themselves are passing through particular life stages. While society has adapted itself to the individual, the individual in turn adapts to society. This is achieved in a way whereby the developmental needs of individuals in a certain age-band integrate effectively with the developmental needs of individuals in other age-groups. For example, the need of adults to become carers should coincide with the child's needs to be taken care of (Miller, 2001).

The idea of 'balance' is important because the individual, ideally, should not adopt an extreme position of values at any stage. Yet, not all individuals are successful in attaining a balance between the two potential outcomes of each stage. If this balance is not achieved, it will lead to problems in future stages. For example, a child who does not develop *autonomy* in the early years will have difficulties in achieving a high degree of self-esteem when entering school, and an adult who did not achieve *intimacy* in young adulthood will be prevented from building up a high level of *generativity* in mid-life. However, Erikson's theory does leave some room for optimism because it does not exclude the possibility that experiences later in life might help to heal the hurt and pain of negative experiences in early childhood.

◉ The theory of Roger Gould

While Erikson saw development as a constant adaptation to society's demands on the developing individual, the psychiatrist Roger Gould (1978, p. 321) is more interested in people's own fears, preoccupations and assumptions, which they acquired during childhood and in their relationship with their parents:

> I've come to understand 'growth' in one special way: As the release from arbitrary internal constraints. I don't pay much attention to what happens after the release – that seems to take care of itself. It's the work of liberation, not prescription, that has to be the focus of my attention.

He proposed a stage theory of transformations that start in the adolescent years and continue until mid-life. In his view, children trust completely in their parents and believe that their parents will always protect and nurture them. When reaching their mid-teens (around 16–22 years of age) they start to realize that this is a false assumption, and that they are required to make their own decisions, and to develop self-confidence: They have *to leave their parents' world*.

From age 22 to 28, young people have learned to take control of many areas of their life. But they are still rather naive, and cling to the false assumption that if only they do things as their parents did, and do so with willpower and perseverance, they will achieve all their goals. They are still convinced that their parents will 'bail them out' if something does go wrong. During this period they have to confront reality and learn that life is not always just, that rationality will not always succeed, and that nobody will (necessarily) do for them, what they cannot do themselves. In the end, they will arrive at the insight that they are '*nobody's baby now*'.

Once young adults have learned that, there is another false assumption they have to confront. Between the age of 28 and 34, they have to get rid of the idea that life is simple and controllable, and that there are no contradictory forces inside them. Up to then, they might have seen the world as black and white, and they might have been convinced that they know who they are, and that they have become what they are by their own choice. Now they begin to realize that things are not that simple and that there are sometimes contradictions between emotions and rationality. They learn to turn their attention to their deeper feelings and more complicated selves. That is why Gould called this period '*opening up to what's inside*'.

While entering the *mid-life decade*, between 34 and 45 years, a new awareness develops. Up to then, most people have been healthy and most of their friends and relatives were still around. So, though everybody knows that human beings eventually die, the reality of death has not entered their lives until now. For that reason, people hold implicitly to the wrong assumption that *there is not really death or evil* in this world. Not only do they have to come to grips with their own and others' mortality, they also become aware that there is betrayal, manipulation and evil in the world – and that they themselves often, willingly or not, conspire in creating evil. For instance, couples can hold unconscious ideas about each other's character and intentions and thus build up a *system* of misunderstandings and wrong interpretations; blaming the other for what in reality is a childhood fear one does not dare to confront.

Beyond mid-life, finally, there are no more false assumptions to be tackled. Now is the time of making meaning for one's life, to become reconciled with the fact that one has made mistakes, and to adjust to and accept life as it has turned out. This includes coming to terms with losses, with the inability to do things as well as before, and with the approach of death, and to value what one still has. The motto for this last period of life is: 'That's the way it is, world. Here I am!' This does not mean that there are no more problems and difficulties beyond mid-life, but that, after having achieved 'contact with one's inner core', one is now prepared to face up to life's challenges without confronting one's own demons at the same time!

Though Gould concentrates heavily on the individual and not so much on society, as Erikson did, there are some similarities in their descriptions of the life course; most of all in the description of the last period in life where healthy development includes acceptance of one's life choices. However, note that the age ranges of their stages, and sometimes the developmental issues described, do differ.

◉ The theory of Daniel Levinson

Another scientist interested in development over the lifespan was psychologist Daniel Levinson (1920–1994). He saw adult development as a succession of periods, which centre on different issues. None of these periods is more important than the other; like seasons in the year, they simply follow one other. Unlike the theories of Gould and Erikson, there are no goals to achieve, and no psychological consequences follow from 'success' or 'failure'. For this reason, he does not talk about 'stages', but of the 'seasons of a man's life'. Initially, he only studied men to arrive at his theory (Levinson, 1978) but later complemented his research by including women subjects (Levinson, 1996).

According to Levinson, two kinds of 'periods' repeatedly alternate over the whole lifespan: A long period of stability, which is then followed by a shorter period of transition. The transitional period often represents a fundamental *turning point* in the life cycle, and can be accompanied by turmoil and stress, and then leads into another period of consolidation and stability. On the basis of his findings, he divided adult development into the following cyclical periods:

Childhood ends with the early adult transition at age 17–22. The young person encounters the turning point of having to leave the parental home and begin an independent life as an adult. As soon as this is achieved, the relatively stable period of young adulthood begins, which lasts until the age of 28 years. Adult relationships are formed, and a basis laid for a future life structure – a period of construction of the dream: A vision of the future.

This period is succeeded by the age 30 transition, which lasts from 28 to 33. The young adult is aware that time is running out, and that commitments and choices have to be made which will have an impact on the rest of their lives. This can be quite stressful for some individuals, until they again reach some form of stability.

This is the time for settling down, lasting from 33 to 40 years. Gone are the insecurities from young adulthood, the individual has gained self-assurance, respect in the community as a fully grown-up citizen and knows where his life is going.

However, when reaching 40, the focus of attention changes to an evaluation of life, so far: Whether goals have been achieved and dreams attained. Depending on the outcome of this assessment, the individual is reassured and settles down or else is thrown into the turmoil of trying to change less satisfactory aspects of life, be it in the sphere of relationships or career. In the media, this period has often been called the 'mid-life crisis'.

The mid-life transition ends when the individual is 45 and enters the more stable phase of middle adulthood lasting to the age of 50. Earlier issues are now settled and the individual can enjoy the achievements gained.

However, by the age of 50, a new period of unsettlement and transition occurs. Individuals become aware of their own mortality, feel a decline in health and strength, and may wish to confront unsolved issues from earlier eras. This period lasts until the mid-fifties.

Again, from 55 to 60 life is more stable, until the next turning point approaches.

With retirement looming, individuals move towards another significant 'shift' in their lives – the late adulthood transition. They now tackle the changes that come with ageing and career loss. For some, this period opens up new horizons, while for others, it signifies the beginning of the end, and might be particularly hurtful. New choices have to be made, until, at the age of 65, individuals settle again into the stable phase of old age, where they finally can let go of commitments.

Thus, according to Levinson, life is an ongoing succession of turmoil around certain turning points followed by periods of stabilization and settlement. The turning points are age-specific, which makes it possible to assign an age range to each 'season of life'.

◉ The theory of Robert Havighurst

While Gould's theory is mainly concerned with the individual's psychological adjustment to life, Erikson and Levinson were more interested in the interaction between the developing individual and social demands. For Erikson, it is crucial that every 'crisis' is resolved, before the individual moves to the next stage, while Levinson regarded each 'season' in an individual's life as independent from the others. Yet another view was presented by Robert Havighurst. In 1953, he proposed that development occurs each time an individual encounters and solves a new 'developmental task'. Developmental tasks are major accomplishments that are required at certain points in life and these are developmentally sequential to some extent, such as starting school, orienting to a career, developing intimate relationships or becoming a parent. He distinguishes three types of developmental tasks: Those that stem from physical maturation, from personal values and from social demands. In his theory there is much less emphasis on pre-defined stages and more concern for the psychosocial forces within a culture. However, Havighurst also divided the lifespan into different periods depending on the prevalence of certain developmental 'tasks' that are expected to occur at certain ages:

During the first 18 years of life, children are mainly occupied with solving maturational tasks, such as learning to walk, and responding to social demands, such as forming relationships.

Early adulthood lasts from 18 to 35 years, and the developmental tasks identified for this period include finding a partner and starting a family, starting a career and taking on civic responsibilities.

Middle-age, comprising the years from 35 to 60, has the individual deal with tasks such as achieving full adult responsibility, maintaining an economic standard of living, assisting teenage children and ageing parents and accepting the maturational changes of middle age.

From 60 years on, developmental tasks consist mainly of adjusting to ageing and coping with bereavement.

◉ A comparison of theories

As an overview, Table 1.1 shows the changes and transitions described for the different age ranges as proposed by the four theories we have described. As we can see, there are some overlaps, but there are also some obvious differences. For example, while all the theories agree that the early twenties is a time for gaining independence from parents, and that old age (approximately being over 60) is devoted to coming to terms with the life one has lived and adjusting to decline and mortality, there is less consensus about when commitments are made, and what mid-life development encompasses.

Further, as already mentioned, there are differences between the theories with regard to the impact of successful or less successful transitions on later life events and on the importance of chronological order of the various stages. However, there is one interesting observation to be made, one that all the theories have in common: Transitions and developmental changes are accompanied by some degrees of turmoil, anxiety and instability. Living a life is not simply a matter of smoothly growing older; it is

Scientist	Erikson	Gould	Levinson	Havighurst
Transitions	Crises	False assumptions resolved	Seasons	Developmental tasks
12	Adolescence: Identity vs role confusion			Learning basic motor and social skills
15		I have to leave my parents' world		
17/18			Early adulthood transition, leaving home	Achieving emotional independence Choosing career Developing an ethical system Deciding on a partner Starting family
20	Young adulthood: Intimacy vs social isolation			
22		I'm nobody's baby now	Young adulthood	
25				
28		Opening up to what's inside	Age 30 transition: Making commitments	Starting an occupation Assuming civic responsibilities
30				
34/35		There is death and evil in the world	Settling down	Changing time perspective
40	Middle adulthood: Generativity vs stagnation		Mid-life transition: Life evaluation	Adjusting family relationships Revising/ continuing career plans
45		Time to make meaning of one's life	Middle adulthood	Making major contributions to society
50			Age 50 transition: Coming to terms with mortality	Adjusting to ageing Dealing with teenage children and ageing parents
55			Middle adulthood: Settling down	
60			Late adulthood transition: Retirement	Retirement Declining health Bereavement New living arrangements/ dependency
65+	Old age: Integrity vs Despair		Old age: Letting go of commitments	Maintaining dignity

Table 1.1 Lifespan transitions according to four different theories

a process full of tasks and challenges, which sometimes are stressful and difficult to cope with. It is these transitions that cause us to change and to develop.

👁 Criticism of the theories

Up to now we have simply described these early theories of lifespan development, without referring to the criticisms that have accrued over the years. What could these criticisms be? Let us start by looking at some modern lives:

There is for example Conchita, a 12-year-old Mexican-Indian street girl. She takes care of her two younger siblings, while begging at night in the streets of San Cristóbal de las Casas. Her drug-addicted mother attempts to nurture a baby, while her father tries to use all the cash he can find for alcohol. Conchita is solely responsible for the daily food her family gets every day. She looks after them all with great care and responsibility, and she knows they would starve if she 'wasted her time' by attending school. Yet, she is fluent in both Quechua and Spanish, and has a good command of English, enough to approach foreign tourists when she begs. She has no problems in calculating her daily income and is able to spend it wisely on the food she can afford.

Then there is 42-year-old Daniel, who left his wife and children in Lesotho to work in the mines in South Africa. He has recently lost his job because of ill health – he has contracted HIV and tuberculosis – and does not know how to get treatment or earn a living. His prognosis is poor. He is very likely to die within the next few years.

We do not even have to consider foreign countries to look at the unusual lives of some people: For example there is George, aged 18 years. He is a so-called young carer, because he has to look after his mentally ill mother and his autistic younger brother. His father has left the family long since because he could not stand the everyday problems of caring. But George had to stay. He had to leave school at 16, but that does not worry him, he was bullied there. He has no future career to look forward to without educational qualifications and with the heavy commitment he has to his family. He can only plan from one day to the next.

Or there is Sabrina, a highly talented gymnast. She represented her country in the world championship when she was only 11, highly committed to her sporting career, training eight hours every day. When travelling to competitions her whole life has been taken care of by her coaches; she did not even hold her own passport. And, of course, there was no time for boyfriends, peers and partying. Now she is 21 and feels she is too old to compete any more. She is retiring from gymnastics this year and has no idea what to do with the rest of her life.

Then you might already have heard in the media of the Indian farmer's wife, Rajo Devi Lohan, who gave birth to her first child at the age of 70. And of course there is Sebastian, a successful academic with a long track record of teaching, researching and publishing. At the age of 76 years, and in spite of the major surgery he is facing, he has no intention of retiring, having a long list of academic and writing tasks to accomplish over the next few years.

What have all these case studies in common?

None fits into any of the life stage descriptions summarized in Table 1.1, and that is where we find the major criticism of all stage theories: They cannot really describe everyone's life. There are far too many exceptions to general stage descriptions for us to accept them as universal theories. They are, at best, broad and general descriptions of lifespan change.

Depending on personal experiences and life events, the life course can be very different for various individuals living in the same country. They go through the phases differentially, some might not experience all the events ascribed to a particular life stage, or experience them earlier or later, and some might even regress temporarily to a previous stage. That means, stage theories are *too general* in describing the life course change.

In countries that are very different from the UK and the USA, developmental tasks are not the same, and so people there have different life trajectories. For example, in some cultures, adolescence does not exist, children move directly into adulthood roles.

Furthermore, in about 50 countries of the world – many of them in Africa – people do not have a chance to experience old age, because their life expectancy is lower than the age of 60, so they do not reach Erikson's eighth stage. Thus, the stage theories we have discussed in this chapter can be seen as *ethnocentric*: They ignore other cultures, and give the impression that life in the Western world is 'normal', while all other lifestyles are 'deviant' (even though over 80 per cent of the world's population does not live in the Western industrialized world).

Changes in societies, such as style of government, the economic situation and the advance of new technologies all have an impact on how people live their lives, which developmental tasks they encounter, and when in the lifespan these occur. Looking at all the theories we discussed earlier, it is quite easy to see that many of the stage descriptions are already *outdated*. The age of leaving the parental home has increased considerably, while the number of people choosing to have children has decreased. There are now other forms of partnerships than marrying an opposite-sex partner, and the high divorce rate has led to many people experiencing the task of 'building a family' more than once in their lives. Hence, of all people who married in England and Wales in 2002, nearly a third had been married before. In 1950, fewer than a tenth of all brides and grooms had married a second time (Office for National Statistics, 2010).

How could such eminent researchers as Erikson overlook facts like this?

First of all, it has something to do with the research methodology employed by these early lifespan researchers. Erikson, for example, based much of his theory on personal observations of his own social environment and on the analysis of the lives of famous people such as Martin Luther. Gould was a psychiatrist, and based his theory on the life stories of his clients. Levinson centred his theory on repeated in-depth interviews with only 40 men. All of the information the scientists in this chapter used to create their theories came from US Americans, often white, middle class and male – and all living around the beginning to the middle of the twentieth century.

Now, it is in itself not an error to base a theory on a few unsystematic observations. After all, a theory is just qualified observation and speculation. What counts is if there are – at the time of the formulation of the theory or later – any facts or empirical evidence to support it. Indeed, many aspects of these theories have been empirically tested, and we will refer to these studies in the following chapters. Unfortunately though, even these studies sometimes repeat the mistake of ignoring individual and cultural variability and are thus of limited value. In other words, stage theories cannot illuminate individual differences, often treating these as 'error variance' when presenting average outcomes. As a consequence, anybody who does not fit into the somewhat stereotypic picture painted by stage theories appears to be somewhat deviant, which can lead to stigmatization. Such age-related stereotypes can lead to self-fulfilling prophecies: If we expect teenagers to act as 'no brainers', middle-aged people to become complacent and conforming, and old people to lose their wits, ultimately they might live up to our expectations. Because of this, scientists have moved away from looking at chronological age as a major variable and instead concentrate – as Havighurst (1953) already posited in his theory – on the impact of different life events on human development.

A second criticism against stage theories is that they are mainly descriptive generalizations. They describe what happens from birth to death, but they do not *explain* how development occurs. How does an adolescent become independent from his or her parents? How does the way they become independent influence further development? Why are some older adults bitter about the way their life progressed while others are happy? What is it that actually happens before, during and after major turning points in life, and what are the influences that affect the outcome?

To illustrate, we would like to borrow Levinson's metaphor of the 'seasons' in one's life: He used this comparison to describe how different periods in life alternate with others, as summer follow spring and precedes autumn. But he contented himself by *describing* how these 'seasons' looked, very much as a poet might describe spring as being full of flowers, and autumn being a time of harvest and falling leaves. While a description like that has value, it does not help us to understand *why* and *how* seasons change. Scientists have become increasingly interested not only in the end product of different stages in human development, but in the *processes* and *mechanisms* that bring about human change. The next chapter will explore some of the major theories that have tried to address this issue.

◉ Summary

In this first chapter we have looked at four different theories that address lifespan development. We noted that there are differences between them, mainly in the various foci that these theories offered: While Erikson, Levinson and Havighurst acknowledged that development occurs when individuals have to deal with different social demands, Gould concentrated more on the individual coming to terms with the disappointment arising from a clash between false assumptions and reality. While Erikson and Gould saw only a few major turning points in an individual's life, Levinson, and particularly Havighurst, saw many issues and tasks that had to be addressed across the lifespan. Only Havighurst was flexible about the age ranges attached to different stages, and only he did not predict any disastrous consequences from failing to resolve any of the lifespan issues people face. However, they all agreed that human development is a lifelong process that continues well beyond childhood or adolescence. Given the fact that even today, courses and textbooks on Developmental Psychology deal mainly with childhood, this was a major advance, drawing scientific interest to issues of mid-life and ageing. Furthermore, they all agreed that dealing with turning points is often a stressful experience, and that after times of turmoil, there are periods of adjustment, balance and stability: We agree particularly with this latter theoretical viewpoint.

All four scientists have been accused of basing their theories on limited observations of biased samples, which led to interpretations that are too general, ethnocentric and quickly outdated. So, in the following chapter, let us turn our attention to theories that have attempted to address these shortcomings.

◉ Further reading

See any up-to-date introductory text on developmental psychology.

Chapter 2

Ecological Theories of Human Development

Summary

This chapter looks at a number of theories that take an ecological, systemic view of human development:

- Urie Bronfenbrenner's ecological model
- Glen Elder's approach to the life course
- Paul Baltes' theory of lifespan development
- Dynamic Systems Theory: An interdisciplinary approach
- A simplified, integration model of lifespan development.

Introduction

In Chapter 1 we showed that stage theories of human development have the limitation that they are rather descriptive – they do not really explain *why* and *how* people change. Neither do they offer universal descriptions of development over the lifespan. Several researchers have tried to find other ways of explaining what happens during the life course, and we explore some of these approaches here.

👁 Urie Bronfenbrenner's ecological model

Urie Bronfenbrenner was born in Moscow in 1917 and moved as a child with his parents to the USA. He studied psychology and music, and was a professor at Cornell University for many decades until his death in 2005. Perhaps because of his immigrant background, he was interested from early on in the influence of culture on child development. One of his first books (Bronfenbrenner, 1970) dealt with the different social contexts in which children develop, comparing the USA to the Soviet Union. Thus, he was sensitive to the ethnocentric approach which some of his American colleagues brought to the study of child development. He was particularly opposed to experimental approaches, in which researchers studied the behaviour of children in a laboratory setting, because he thought that the results did not reflect what happens in the real world. In a famous quote, he referred to developmental psychology as:

> the science of the strange behavior of children in strange situations with strange adults for the briefest periods of time.
>
> (Bronfenbrenner, 1977, p. 513)

Bronfenbrenner claimed that, as development demands social experiences, it has to be studied in context. Over the years, he developed a new model to explain what happens when individuals – not only children – interact with the social world around them. He called his theory the 'ecology of human development' (Bronfenbrenner, 1979). The word 'ecology' is borrowed from biology, where it refers to the various interactions of living organisms with their environment. You may have heard the word 'ecosystem', which describes a biological community and its surrounding physical environment. For example, a coral reef represents such an ecosystem, where all organisms living there – corals, fish, snails, crabs and so on – depend on one another and on the temperature, light and salt contents of the water around them. Because of the interdependence of all the animate and inanimate elements of the ecosystem, the system can easily be disrupted if just one element changes. For example, if one species of coral dies because of a higher water temperature, all organisms that depend on this for food or hiding places can no longer live there. This will then affect all organisms that require their presence for their own survival – and so on.

Bronfenbrenner thought that the conditions under which humans grow and develop are very similar to such an ecosystem. As human beings are social beings, their development depends on the relationships they form during their lives. Some of these relationships are immediate and direct, while others are more distant and indirect. The individual might not even be aware of all the relationships within which they exist! All these relationships can be described as different systems, each offering different roles (such as leader, follower, carer), rules and boundaries (such as what is allowed and what is not), and norms and expectations for the different individuals within these systems.

Thus, individuals are not only affected by their relationships, they also powerfully affect these relationships. For example, developmental psychologists have long been interested in the influence parents have on the development of their children. According to Bronfenbrenner, this is a one-sided perspective because it does not examine the influence of children on their parents and the two-way reactions and interactions; or, as a social scientist would say, the bi-directional influence.

However, the relationship with parents is not the only relationship to which the child belongs. There are many others, and they all interact with one another in some way. Bronfenbrenner described relationships on different levels as systems that are nested within one another, rather like a set of Russian dolls (Bronfenbrenner, 1979).

Apart from the immediate contexts in which the individual exists, such as his or her family or peer group (i.e. the *micro-systems*), there are other influencing systems. For example, if members of one micro-system (such as the parents) interact with members of another micro-system (such as schoolteachers), this will have indirect effects on the development of the child: for example, the child might then be confronted at home with conflicting values about schooling.

Similarly, the relationship of your romantic partner to your parents will influence you strongly, whether you wish this or not. Interactions of members of different micro-systems with each other occur in the *meso-system*.

Furthermore, persons within one's micro-systems are *themselves* affected by persons in their own particular micro-systems, of which the individual is *not* a member and about which they might not even be aware (such as the child's parents and their working colleagues): This is called the *exo-system*. These interactions can also have indirect effects on the developing individual.

Finally, the wider culture, with the laws and norms of the particular society in which the individual lives, has a powerful influence on all levels of the system (i.e. the *macro-system*). For example, at the time of writing, ongoing economic changes alter our lives profoundly. The British government reacted to the credit crisis by cutting the budget for higher education and by increasing study fees, at the same time as youth unemployment was at a record high. Another policy change has been the increase in retirement age. No doubt, these measures will have a profound effect on everyone – children, teenagers, young adults, the middle-aged, old people, families, relatives, businesses and professionals and policy-makers of all kinds.

The 'ecological' key to Bronfenbrenner's theory is not the division of influential environments into systems, but rather that the interactive influences are *multi-directional*. Individuals affect the surrounding systems as, in turn, they are affected by these systems, so that 'the characteristics of the individual function both as an indirect producer and as a product of development' (Bronfenbrenner & Morris, 2006). At the same time, the various systems are interdependent on one another – affecting and being affected. Development is not something that just 'happens' to the individual, but an interactive, dynamic process that involves all the system levels of a society.

As an example: The bad mood of a teenager, caused by problems in school, can affect his parents' behaviour in their workplaces. In turn, their attitudes towards his moodiness are shaped by what their working colleagues say. So, they might treat a colleague unkindly because they are still angry from the last confrontation at home, and this might cause the colleague to act differently to his or her own children. Meanwhile, the teenager's rebellious moods might develop into a general negative attitude towards authority, which, in turn, might concern adults so much that they agitate for new anti-social laws. Thus, there are interactive changes going on within micro-, meso-, exo- and macro-systems, initiated by minor events such as reactions to poor school grades, which themselves are caused by a wide range of interacting factors. Hence, it is impossible to find simple, one-variable cause-and-effect explanations to developmental issues. That is why Bronfenbrenner called his theory 'ecological'.

Glen Elder, the Great Depression and the life course

Up till now, we have discussed the individually-based theories of psychologists and psychiatrists, while, traditionally, sociologists are interested in what Bronfenbrenner would call the macro-system, how society and social groups function.

Glen H. Elder Jr had a reason to mix these two approaches (and he had both Psychology and Sociology degrees). Around the time he was born, America and the world was shaken by what was called the 'Great Depression'. The stock market had failed, and the economic crash that followed from 1929 led to an extreme rise in unemployment (up to 25% in the USA, even more in other countries), crop prices fell and personal incomes dropped. A societal change like that (that's the sociology bit) is most likely to have a lasting effect on the people experiencing it (which is the psychological part of it).

As a young scientist, Elder was compelled to find out what effect a social change like this would have on individuals – and he was lucky, because there existed a longitudinal census, capturing great amounts of data from the people who lived through this period, ranging from socio-economic figures to measures of psychological well-being. So, he set out to study these data in detail. And the results were amazing (Elder, 1972, 1998a).

For example, one of the answers to the question of how an economic crisis affects the people was that some were not affected at all! Some had been lucky to keep their jobs, or even got richer by buying property cheaply from people who were forced to sell. Those who did experience economic problems showed a range of different behavioural and psychological reactions.

Economic adjustment strategies that involved an element of loss – such as selling possessions, reducing purchases or using up savings – had a more negative psychological impact on families than other arrangements, such as growing one's own vegetables, mothers working part-time or the men doing overtime whenever possible (Elder et al., 1992). The 'children of the great depression' were usually not affected directly by economic hardship, but indirectly, through the reactions of their parents (Elder et al., 1985; Flanagan, 1990; Lempers et al., 1989; Skinner et al., 1992). Typically, it was the father who responded to economic difficulties with increased hostility and acted more negatively towards his spouse. Negativity within the marital relationship, coupled with financial difficulties, led in many cases to more punitive, arbitrary and rejecting parenting styles. In turn, these changes in parental behaviour could result in more temper tantrums and difficult, irritable behaviour in children, and could increase the risk of aggressive behaviour and depressive feelings among adolescent boys and girls. However, if parents' marital relationships were unaffected, or even strengthened, by economic difficulties (this was particularly the case with couples who had strong bonds before the crisis), this downward spiral was not initiated and children did not suffer in the same way.

This is only one example showing how extremely complicated are the relationships between certain events and certain outcomes in real life. The same event, an economic crisis, brought about either a positive, neutral or negative outcome for the individuals involved, depending on their coping behaviours, their age and gender, the quality of their parents' marriage and even their looks! These results caused Elder to formulate a new theory of human development across the life course. In detail, he proposed the following four principles of life course theory (Elder, 1998b; Elder & Shanahan, 2006):

The principle of historical time and place: The life course of individuals is embedded in, and shaped by, the historical times and places they experience over their lifetime. For example, the same event can have completely different consequences for the individual, depending on when and where in the world it happens. A child born out of wedlock can be a very happy event for a Scandinavian mother in this century, but it was a catastrophe 100 years ago, and it is still a disaster for many women in some countries in the world.

The principle of timing in lives: The developmental impact of a succession of life transitions or events is contingent upon when they occur in a person's life. For instance, in the example above, even in Sweden this birth would be slightly problematic if the mother is in her early teens.

The principle of linked lives: Lives are lived interdependently, and social and historical influences are expressed through this network of shared relationships. This principle is similar to Bronfenbrenner's ideas discussed above. When some people argue that their decisions only affect their own life, and others should not interfere, they do not see the whole picture. Whatever we do, or what happens to us, will also have an effect on others, yet we might not even be aware of it. Just think how little your ancestors thought of what it means for your life that they settled in a certain place or married a certain person. Falling in love seems to be very much a private affair between two people. Yet, these decisions – to engage in a long-term relationship or have a brief encounter, to break up or to become parents – have a 'ripple effect' on many others. Parents might have to cope with an adult child moving away from the family home, or, alternatively, to make room for an adult child returning home after a divorce, or to be cast in the role of baby-sitting grandparents. Children might have to face up to the divorce of their parents and one or other of them remarrying, or find themselves cast in the role of carer for a parent who cannot cope independently, or see their hoped-for inheritance being spent on expensive cruises as part of a parent's second or third honeymoon!

The principle of human agency: Individuals construct their own life course through the choices and actions they take within the opportunities and constraints of history and social circumstances. This means, human beings are not passive products of their environment, but as they choose pathways, they change their environment, which then will have repercussions for them. For example, the choice of dropping out of education or not is *affected* by earlier experiences in the school system, by intelligence, by parents and peers, yet it is an individual decision with future consequences.

To summarize, not unlike the scientists we discussed in Chapter 1, Elder sees the importance of 'life transitions' in shaping development. However, in contrast to them, he does not want to focus certain events on particular age-stages, but regards them, and individuals' differential reactions to them, as a function of historical period, place and timing in the life course. Furthermore, in line with Bronfenbrenner's ecological model, he emphasizes the interdependence of lives within mutual micro-systems.

⊚ 'Use it or lose it': Paul Baltes, ageing and the lifespan

Around the same time as Glen Elder was developing his theories in the USA, Paul Baltes (1939–2006) and his colleagues (Baltes & Goulet, 1970; Baltes *et al.*, 1980) in Germany began to elaborate their particular approach to lifespan developmental psychology. Baltes was fascinated by ageing, and by the clear evidence for continuing development even in the later years of life. From his research, he formulated the following central tenets of this approach, as outlined by Smith and Baltes (1999):

Development extends across the entire life course, and lifelong adaptive processes are involved. Apart from a certain temporal priority of earlier events in life, changes can have the same powerful impact on development throughout the lifespan. Both slow and continuous (cumulative) or sudden, discontinuous (innovative) developmental processes occur. With this, he tries to reconcile stage theories and anti-stage arguments: both are possible.

Similar to Elder, also Baltes *et al.* (1980) claim that *development is embedded in larger historical and cultural contexts*. They distinguish three sources of contextual influences: normative age-graded influences, normative history-graded influences and non-normative influences.

Furthermore, Baltes (1987) postulates the concepts of *multidirectionality* and *multi-finality*. As with Elder, this means the same event can have different outcomes (multi-directionality) or that very different experiences in a person's life can lead to similar outcomes.

Development always involves losses as well as gains. Sometimes, an individual has to lose flexibility in order to gain specialization (over time, a small child loses the ability to produce certain sounds, which will help him or her to become fluent in their native language, but can hinder attempts to learn a foreign language later). Sometimes, gains in one domain are accompanied by losses in another. For example, retirement opens up possibilities for exploring new activities, but might be accompanied by loss of work-related self-esteem. Losses, deficits and limitations are seen as serving as catalysts for positive change, because they cause the individual and/or the environment to respond. Thus, they can bring about an adaptive ability, which means they can help individuals to adjust to changes in their lives. Successful development is, accordingly, defined as the 'maximization of gains and the minimization of losses' (Baltes *et al.*, 2006).

Finally, there is the basic concept of *plasticity*. This means there is a difference between what a person can do ('baseline reserve capacity') and what he or she could do with training or help ('developmental reserve capacity'). This term was introduced to explain why older people in some research studies perform less well in cognitive and motor tasks than young people. Baltes *et al.* (2006) argue that these results look too pessimistic, as they only reflect the *actual* performance of the participants, and not what would be *possible* at their age, if an effort was made to train these skills.

The resources an individual possesses are, according to Baltes (1997), allocated differently across the lifespan. In early life, they are allocated to functions associated with growth (reaching higher levels of functioning). During adulthood, they are directed towards maintenance (sustaining normal levels of functioning in the face of contextual challenge or a loss in potential). In later old age, they are allocated to the regulation of loss when maintenance or recovery is no longer possible. In this context, individuals seem to prefer avoidance of loss rather than enhancement of gains. Baltes *et al.* (2006) suggest a model of development involving a selection (of developmental goals), optimization (generating and activating goal-related resources) and compensation (functional responses to the environmental- or age-related loss of goal-related resources). The strategies for successful ageing are presented as follows:

Selection: In advanced old age, individuals may be faced with increasingly drained resources. Deterioration in hearing, seeing or memory capacities, for example, needs increasing compensatory efforts, which can lead to the difficulty of trying to do too many things at the one time. This may lower stress tolerance because too many stimuli can easily become overwhelming for the individual. One way to counteract these shortcomings is to evaluate the choice of goals and drop some of them, in favour of other more important ones. Thus, energy can be canalized into fewer projects which can be accomplished satisfactorily.

Optimization: This involves the means of achieving desired outcomes. For instance, the time and energy saved by selecting only a few targets is now freed up to be concentrated on the remaining goals (such as having more time to dedicate to training).

Compensation: This denotes a response to a loss in resources used to maintain desired outcomes by counterbalancing them with other resources (such as using a walking stick, or leaving the house earlier in order to catch a bus).

To summarize: For Baltes, development is the result of the successful confrontation of contextual life challenges and/or losses and deficits. What exactly these challenges are, and how they will impinge on the individual, will vary with context, age and culture. Whether or not they are met successfully is dependent on a wide range of factors, amongst others, on how easily individuals can adapt to changes. As with other theorists, Baltes and his team see a challenge as a necessary trigger to development. This challenge, however, does not have to originate in the individual's social environment. It can also be a loss of function or a deficit in the individual that calls for action and, thus, possible growth and development. Like Bronfenbrenner and Elder, Baltes sees development as a lifelong, dynamic process of the interaction of elements within the individual, and between the individual and specifics of the context.

From atoms to the universe: Dynamic Systems Theory

Being *social* scientists, scholars such as Bronfenbrenner, Elder and Baltes describe development from a macroscopic point of view. Though they emphasize that any developmental event is better described as a process than a single event, they do not often try to explain in detail how the process of change comes about. Elder (1998b), for example, described how an 'event', such as teenage pregnancy and its outcomes, consists in reality of a whole range of different processes involving several possible 'turning points' (such as deciding to have sex, whether or not to use contraception, whether or not to have an abortion, whether or not to marry and so on). Each of this these 'turning points', however, is again a process consisting of various interacting elements (the decision to marry, for example, is surely a process extended over some time and involving different systems!). Further analysis of the components of the process of change will reveal increasingly microscopic elements of behaviour, interacting with one another and with parts of the environment, forming a so-called open system, a system that can interact with other systems.

Such ideas now lead us to have a closer look at Dynamic System Theory, which attempts to explain what it is that brings about change in systems, and thereby leads to development.

Unlike all the other theories we have discussed so far, Dynamic Systems Theory does not originate in the Social Sciences. It stems from ideas developed in Physics and Applied Mathematics, but has recently been highly influential in other disciplines, such as Genetics, Neuroscience, Human Movement Science and, yes, also in Psychology. Some scientists have even expressed the hope, that Dynamic Systems Theory might be the one approach that can unite the disciplines (Lewis, 2000; von Bertalanffy, 1951; Witherington & Margett, 2010). So, what is it all about?

As the name says, it deals with systems, a word that we are already familiar with from Bronfenbrenner's theory. Remember, a system was an entity comprising elements that all interact with one another and with other systems. While Bronfenbrenner's systems contained relationships between people, Dynamic Systems Theory observes many more elements on many more levels. The hormonal system within a body is as much a system as the political organization of a country and the constellations of solar systems in the universe – and they are all interdependent with one another. Each component is both a system in itself and a part in a larger system. To cite a practical example (Adolph, 2008): When a child learns to walk, it is part of a system that consists of elements such as the length of its legs, the weight of its body, the surface of the floor, the presence of other people and their actions, surrounding furniture, attractive objects around, past experience, role models and so on. Sometimes it is the presence or absence of just one of these elements that determines success in this instance, sometimes it is a combination. A rail to hold on to, a teddy out of reach, or supportive comments from a carer might not be enough to encourage walking if the surface is too slippery or the legs too weak to support the body. Thus, change is the product of many different elements. Dynamic Systems scientists claim that all human change follows the same rules and includes the same developmental processes and mechanisms as in this example of a child learning to walk.

One of the most important principles in Dynamic Systems Theory is the principle of *self-organization* (Thelen & Smith, 1998, 2006). This means the way a system is structured, and how its elements are coordinated, is not the result of some innate maturational programmes or some organizational power from outside: It happens through the interactions of the elements in the system itself. First, this interaction seems to be chaotic, but eventually each element finds its place, role or form, and a new organized system emerges. We will illustrate this with a range of examples:

You might have heard of the latest book by Stephen Hawking (Hawking & Mlodinow, 2010), which caused a media uproar because the two physicists used the principle of self-organization to explain the origins of universes, claiming that the elements of which universes consist organize themselves following physical rules and without the need of any divine intervention:

> As recent advances in cosmology suggest, the laws of gravity and quantum theory allow universes to appear spontaneously from nothing. Spontaneous creation is the reason there is something rather than nothing, why the universe exists, why we exist. It is not necessary to invoke God to light the blue touch paper and set the universe going.

At the microscopic level, you might have heard of stem cells. Embryonic stem cells are the first cells that emerge, when a fertilized egg divides in the womb. These cells have a special characteristic: They can develop into any body part. Nothing inside them makes them become a cell in an arm, or the brain, or the liver. However, when cells go on to duplicate, they start to become increasingly differentiated, depending on different micro-environmental conditions, until different types of body cells develop (Qu & Ortolewa, 2008). Similarly, when small water droplets freeze because of their electrical loadings, the water molecules rearrange themselves in such a way that geometrically-formed crystals in many different shapes evolve. Thus, self-organization can be observed everywhere in the natural world from microscopic to universal systems.

In recent years, psychologists have begun to observe self-organization in human behaviour and human development. For example, imagine a group of students who do not know one another, and who have just moved into a university hall of residence. In the beginning, nobody knows their place in the hierarchy, the roles and expectations of different group members, and whom they will like and dislike. Over the days, and depending on the characteristics and interests of each member, it will become clear who usually cleans the kitchen, who annoys others by playing loud music, who becomes a friend, who is good at helping with course work, and so on. Organization and structure comes to the group, evolving out of the interactions of group members themselves. This structure is quite stable until some influence from outside brings change: a new boyfriend, a failed exam, an illness, for instance, can disturb the group dynamics and force the group to adjust and reorganize. Sometimes these adjustments can be minor, but at other times it can mean the whole group disintegrating.

Over the lifespan, an individual belongs to many different systems which are all constantly changing, and so do the members within them. One single factor is seldom responsible for a change. Rather, it is the sometimes abrupt, sometimes gradual, intricate interactions of many different elements that produce outcomes. For example, we know that certain genes are associated with conditions like alcoholism and schizophrenia, that social class has an effect on health, and that the number of years one spends in education correlates highly with later earnings. But not all carriers of these genes will become alcoholics, not all working-class members are unhealthy, and not only highly educated people earn high incomes. All these are generalizations, averages.

Dynamic Systems Theory sees the life course of every individual as unique – as a result of the distinctive combination of all the individual's different systems. They are more interested in investigating the processes and mechanisms of change than looking at the outcomes. So, there are no stages with rather static outcomes, but there are periods of relative stability where not much happens, interspersed with periods of turmoil. The turmoil is caused by a change – a new task, an illness, a new person in one's life, a loss, bodily changes or changes in the environment, and so on – which disturb daily routines and force the individual to adapt. In their terminology, they would say the system has lost its balance, and it takes some time for all the elements to reorganize until the system is relatively stable again.

Interestingly, many stage-theorists have said something similar. Piaget talked about 'disequilibrium', losing cognitive balance when a child encounters a novel task, and 'equilibrium', the re-achieving of balance which he or she has mastered by solving the task. Erikson described each of his stages as a 'crisis' that had to be resolved. The difference between stage theorists and dynamic system theorists is that the latter would not assign particular age ranges to periods of change, but postulate that there are myriads of smaller and larger changes happening all the time; that each individual follows their very own pathways, so that it is impossible to construct a general description of development, valid for all human beings.

👁 Resources, challenges and risks: Hendry and Kloep's Lifespan Model of Developmental Change

Inspired by these ecological theories, we developed a simplified model of our own to examine human change (Hendry & Kloep, 2002). We started by trying to find out what it is that makes human beings so similar in their development – and, conversely, what it is that makes them so different. On the one hand, all normal babies develop into humans with two legs and two arms, they all learn to walk and to talk, they will all become adults, who eat, love, work and interact, and eventually they will grow old and die.

On the other hand, some of them will become parents, some will not, some will be outstanding in intellectual endeavours, others will hardly learn to write, some will spend most of their lives in prison, others in a castle, and still others in a tin hut in the forest or an urban slum.

We distinguished between three kinds of *developmental shifts* that can occur during the life of human beings. The first group are 'maturational shifts' – changes that happen to everybody, due to biological influences. These are body changes such as physical growth, puberty and ageing.

Because they are experienced by everyone, they account for similarities in the development of human beings as opposed to other species of mammals.

Then, there are 'normative-social shifts'. These are changes prescribed by the individual's culture, often by law, religion or social norms. These are, for example, school attendance, military service or retirement. Because of these normative shifts, individuals within the same culture are more similar to one another than to members of a different culture.

The last group of shifts, however, is what makes every individual unique. These are the 'non-normative shifts', the changes that do not occur to everyone, but which are different for each individual.

All these shifts present the individual with many different challenges, as they have to adapt to new situations. In order to cope with these challenges, resources are needed. All healthy children are born with a certain range and level of fairly similar resources that will help them to develop into *adult human beings*, and to cope with life challenges. Importantly, these resources will change and alter over the life course. Furthermore, all babies get bigger, all have a predisposition to learn to walk and speak a language, to see, to hear and to smell, to learn new things and to feel varying emotions. Consequently, Indian and Russian, British and Maori babies behave much in the same way, as do babies in rich and poor families, as did you and your mother and even your Celtic ancestors when they were small.

But accepting these similarities, we are also very different from one another from birth onwards, and even before that as foetuses in the womb. Many of these resources are innate, such as certain reflexes. Others are learned, since learning starts in the first seconds of life and will go on until death. Still others are structurally determined, such as nationality or social class. Just as certain potential resources exist for every individual from the very first moments of life in the womb, so too does the inequality in their distribution amongst individuals. We can consider the array of resources an individual can draw upon as their 'resource system'. It is an open system that consists of a variety of interacting items of resource. The number and kind of resources can vary at any moment in time, and over the lifespan. New resources are added, others disappear, and some characteristics become resources while others are gradually lost. None of the variables within these different categories can be seen in isolation from the others, rather they should be regarded as highly interactive.

Up to now, we have discussed the 'shifts' and challenges that occur in an individual's life course, together with the resources the individual has to cope with them, as if they were two separate entities. In fact, they are not. There is no boundary between 'individuals' (and their resources) and 'environment' (and its challenges). No potential resource is a resource in isolation. For instance, no one can tell whether the Ace of Spades is a good or a bad card to play, without knowing what the card game is! Similarly, any characteristics of the person can be a *resource* (e.g. being tall as a high jumper), *irrelevant* (being tall and trying to solve a mathematical problem) or a *disadvantage* (being tall and trying to sit comfortably in an economy class transatlantic flight). In other words: Any of these potential resources only become actual resources *in interaction* with the kind of task or challenge that has to be met. Thus, while the task determines what a resource *is*, the number and kind of potential resources within an individual's resource system determine whether or not the particular task the individual meets turns out to be a routine chore, a challenge or a risk.

A challenge can be a clearly positive experience, or it may contain negative elements that nevertheless lead to growth. Something as undesirable as having a physical handicap has for some people been the antecedent for enormous personal growth. On the other hand, something as apparently desirable as winning a large amount of money can turn out to be disastrous for people who cannot cope with new-found wealth.

Another important variable affecting the 'goodness of fit' between resources and challenges can be the number of different challenges the individual has to cope with *at the same time*. The 'goodness of fit' between potential personal resources and certain challenges is different *between* individuals, but also *within* individuals, because of situational factors. Something that is easy for one person is not necessarily easy for another; something that was too difficult for someone yesterday might be relatively easy tomorrow.

Dealing with a challenge can add to the person's resources and lead to further development. However, it can also drain resources, and thereby make it more difficult to deal with future challenges. When potential challenges are too extreme and difficult to be met by existing resources, then the situation or event facing the individual can be termed 'risky' and may possibly lead to further decrements in the resource system. If an individual assesses his or her resources as being inadequate for solving a certain challenge, anxiety will arise, and the individual will try to avoid meeting the challenge. On the other hand, if the resource system is perceived as sufficient in relation to the task, this will enhance feelings of security and efficacy.

Thus, if the resource system is relatively full, a state of contentment, a feeling of security, is accomplished. This in itself is a pleasant state of well-being which, however, after some time can lead to feelings of boredom. If this state of boredom occurs, the individual might set out to find a new challenge to overcome, and thereby add new resources to the resource system. These challenges that people might seek out if they feel 'boringly' secure can be anything from small *daily tasks*, such as trying to repair the bathroom light or experimenting with a new recipe, to more *sensation seeking* ones as going on an adventure holiday, to real *'life shifts'* like selling one's home and going to live on a house boat or in another country. Thus, in trying to find the right balance between security and boredom, on the one hand, and anxiety and risk, on the other, a dynamic and accumulative process occurs: The more and better potential resources individuals can count on, the more daring they will be in relation to new challenges. As a consequence, they will be more willing to seek out new tasks, and, if they meet them successfully, will add even more resources to their systems.

Similarly, a downward spiral can occur. The fewer and weaker resources individuals have, the higher will be their anxiety when confronted with new tasks and the lower the probability that they will voluntarily seek out new challenges. As they add few new resources to their resource system, their capacity to solve tasks successfully will decrease further in the future. 'Developmental stagnation' is a period of time where no new resources are gained.

We would postulate that individuals can stagnate in their development at any phase of their lives, if their potential resources do not match up to the challenges they meet. Further, it is possible to stagnate in one life domain and to continue developing in others. The individual's resources can be almost completely drained within one life domain (e.g. being unskilled in physical activities), be just sufficient to be happily stagnated in another (e.g. in one's social life) and continue to develop in a third (e.g. doing one's job efficiently). These different lifespan states are temporary, and can be reversed at any time. As mentioned repeatedly, there is no steady or static state in open dynamic systems, rather there is a continuous ever-changing interaction among the elements of these systems.

◎ Summary

In this chapter, we have considered ecological approaches explaining human development and change over the life course. All these theories have in common that they are not particularly interested in static developmental outcomes, such as fulfilling the goals of a stage, but investigate the processes and mechanisms that lead to developmental change. They do not believe in a prescribed, normative sequence of developmental steps that unfold independently of culture and environment. Instead, they describe development as a constant interaction between and within different systems. There is no 'goal' to be reached, and development never ends, as there will always be change to which individuals constantly adapt. Further, they do not accept simple 'one-variable' explanations of change, but rather insist that all interactions are multi-directional, and that development always consists of both losses and gains.

◎ Further reading

Hendry, L. B., & Kloep, M. (2002). *Lifespan development: Challenges, resources and risks.* London: Thomson Learning. This book extracts the common elements in the major traditional theories of human development, and utilizes these principles to construct a simplified ecological theory around the concepts of 'resources', 'challenges' and 'risks'. The model is then applied to gaining an understanding of human change from birth to old age.

For a description of the most modern theories of Human Development, particularly on Dynamic Systems Theory, see:

Murray, T. R. (2001). *Recent theories of human development.* London: Sage.

For a very comprehensive overview of theories, sometimes difficult to understand, but if you are ambitious, go for it:

Lerner, R. M. (2002). *Concepts and theories of human development.* 3rd edition. Mahwah: Laurence Erlbaum.

Chapter 3

What Is Adolescence?

Summary

In this first chapter about adolescence, we will:
- Outline difficulties in defining adolescence
- Detail the major changes of puberty
- Consider the search for identity
- Examine the so-called 'storm and stress' of adolescence
- Explore various aspects of risk-taking and thrill-seeking behaviour, such as substance use, delinquency, reckless behaviour and unprotected sex
- Discuss what is known about brain research and stereotyping.

Introduction: What is adolescence?

What is adolescence? Although we talk about our own teenage years and tell of our adolescent exploits, and comment about what adolescents are like today, technically, adolescence is difficult to define. Actually, the whole concept of 'adolescence' did not even exist until the twentieth century (Demos & Demos, 1969). Within the teenage years, the adolescent becomes physically and sexually mature without necessarily being seen to assume fully adult social roles. Adolescence, as a time set aside for developing and maturing and for accomplishing the transitions and transformations between childhood and gaining adult status, is an extended phase of life for today's young people. However, no one is entirely sure when adolescence begins. Some may consider it to be at 13, the first 'teen' year, while for others it may be the start of secondary schooling. For those who want to equate it with the teen years, does it end at 19? When are the transitions to adulthood and full adult status completed and achieved? How do we know this assuming of adult social roles has actually been gained?

For those who prefer a physical 'marker', the commencement of puberty is the obvious moment when adolescence begins. Yet, as we shall see, puberty itself is a complex process involving various elements – the growth spurt, menarche and so on – all occurring at different times.

The picture is further complicated by the so-called 'secular trend' in puberty: it is suggested that its occurrence has been approximately one month earlier in each decade of the twentieth century in Western industrialized societies. Today's children mature to puberty earlier than their parents and grandparents, and become aware of global affairs through modern technologies such as the Internet. Compulsory schooling has been extended and pressures to become better qualified have put a premium on 'staying on' at school and preferably going to university. The delay in gaining an income is just one of the factors which seems to defer transitional passages to early adulthood. The erosion of traditional roles and values has resulted in a fragmentation of adolescent transitions.

Puberty

Since puberty has a role in adolescent transformations, how does it unfold? Puberty is normally considered to date from the onset of menstruation in girls and the emergence of pubic hair in boys. However, these two easily observable changes are each only a small part of the total picture, since puberty is in reality a complex *process* involving many bodily functions and associated with sexual maturation. Puberty is accompanied by changes not only in the reproductive system and in the secondary sexual characteristics of the individual, but in the functioning of the heart, and thus of the cardiovascular system; in the lungs which in turn affect the respiratory system; and in the size and strength of many of the muscles of the body. Puberty must be seen, therefore, as a process with wide-ranging implications.

Pubertal changes are initiated by hormone signals to the ovaries and testes, which in turn release a wide range of different hormones that stimulate other body changes. Social and nutritional circumstances affect the timing of puberty: For example, it occurs later in less developed communities around the world (Parent *et al.*, 2003). In girls, it usually starts about two years earlier than in boys, and one of the first signs is the 'growth spurt'. This term is usually taken to refer to the accelerated rate of increase in height and weight that occurs during early adolescence, with considerable individual differences in the age of onset. In Western industrialized societies, the growth spurt in boys may begin as early as 9 years of age, or as late as 15, while in girls the same process can begin at 7 or not until 14 years of age.

Box 3.1: Cultural differences: Orthodoxy or deviancy?

Once upon a time, results from research conducted in the USA or in the UK – incidentally, mainly with male subjects – were then used to explain human development in many different countries of the world. Sometimes, even tests developed for use in one country were then simply translated and applied in completely different cultures. Fortunately, of late, more and more researchers in this globalized world are interested in differences and similarities between people in different cultures. Nevertheless, there is still a whiff of ethnocentricity in the air.

Research cross-culturally and in other societies carries a range of difficulties and limitations. To give you an example from our own research, some years ago we were carrying out a number of pilot studies in order to devise a theoretical framework of risk-taking behaviours based on empirical data, since we considered that researchers used the term 'risk-taking' rather loosely in their writings (see Chapter 3). When we tried out our framework on a Turkish sample, asking them to give examples of typical risks, we were surprised to find that 'preparing a meal for in-laws' was seen as a very risky behaviour. However, a typical risk behaviour often cited in Western studies, namely, riding a motorcycle without a helmet, did not feature at all: None of our Turkish participants could afford a motorcycle to ride.

Some pitfalls in cross-cultural research:

- Commonplace phenomena in Western societies do not necessarily exist in another culture, or else they appear in completely different forms. Teenage pregnancy, for example, is regarded as non-normative and problematic in Britain, but in some other cultures, it is normative and even culturally desirable, and the teenage mothers are usually married – so we cannot compare the findings. Even something seemingly as simple as how many hours of TV teenagers watch in a normal day might be difficult to compare cross-culturally: In some countries, the television is switched on all day, with nobody really paying attention to it, while family members carry out many other concurrent tasks. That is a very different scenario from forgoing other leisure activities in order to watch particular programmes.

- Test-scales measuring intelligence, personality, well-being or attitudes are often constructed and validated in a certain country. They may measure something completely different when used on a different cultural population. For example, the query 'Are you inclined to keep in the background on social occasions?' is aimed at measuring introversion (a personality trait of having a tendency to prefer one's own company to that of others). However, it is not difficult to imagine that an affirmative answer given by a woman in rural Afghanistan would tell us nothing about her personality – more likely much more about the social norms of her country.

- The reasons why we would want to do cross-cultural research also need to be analysed. Much of the published research has a tendency to use data from other cultures as weird examples, trying to point out how 'strange' others are compared to our 'normal' selves, and thus they add to ethnocentric stereotypes and prejudices, rather than reducing them. Other studies more or less haphazardly compare countries on some measurement, without clarifying a reason why these particular countries were selected. If we want valuable results from cross-cultural comparisons, there has to be a clear research question as to why such a comparison would add to our knowledge. For instance, this could be to show that some phenomena are universal (e.g. education has beneficial effects on life quality, regardless of country); or an attempt to tease out which cultural factors lead to differential effects (e.g. Why do Scandinavian teenagers drink far less alcohol than young Britons?); or to show that certain theories are not applicable to other cultures (see Chapter 5 on emerging adulthood).

Both genders gain weight. However, for girls, weight gain is mainly due to an increase in fatty tissue, while for boys, it is fat-free tissue that increases most (Rogol *et al.*, 2002). The next step is a change in the reproductive organs, which start to grow and mature, alongside the development of secondary sex characteristics. This is usually accompanied by the appearance of body hair. Much to the distress of young people, hormonal changes also cause acne and increased body odour.

Young women and young men experience puberty somewhat differently. Martin (1996) interviewed male and female teenagers about their experiences, and found that puberty means that boys look forward to becoming men: Gaining strength, freedom and status. By contrast, for young women, puberty has an ambivalent, if not negative, value: Implicit social values still assign lower status to women, and identifying with adult female roles means having to accept that. Then there is a restriction on freedoms, because the developing female body now has to be guarded against dangers such as rape, pregnancy and harassment, while at the same time it has to be extremely beautiful. While the shame associated with menstruation and menarche in earlier generations (Brooks-Gunn & Petersen, 1983) is slowly giving way to more positive attitudes towards sexual maturation in the narratives of young women (Lee, 2009), many still develop a range of depressive symptoms with the onset of puberty. The extent of depression amongst girls, which before puberty did not differ from that for boys, becomes significantly higher and stays at that level for the rest of their lives (Vogt Yuan, 2007).

One reason that depressive symptoms increase for girls but not boys lies in the perception of the ideal body. While both boys and girls gain weight during puberty, this is regarded by boys as desirable, but not by girls. With body shape being of such importance, it is not surprising that teenagers of both genders try to slim, or to build their muscles in gyms, sometimes using illegal drugs to aid their 'body sculpting'. Nevertheless, worry about appearance is largely a female concern, with scores for 'negative body image' being one to two standard deviations higher for girls than boys beyond 13 years of age (e.g. Kloep, 1998, 1999; Wichstrøm, 1999). Body satisfaction is highly correlated with depressive symptoms and most adolescent girls perceive themselves as *too fat*, even when they are of normal weight (Kim & Kim, 2001; Shucksmith & Hendry, 1998).

Gender differences in depression are particularly accentuated for those adolescents who enter puberty earlier or later than their peers. For girls, early puberty is associated with higher depression rates, while for boys, a late onset of puberty is more likely to predict depression (Conley & Rudolph, 2009). Early maturing girls are also at a higher risk of other psycho-social risks, such as delinquent behaviour, substance use, social isolation and early sexual behaviour, though by early adulthood, the differences with 'normal' maturers tend to disappear for most of these problems (Copeland *et al.*, 2010).

Technological advances within neuropsychological research have yielded interesting findings about brain development. In a child's brain, neurological pathways are formed between brain cells each time the child learns something new. Repeated behaviours and experiences lead to a strengthening of these pathways, while at the same time, pathways that are not used disappear. Areas with few established connections are called grey matter, while regions in which pathways are strengthened (and unused ones 'pruned' out) are called white matter.

With increasing age, the amount of white matter augments, and the amount of grey matter decreases. This can now be observed by using a technique called magnetic resonance imaging (MRI). Studies using this technique show that this process continues at least until the mid-twenties, maybe even across the whole life course (Sowell *et al.*, 2003), and it occurs at a different pace in different areas of the brain (Giedd *et al.*, 1999; Hofman, 1997).

Some researchers claim that the adolescent brain is still immature, because the increase of white matter in an area in the front of the brain, called the prefrontal cortex, which is thought to be involved in planning complex cognitive behaviour, decision-making and governing social control, does not begin before late adolescence (e. g. Steinberg, 2008).

However, most researchers agree that it is premature to draw such conclusions, as work in this area is still in its infancy and all implications of these observations are seen as sheer speculation (Blakemore & Choudhury, 2006; Keating, 2004; Sercombe, 2010). For example, nobody has yet been able to establish any *causal* link between brain structure and behaviour, and there are also tremendous differences in the development of brain structures between different individuals (Johnson *et al.*, 2010; Males, 2009, 2010). However, this has not stopped the media over-interpreting every tentative research result, and describing adolescents as unstable, dysfunctional, brain-damaged individuals (Payne, 2010). This is one example where puberty takes its meaning not only from physical changes, but also from the social implications and interpretations of these changes.

⊙ The search for identity: Who will I be?

As described in Chapter 1, Erikson (1950) saw the adolescent period as the time of forging one's identity. He described identity as an unconscious striving for a continuity of personal character and maintenance of an inner solidarity with a group's ideals. There are three interacting elements that constitute one's identity: One's biological characteristics; one's own unique psychological needs, interests and defences; and the cultural milieu in which one resides. Optimal identity development involves finding social roles and niches within the larger community that provide a good fit for one's biological and psychological capacities and interests. Typically, adolescents experience a 'crisis' while they solve the dilemma of who they are, who they will become, and who they do not wish to be. As we see, Erikson has been somewhat vague in his definition, and now there are several different interpretations, research approaches, definitions and explanations of identity.

The most influential interpretation of adolescent identity is Marcia's (1966) theory of identity status. He postulated that identity development happens in four stages:

First there is *identity diffusion* – the young person has not yet started to explore identity questions in a variety of life domains such as vocation, religion, relational choices and gender roles. There is no investigation of possible selves, and no commitment to any values.

The next identity status is *foreclosure*, which means the adolescents commits to certain values, but without exploring different alternatives. Often, this commitment is a result of parental or peer influences, and not a conscious, personal decision.

Then there is a time of *moratorium*, which means a delay in decision-making. This is the actual 'crisis' period, during which different options are explored, before a firm commitment is made. Young people may change their opinions often and rapidly, trying out different identities, values and lifestyles.

When they finally commit to certain values and decide who they want to be, they have reached the most mature stage of *identity achievement*. This occurs, according to Marcia (1980), between the ages of 18 and 22 years. A well-developed identity gives the individual a sense of one's strengths, weaknesses and uniqueness. Thus, identity is formed through crisis (i.e. a time when one's values and choices are being re-evaluated) and commitment.

Since Marcia's first formulation of identity status theory, scholars have pointed out various shortcomings, even stating that his description of identity formation does not qualify as a developmental theory (e.g. Meeus *et al.*, 1999; Waterman, 1982, 1999). Some of these identity theory controversies are reminiscent of the debates between stage and ecological theorists that we described earlier.

Is there a 'general identity' or is identity status domain-specific?

When discussing identity development, researchers do not always make it clear whether identity is a construct, strived for and attained as a whole, or whether it consists of several domains. For example, will a young person achieve identity in different domains, such as religious, social, sexual and work orientated values at the same time? Alternatively, is it possible to be in diffusion in one of these domains, in moratorium in another, and in achievement in a third?

Solomontos-Kountouri and Hurry (2008) investigated this question with a nationally representative sample of young Greek-Cypriots. Results showed that young people were not in the same status across their global, political, religious and occupational identities. The results also demonstrated the impact of context: Greek-Cypriot people spent little time exploring different religious values before making their commitment – a fact easily explained by the prevailing religious climate in the Greek sectors of Cyprus, with the orthodox Christian religion forbidding explorations of other beliefs. This now leads to the next question.

Is the theory valid cross-culturally?

Though Marcia (1966) initially proposed a theory that he expected to be valid globally, he soon had to accept that this was not the case. When investigating identity formation in non-western countries, he found that in cultures that do not encourage individualism, but rather emphasize group cohesion and collectivism, identity formation follows a different pathway. For example, university students in India (Marcia, 1996) rarely reach *identity achievement*, and are most often in a state of *foreclosure* – that is, they have made early commitments based on tradition, not personal exploration and choice. So, Marcia had to admit that his formulations of identity development do not apply to all cultures.

Do the stages described by Marcia always occur in the same sequence?

Originally, the four identity statuses were meant to represent different degrees of maturity, with diffusion being the lowest and achievement the highest status (Marcia *et al.*, 1993). However, research has shown that young people do not always progress through the four stages in the same sequence: They might skip a stage or regress to an earlier one during the process. Nowadays, there is a strong agreement among researchers that the four statuses cannot be rank-ordered along a developmental continuum (e.g. Goossens, 1995; Waterman, 1999). A review of longitudinal analyses of identity formation shows clearly that there are several different trajectories of identity development, and the end-point is not always achievement (Meeus *et al.*, 1999).

Identity is also influenced by context, and as such can change within short periods of time. As Hendry *et al.* (2007) show, young people have different commitments to national identity depending on whether they see it in the context of sports, in comparison to rival nations; in terms of their own life and career trajectory; or as an expression of belonging to friends and family. For these reasons, research now tends to investigate identity formation as an ongoing process, focussing on its transitional and contextual nature, instead of emphasizing the attainment of end-goals.

The search for identity as a dynamic process

Theory development is an ongoing process: A theoretical hypothesis is formulated and then tested in empirical studies. The results then inform the theory, and might lead to a reformulation. Marcia's theory on identity statuses is a good example for this. Given the criticisms, and the results of many studies, Marcia changed his theory to accommodate his critics (Stephen *et al.*, 1992). Identity statuses are no longer seen as 'end-points', attained by early adulthood, but as sequences that can be brought out of balance at any time. So, even if a commitment is reached, something might happen, forcing the individual to rethink his or her position, to explore again, and to find a new commitment and period of consolidation after a while. This is in line with the process-perspective.

Many modern researchers, including those who suggest a dynamic systems approach, argue that identity formation is an ongoing, lifelong process where periods of stabilization and commitment alternate with periods of instability, triggered by changes in person-context interactions. Whenever a commitment is no longer adaptive to the context, the individual needs to change. This can be done either by changing the perception of the environment (assimilation) or by rethinking one's identity (accommodation). The latter takes more time, and can be a painful process, though facilitated if the person is open to change and has environmental support. Examples of situations that might elicit such an identity crisis could be: If one's ideological convictions are questioned by changes in a political system, as happened in the countries of Eastern Europe in the 1990s; when one's social identity is threatened by divorce or death in the family; or when one's self image needs to be adjusted to age-related bodily changes. In all these cases, conflict is the trigger for action and development. In contrast to Marcia's original idea, exploration is not necessarily needed to solve the dilemma. There is broad consensus amongst researchers regarding this description of identity formation (Adams & Marshall, 1996; Bosma & Kunnen, 2001; Hendry & Kloep, 2002; Kroger, 2000, 2004), so the idea of an 'identity crisis' in adolescence needs to be modified: There is likely to be more than one crisis, as there are many domains of identity, and this is a recurring, lifelong process, not simply a feature of the adolescent years.

◉ Storm and stress?

In 1904, the American psychologist Stanley Hall published a two-volume work called *Adolescence*. He was one of the first psychologists to turn his attention to this life phase between childhood and adulthood. He saw it as a time of turmoil and biologically determined development, with inevitable emotional upheaval. According to him, normal adolescents had to go through a phase of extreme stress, rebelliousness and powerful mood swings – from being excited and euphoric to suddenly becoming lethargic and melancholic. These mood swings were seen as a consequence of an internal struggle between childish selfishness and adult social care.

Initially, his theory was widely accepted by scientists and laymen, but, while parents and teachers still tend to endorse this description of teenagers as moody rebels (Hines & Paulson, 2006), over the decades, researchers have begun to question the validity of such a picture. Rutter *et al.* (1976), in a large-scale study of 14-year-olds on the Isle of Wight, found few indicators of psychiatric disturbance and parent-child alienation, while Bandura (1972) claimed that young people's struggle for autonomy was more a problem for parents than for teenagers. Both concluded that the concept of adolescent turmoil was more fiction than fact!

Nevertheless, the issue still occurs regularly in academic discussion and in the media. Because of this, we will take a close look at recent research in three of the main areas in which 'storm and stress' are said to occur: Psychological problems, depression and mood swings; conflicts with parents; and reckless behaviour (Arnett, 1999).

Psychological problems, depression and mood swings

What evidence is there about adolescence being a time of psychological problems and mood swings? Csikszentmihalyi and Larson (1984) developed a unique research method that allowed them to follow adolescents in their daily lives: Adolescents were given a 'beeper', programmed to signal at random times during the day. Each time the signal occurred, adolescents were asked to write down what they were doing *just then*, and how they felt at that moment. This was a very effective technique for getting descriptions of what young people were doing *as they experienced it*, rather than reporting retrospectively. Though the results showed some of the expected mood swings in young people's daily lives, there were no signs of general unhappiness or psychopathology.

To try to find an explanation for these mood swings, Larson & Ham (1993) conducted a large study with teenagers between 10 and 15 years of age, in which they asked them for negative and positive events in their lives, and measured their daily mood. They found that older adolescents do encounter more negative events such as changing schools, being disciplined, receiving poor grades, breaking up with a boy- or girlfriend and family disruptions than do younger teenagers, affecting their moods negatively. Moreover, they perceive personal events more negatively than their younger peers. In other words, negative moods and stress could be seen as a result of growing responsibilities that come with increasing age, as does an increase in feelings and sensitivity in evaluating events in one's life.

As for major disorders, there is some indication that rates of mental health problems increase as adolescence is reached (from around 10 per cent to 13 per cent in boys and from 6 per cent to 10 per cent in girls, Office for National Statistics, 2010), particularly rates for depression and negative well-being. However, the key point is that these rates do not decrease again after adolescence, but increase until mid- to late-forties (Blanchflower & Oswald, 2008; Lewinsohn *et al.*, 1986). The onset of common mental disorders does not vary with age (Singleton & Lewis, 2003). Hence, being unhappy, depressed and having mental problems is not unique to adolescents. Research has yet to find convincing evidence that adolescents are 'victims of their raging hormones' as some scholars claim (Buchanan *et al.*, 1992).

Conflict with parents

Fewer than 10 per cent of adolescents experience serious difficulties with their parents (Holmbeck, 1996), and these conflicts often have their origins before adolescence (Collins & Laursen, 2004). Disagreements are often about mundane day-to-day issues (Smetana & Gaines, 1999) and decrease in frequency from early adolescence onwards (Laursen *et al.*, 1998). Furthermore, conflict with parents does not figure as a major worry for young people between 12 and 18 years of age, especially when compared with concerns about romantic relationships (Kloep, 1999).

Parents, on the other hand, perceive adolescence as the most difficult time in child rearing, experiencing conflicts that occur as more stressful than when children were younger (Buchanan *et al.*, 1990). However, in a study of 15-year old-girls by Lichtwarck-Aschoff *et al.* (2010), they found the average number of conflicts with parents over a nine-week period to be lower than one per participant. In contrast, when mother and toddler interactions were observed, between 3 and 15 conflicts per hour were counted (Dix, 1991; Klimes-Dougan & Kopp, 1991). Maybe parents perceive more stresses because they are less likely to win, as adolescents become physically mature and more skilful in arguing. As for adolescents, conflicts with parents can be the necessary trigger for developing a sense of autonomy (Lichtwarck-Aschoff *et al.*, 2010). In sum, while many parents seem stressed while parenting adolescents, most young people cope well and do not reveal any particular anxieties about disagreements with parents.

Risk-taking

'Risk-taking' is a relatively vague concept. From the research conducted, it is possible to note many different behaviours subsumed under this heading, ranging from dangerous extreme sports, through unhealthy lifestyles (substance abuse, unhealthy eating, lack of exercise) to criminal, anti-social activities and unplanned, thoughtless, spontaneous behaviours such as climbing onto your girlfriend's balcony to leave a bouquet of flowers, setting off the alarm and bringing the police to the 'scene of the crime'! These risky behaviours can have different purposes, and individually they can be positive or negative in the young person's development. So, being scientific, we should look at different categories of risk-taking separately, and see whether or not young people are more prone than other age-groups to engage in them.

In an effort to differentiate categories of risk-taking, Kloep and Hendry (1999) offered the following theoretical types:

Firstly, activities that could be called *thrill-seeking*: These are exciting or sensation-seeking behaviours which challenge and test the limits of one's capacities and capabilities.

Secondly, there is *audience-controlled risk-taking*. In order to be accepted, to find and establish a social position in the peer group (and receive social support and security), individuals have to demonstrate certain qualities. In some circumstances, this might imply taking certain risks, as 'chickening out' might lead to a loss of status. Indeed, some adolescent *and* adult groups have 'initiation ceremonies' to test novices before they can be granted entrance to the group.

Thirdly, there are risk-taking behaviours which are simply *irresponsible behaviours*. These are not performed *because* of the risks, but *in spite* of them, in order to achieve desired, perhaps more immediate, goals. Such irresponsible behaviours demonstrate the inability of individuals to see long-term consequences, or, if these are apparent, to be unwilling to delay because of perceived short-term advantages. It is obvious that behaviours such as getting drunk or failing to use condoms are not pursued because they are risky, but for other, more immediate reasons.

Following a study of risk-taking among Turkish adolescents, Kloep *et al.* (2009) added a fourth category: Risks that are taken in order *to pursue a future goal*, such as applying for a high status job, moving to another country for better opportunities, or dating a girl/boy friend against parental wishes. This category of 'calculated risk' emphasizes actions taken *after* considering the advantages and disadvantages of a planned strategy, and deciding it worthwhile.

Thus, different forms of risk-taking meet different needs, and cast doubt on the idea that it is always and only young people who engage in risk-taking. Let's look at some prominent examples of risk-taking and their functions in order to examine this question.

Smoking and drinking

Substance use in adolescence is important, since unhealthy lifestyles at a young age can seriously affect health. Nevertheless, the picture of adolescent smoking, drinking and drug misuse painted by the media is exaggerated. In the UK, 80 per cent of 15-year-olds do *not* smoke, 60 per cent do *not* drink and 70 percent do *not* use cannabis (HSBC, 2001/2002). The age-group most engaged in these pursuits are the 20- to 24-year-olds.

However, it might be useful to understand why a minority of young people *do* engage in these behaviours. Engels and van den Eijnden (2007) have provided a comprehensive review of the research and list the following contributory factors:

Alcohol facilitates social interaction. Young people often quote this aspect as an important reason for drinking, particularly with regard to dating and romance (Kloep *et al.*, 2001). Several studies have shown that young people who never drink, or who start to drink later than others, have lower self-esteem, higher depression rates and fewer friends than others (Pape, 1997; Pape & Hammer, 1996).

Drinking and smoking are admired adult behaviours. Living in a culture where alcohol and cigarettes are associated with 'being cool' and relaxed, and where these adult attributes are portrayed in advertising, they become important status symbols. For the teenager, being allowed to order a drink in a pub seems more important than having the actual drink (Kloep *et al.*, 2001).

Drinking, particularly in the company of peers, is helpful in relieving stress. The demands of modern society, with its instability and uncertainty, might well contribute to drug usage in easing stress (Wagner, 2001).

When encouragement to engage in smoking, drinking and drugs do start to feature in adolescence, this may be to some extent an acceptance of adult values and norms, rather than teenage rebellion or experimentation (Berndt & Zook, 1993). While for some young people, experiments with recreational substances are just a part of growing up and becoming socialized into adult society where drugs are seen as 'normal' (Jessor, 1987), for others, they become the main source of coping. It is the latter group that has the greater risk of developing into problem drinkers (Beck *et al.*, 1993).

When looking at the main reasons for adolescent substance use, they seem to be no different from the reasons adults would give for these behaviours. Furthermore, adults who smoke, drink or use drugs often start their habit when below the age of 24 years (Coulthard *et al.*, 2002), indicating that these are mainly adult behaviours that commence, for some, during the transition from adolescence. This makes it problematic to regard them as part of adolescent 'storm and stress'.

Crime

There is a widespread consensus among youth researchers that crime and anti-social behaviours are mainly engaged in during adolescence. For example, Coleman (2010, p. 197) writes, 'Why is it so closely associated with the adolescent period? Why does it decrease markedly as young people reach adulthood?' Steinberg (2007) asks similar questions. But is their claim that criminal behaviour increases in adolescence, and decreases thereafter, an accurate one? At first glance, it looks as if they are right. The number of offenders who are cautioned peaks in mid-adolescence and then declines.

But crime peaks again in the mid-thirties, though this is hardly ever mentioned (McVie, 2005). Using the age-crime curve as support for the claim that adolescence is the time of aggression and crime is seriously flawed. Consider this: Most of these statistics are based on the numbers of 'cautioned' or 'arrested' individuals, or even the number of *arrests* (where the same person can be re-arrested and thus counted into the statistics several times). Perhaps it is not so surprising that fewer experienced adults than adolescent novices are arrested, particularly as policemen tend to keep a particularly vigilant eye on young people.

Further, statistics do not usually discriminate between types of crime. Where different crimes are looked at *separately*, the age-peaks vary considerably (McVie, 2005). Further, crimes that are most frequently presented statistically are criminal damage, theft, violence, public order and motoring offences (Natale, 2010). These offences are all presented equally in combined statistical tables, as if painting graffiti on a public wall is as serious as murder! Hence, petty adolescent offences are often equated with *really serious* adult crime. Some offences are only offences because they are committed by a certain age-group (such as underage drinking), while others are not recorded as criminal offences because the perpetua-tor is not of legal age. For example, acts of physical aggression peak at the tender age of two, and then decline steadily (Tremblay & Nagin, 2004).

Distorting the picture even further, offences of great significance, highly unlikely to be committed by teenagers, are not included in these statistics, such as large-scale tax evasions, corporate crime, causing global economic crises or environmental destruction, or ethnic cleansing.

Realistically, if we look at the issue from this perspective, most studies show that between 70 and 80 per cent of young people are *not* delinquent (Roe & Ashe, 2008). A further 5 per cent do break the law consistently, but they have been doing so from childhood and are likely to continue to do so for the rest of their lives.

Only about 20–25 per cent fit the description of 'wild and reckless' teenagers: They start offending in their early teens, but become law-abiding citizens when they become adults. Moffitt (1993) called them 'adolescent limited offenders' as compared with 'life-course persistent offenders'. So, again, we need to emphasize that 'storm and stress' is not a description of normal adolescence, but only of a small group of young people who – in the case of criminal offending – are likely to be male (Office for National Statistics, 2010).

Exploratory risk-taking and thrill-seeking behaviour

It has been argued that an increase in exploratory and risk-taking behaviour can be observed in most species since it serves important developmental functions: Namely to allow the young to learn about their environment and become independent from parental protection (Johnson *et al.*, 2010). But why would such activity not be equally functional for mid-life and older adults – indeed all ages – to explore their environment and consequently become more skilfully adapted?

Is there evidence in day-to-day living that young people engage in more reckless behaviours than other age-groups? The reason car insurance is so much higher for young drivers is that insurers take statistics into account, and these show that young men are greatly over-represented amongst drivers involved in car accidents. In the literature, this fact is seen as proof of young people's reckless risk-taking (e.g. Arnett, 1999).

The problem with this interpretation is that accidents in *themselves* are not risk-taking. If anything, they might be an indication that risk-taking has occurred. However, they could also be the result of inexperience, poorly-serviced cars or dangerous roads. Indeed, Males (2009) stated that it is unfair to compare young inexperienced drivers, who often drive old unreliable cars on bad roads, with mature experienced drivers who drive better quality cars on good roads, and then accuse young people of reckless driving.

Other indications of adults engaging in risk-taking in traffic can be drawn from motorcycle accidents, in which adult men over 30 years of age are most often involved, and the over 21-year-olds, who are nearly twice as often involved in alcohol-related traffic accidents than younger males (Males, 2010).

Research evidence focusses on young people, and does not often offer comparisons with adult risk-taking, though one comparative study that looked at online sexual risk-taking, such as giving out address or phone number or sending sexually explicit photos to unknown recipients, showed that adults did so as often as adolescents (Baumgartner *et al.*, 2009). Moreover, nearly half the mountaineers trying to climb Mount Everest are 40 years and older (Huey *et al.*, 2007). Accordingly, travel companies now market particularly to the over-fifties, extreme sport holidays (such as white water rafting, bungee-jumping and parachuting) and globe-trotting holidays.

There is little evidence for the assertion that risk-taking increases during adolescence compared to childhood. Children have a natural curiosity that leads them into potentially dangerous situations when they explore their surroundings. They try to climb up and down stairs, fountains, rocks and garden-frames, they do not attend to passing cars and do not hesitate to touch unknown objects such as razor blades, needles, cigarette butts or pills, and inspect them by putting them in their mouth. Nearly 40 per cent of home accidents involve young children, with falls, poisoning, scalding, suffocating and drowning being the most frequent reasons for injury and death (Department of Health, 2004). With the advances in medicine to treat childhood illnesses, injuries are now the greatest threat to children's health (Scheidt *et al.*, 1995). The leading single cause of death in all age-groups between 1 and 44 years of age is unintentional injury (Office of Statistics and Programming, 2007). The evidence is clear that risk-taking is an all-age phenomenon!

To sum up, what distinguishes adolescent thrill-seeking from the risk-taking activities of younger children is that adolescents have increased material resources, are less supervised, and the risks they take are sometimes also dangerous to others. By comparison with adults, teenagers often chose different kinds of risks, and, moreover, have limited experience of their own capacities and the actual risks undertaken. Nevertheless, risk-taking is a way of learning the skills of assessing the 'goodness of fit' between one's abilities and the demands of a situation at all ages.

Unprotected sex

Young people under 25 years are the age-group with the highest rate of sexually transmitted infections (STI) apart from HIV. This has led to a range of interventions to encourage young people to use condoms. However, if we take a closer look at statistics, we discover a paradox: Adolescents already use condoms and use them much more than adults! So how do we explain their high rate of STIs? Could it be that young people engage in intercourse more often than adults? That is not true, either. The age-group in which most people report having had intercourse in the previous month are the 25–30-year-olds, while in the adolescent group, as many as 48 per cent state that they did not have a sexual partner at all.

However, if we ask with *whom* people have sex, we get a partial explanation for the heightened risk of infection during adolescence: Those under 25 who do have sex, do so more often with casual and changing partners than older adults. Older adults, particularly women, are often in long-time relationships with one partner, and thus are not at the same risk of being exposed to infection. Actually, having *unprotected* sex with *casual* partners can most often be found among men in their fifties!

Another reason for increased vulnerability to STIs, particularly among young women, has nothing to do with risk-taking behaviour, but has medical explanations. One is that the cervix of young women is highly susceptible to infection, and another is that anyone who has not had intercourse before has not yet developed immune reactions to infections. As it is mainly those under 25 years of age who experience intercourse for the first time, it is not surprising that there are more infections in this age-group.

One consequence of young people becoming sexually active is the risk of pregnancy. The UK has the highest rate of teenage pregnancy in Europe, with slightly more than 4 per cent of girls younger than 18 getting pregnant. About half of these pregnancies end with an abortion, suggesting that the pregnancy was not planned. Abortion rates are highest in the 20–24 year age-group (3.2 per cent of women in that group), but still remain high in the 25–29 year age-group (2 per cent). This latter figure should be viewed in combination with the fact that more children are born to 25–34-year-old mothers than to younger women. These women are also more likely to be in stable relationships and economically more able to take care of a child, which might affect their decision not to abort an unplanned pregnancy. In other words, there are no strong indications that women under 25 risk unplanned pregnancy more often than other women.

On a closer inspection, there seem to be two groups of young women who get pregnant: Those for whom the pregnancy was an accident, and those who planned it or at least did nothing to avoid it. In the UK, teenage pregnancies are widely regarded as a problem as they are associated with single parenthood, dropping-out from education and reliance on benefits (Dennison & Coleman, 1998). In addition, the young mother, rather than the father, has most often to cope with the burden of single parenthood, with all its economic and social implications. Single mothers of all ages have been shown to be the group in society with the lowest life quality, because of economic problems and social isolation (Cater & Coleman, 2006). So, why do some girls wish for an early motherhood?

Cater and Coleman interviewed young parents and found that they thought they had made a rational choice. Most young people saw pregnancy as a way to escape their dysfunctional homes or adverse school experiences and a chance to construct a new and positive identity. Both young fathers and mothers aimed to create a loving family in contrast to their family of origin. Further, young women preferred motherhood to low-paid, low-status jobs. Obviously, in these cases the pregnancy is not a result of hazardous risk-taking, but a well-planned event.

Phoenix (1991) also pointed out that an early pregnancy does not necessarily have a negative impact on the young mother's future development. Some of the research pointing to teenage pregnancy as the cause of dropping-out from education and other problematic consequences is flawed because it is often cross-sectional and cannot establish clear causal relationships. In a longitudinal study, Ferguson and Woodward (2000) showed that, in many cases, girls lived in economically dire circumstances and had often left education *before* they fell pregnant, suggesting that rates of teenage pregnancy might be elevated among young women who leave school early, rather than rates of early school leaving being elevated among young women who become pregnant during their teenage years. Similarly, the outlook for most of the teenage mothers in Phoenix' (1991) study was discouraging and rather bleak before the birth of their child, and the pregnancy was a consequence rather than the cause of their problems.

Actually, many teenagers cope well with their role as a mother, often in spite of enormous difficulties (Phoenix, 1991). It was easier for some young women from deprived backgrounds to return to education years after they dropped out if they had their children early, than for drop-outs who became mothers later in life. This was possible because they were still young when their children started school and could devote time to their own studies (Rich & Kim, 1999).

To sum up: Young people under 25 years of age do use condoms (and other methods of contraception) more often than any other age-group. Nevertheless, they are the age-group most susceptible to STIs, partly due to biological reasons and partly because they do not yet live in a stable partnership, often having multiple partners. Four per cent become pregnant (while 96% do not), and some of these have planned to conceive. The abortion rate in this age-group suggests that a high percentage of young women consider possibilities, plan carefully and act to ensure that their future is not compromised. So, though teenage pregnancy as a phenomenon may offer problems for adult society, it is neither a problem for the vast majority of teenagers, nor is it proof of mindless risk-taking.

Brain research and stereotyping

Having shown in the sections above that adolescence might be a precarious time because there are many developmental challenges to meet, it is by no means a time of 'storm and stress'. Adolescence is no more filled with conflicts, depressions or taking risks than later life phases. Only a minority of young people, often those with other problems, are involved in so-called reckless behaviours. Coleman and Hendry (1999) emphasized that it is the young person who has to deal with more than one issue at a time who has most adjustment problems. For example, an adolescent faced with intra-family issues, living in poverty, mixing with delinquent friends, in addition to dealing with school attainment concerns and behaviour-management difficulties, will have great problems in resolving such an overload of developmental challenges. On the other hand, the majority of teenagers are able to deal with developmental tasks one-at-a-time so that, when a personal, social or relational issue (such as gaining a degree of independence from parents or relating to peers) comes into focus, it is dealt with, and fades into obscurity to be replaced by another challenge later in the individual's developmental transition. Hence, most researchers now agree that the idea of describing the adolescent years as stormy and stressful for most young people is a distorted, biased view of adolescence. (However, see Arnett, 1999, who argues otherwise).

Perhaps more astonishingly, some researchers have recently started to use the first tentative results from modern brain research to rekindle the old notion of young people as reckless, incompetent and irrational. Steinberg (2008), for instance, devotes a whole article to the questions: 'First, why does risk-taking increase between childhood and adolescence? Second, why does risk-taking decline between adolescence and adulthood?' – based on the unsubstantiated idea that risk-taking DOES increase during adolescence – and then goes on to cite provisional findings from magnetic resonance imagining, which at present can only show that the adolescent brain looks different from the adult brain (see above). However, these observations can be interpreted in several ways: As some lack of maturity in the adolescent brain; as increasing decay and inflexibility in the adult brain; as the result of shared experiences within an age-group; or none of these. Brain researchers themselves admit that any conclusions presented regarding the connection between brain structures and behaviour would have to be tentative and would be premature since brain research itself is still in its infancy (Johnson et al., 2010).

Despite the lack of evidence linking brain development to adolescent behaviour, the media have been eager to accept preliminary results and exaggerate them widely, going so far as describing adolescents as 'insane, unstable and dysfunctional'. This is a serious issue because it can lead to the negative stereotyping of young people, and create and strengthen a self-fulfilling prophecy. If adults expect young people to behave childishly and irresponsibly, and, as a consequence, restrict their freedom to act and the opportunities to demonstrate their abilities, this might well create the very conditions that will encourage young people to behave irresponsibly. Many authors have pointed out that adolescence research, conducted by adult researchers, is extremely biased in concentrating mainly on problem behaviour and in interpreting results in a negative way, thus demonizing and 'scapegoating' young people (Ayman-Nolley & Taira, 2000; Males, 2009, 2010; Payne, 2010; Sercombe, 2010). Little that is positive about adolescent lifestyles has been investigated by researchers, and most writing about teenagers concerns the risks they are perceived to take (though see Roker et al., 1999). Others even advocate legislation to prevent adolescent risk-taking in order to protect them (Johnson *et al.*, 2010; Steinberg, 2008). There is an ongoing heated debate between the two camps of researchers (for example, see the special edition of the *Journal of Adolescent Research*, 2010, 25, 1).

⊙ Summary

To conclude, adolescence may be a difficult time for some young people, especially those who have already suffered from a range of problems in childhood, or who are confronted by too many concurrent issues. These distressed young people are in the minority. Hence, the idea that adolescence is a time of 'storm and stress' for most teenagers is a biased, negatively stereotypical view, reinforced by the media and little supported by statistical and empirical evidence. As we will discuss in some detail in the next chapter, most young people manage to meet the developmental tasks of educational demands, changed relationships with parents, peers and romantic partners, and an increase in personal and social responsibilities extremely well.

⊙ Further reading

Jackson, S. & Goossens, L. (2006) *Handbook of adolescent development.* Hove: Psychology Press.
This is an edited book looking at adolescent development from a European point of view to offset the predominant views of USA-centred research. It covers topics such as puberty, emotion, cognition, self-esteem, moral development, family, peers, school and leisure in chapters written by leading European adolescent researchers.

Chapter 4

Social Teenagers

Summary

This chapter on teenagers as social actors looks at:
- Relationships within the family
- Young people's relationships with friends and peer networks
- Communication and the Internet
- Gender differences in peer relationships
- School as a context for relationships
- Leisure transitions and transformations
- Young people's community participation and citizenship.

Introduction

Experimentation is a significant aspect of adolescent transitions to adulthood (Coleman & Hendry, 1999), located within wider economic and social contexts (Furlong & Cartmel, 1997). Beyond the development of selfhood and individuality described in the previous chapter, learning conformity and acceptance of society's norms and values involves socialization within a variety of relationships during adolescence.

Adolescents engage in a complex network of relationships which form a continuum from family, through best and close friends, acquaintances and peers, to romantic relationships. At times, encounters with adults in authority can be ambivalent and confrontational, whether they are parents, teachers or the police – and even peer interactions can become problematic. At other times, relationships with adults or peers can constitute a lifeline to help young people overcome risks and challenges in their lives. Hence, in this chapter, we examine some of the major relationships in which adolescents engage on their journey towards adulthood.

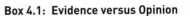

Box 4.1: Evidence versus Opinion

When we are looking for supporting findings for our theories and ideas in writing scientific papers or books, where do we look? When we talk with our undergraduate students about searching for genuine evidence, they often say, for instance, 'But I read a report in the Guardian' or: 'There was an article in the Sunday Times Colour Supplement mentioning a study by Dr George Michael', or: 'Professor John Lewis, a well-known expert in his field, believes....' Now, are these opinions reliable facts, or scientific evidence? The academic community uses a few criteria to determine whether or not 'information' is acceptable scientific evidence:

You need to differentiate between opinions and facts. Even the opinion of the most intelligent or famous person in the world is still an opinion. If it is a well-formulated opinion, we sometimes call it a theory – but it is not a fact! For this reason, an opinion cannot be used to back up an academic argument. For example, if a famous theorist has formulated the belief that owning a teddy bear is bad for children, you should not take their teddies away, *just because he thinks so*. A belief is not a fact, no matter who voices it. In other words, the beliefs of Professor John Lewis are of no significance.

This is the point where research comes in. Some clever people have formulated some ideas that might be true. These are theories. In order to find out whether they really are correct, we have to find evidence to support them. If we stay with the theory of teddy bears, researchers would now look at the situation and say: If this idea is true, then children who own a teddy bear would show some unfavourable symptoms, which children without teddies would not have. This is called a hypothesis. The next step would then be to show that this is actually the case (or not) – by using an experiment, or a survey, or an interview study or another method of data collection. The results of these studies then are *facts*, also called empirical evidence, and usually published as a research article.

In order to make sure that the data were collected and interpreted correctly, the academic journals which publish research articles first check them thoroughly, usually by letting other researchers evaluate them (they call this 'peer review'), before they publish them. Though it might still be possible that some mistakes escape their critical eyes, this procedure ensures that the published results are highly reliable. For this reason, whenever scholars use facts to support an argument, they quote research results published in these journals (and that is why you find so many names in parentheses behind many of the statements we make - this is to show what facts we use to support our argument).

Journalists often hear about research studies, and sometimes write a story for a magazine or a newspaper around them. However, journalists are not academics. It is uncertain whether they have understood these academic studies correctly, whether they take a biased position and only report results that support one side of an argument or even exaggerate some findings in order to make a story more sensational. The same happens on web-pages, particularly if they are from a commercial organization or an interest group. For that reason, these sources are not regarded as trustworthy by the academic community (and both the Guardian and Dr Michael are discarded as reliable sources).

There is a valuable lesson to be learned from this that can be used beyond the academic context: An argument, whether spelled out in a scientific journal or voiced in a pub, does not become better by being repeated or yelled, and whether you 'strongly believe it', or 'feel' that in 'your opinion' it is true, it only becomes convincing when you have reliable facts to support it. So, what are your views about teddy bears now?

👁 Relationships within the family

Most adolescents acknowledge that their closest relationships are with family members, including parents, siblings and grandparents (e.g. Hendry *et al.*, 1993; Phillip & Hendry, 1997). While peers can be the major sources of support in day-to-day matters, the assistance provided by parents is crucial in emergencies and in future planning, and sibling relationships are essential in developing social skills and as a source of social support. Several longitudinal studies have shown that receiving sibling support is associated with better peer relationships and social skills, and less loneliness, depression and problematic behaviour (Branje *et al.*, 2004; Hsiu-Chen & Lempers, 2004; Kim *et al.*, 2007). Conversely, conflict with siblings increases problem behaviour, more frequently for the younger sibling (Slomkowski *et al.*, 2001).

Family relationships are, of course, so intertwined and interconnected that between-sibling relations are affected by those with parents, and vice versa. Often, children perceive that parents treat them differently from their siblings, and this can have an impact on their psychosocial adjustment. Those who believe that they are less favourably treated can develop psychological and behavioural problems, particularly if they compare themselves with a same-gender sibling with whom they have a poor relationship. Again, younger siblings are more vulnerable to perceptions of differential parental treatment (Plomin *et al.*, 2001; Scholte *et al.*, 2007; Shanahan *et al.*, 2008).

For a long time, researchers believed – and this was eagerly picked up by the media – that parental control was the most important variable for predicting young people's adjustment. This was because measurements of parental control – whether parents knew their offspring's whereabouts, their friends, and what they did with friends – correlated highly with young people's good (or bad) behaviour. Therefore, these results led to recommendations to parents to monitor their adolescent children's behaviour closely. There was consensus about this until the ground-breaking longitudinal studies of Stattin and Kerr (Kerr *et al.*, 2010; Stattin & Kerr, 2000), which showed that it was not the knowledge of teenagers' behaviour itself, but the way this knowledge was acquired, that made the difference. If parents 'closely monitor' their children's behaviour by spying on them and interrogating them, teenagers are more likely to be secretive about their pursuits, or indeed, to give downright lies about what they are getting up to. Furthermore, if young people perceive their parents' attempt at monitoring as invasion of their privacy, they are likely to rebel; and there is a risk of parent-child conflicts escalating across the teenage years (Hawk *et al.*, 2009). However, in families where adolescent-parent relationships are sound and young people voluntarily disclose details about their leisure activities, such as places, peers and risk-taking, to their parents, they are also more willing to take parental advice and avoid engaging in too much mischief.

The way parents interact with their children has a strong impact on children's behaviour, well-being and success in later life. In the late 60s, Baumrind (1967) suggested from her research that there are three main parenting styles: authoritarian, authoritative and permissive. Authoritarian parenting is characterized by a high amount of control and very little warmth in the relationship; permissive parenting offers a lot of warmth, but lacks the control element; while authoritative parenting balances the two elements by providing both warmth and control. Later, Maccoby and Martin (1983) added a fourth style, that of 'neglectful' parenting, describing this style as lacking both warmth and control. Parenting styles have changed since Baumrind first described them. For instance, UK research by Shucksmith *et al.* (1995) found that 'permissive' parenting is now the style most frequently observed by teenagers.

In many different research studies, sometimes using different terminology, these parenting-style classifications have been used, showing clearly that they have a differential effect on young people's development. Parental influences can operate in an indirect way, for example by influencing young people's choice of friends. Durbin *et al.* (1993) found that:

- Teenagers who characterized their parents as *authoritative* were more likely to be oriented towards peer-groups that rewarded both adult- and peer-supported norms (e.g. 'brainy,' 'popular')
- Girls, and to a lesser extent boys, who characterized their parents as *uninvolved* (neglectful) were more likely to be oriented towards groups who did not endorse adult values (e.g. 'druggies')
- Boys who characterized their parents as *indulgent* (permissive) were more likely to be oriented towards groups with a 'fun–culture' orientation (e.g. 'party-goers').

Parents are not the only adults who have an impact on young people's lives. Philip and Hendry (1997) and Spencer (2007) have highlighted adult mentors' emotional connections with their adolescent protégés, and the ways these relationships provide 'safe' contexts of support in helping young people resolve problems, develop social strategies and manage their feelings more effectively. Mentors come in all types and roles, ranging from 'professionals' such as teachers, youth workers, sports and hobby coaches and leisure leaders to friends' parents and neighbours, older friends, and even the occasional charismatic figure who is a reformed offender. Mentoring relationships provide adolescents with adult role models in developing relational skills and interpersonal strategies.

◉ Friendships and peers

Close friendships are the rule during the teenage years. They develop by choice, by mutual preference of characteristics and collaborative activities, and, in a sense, allow young people a re-affirmation of their chosen identity whilst enabling them to perceive, understand and accept the values of their chosen group. Most teenage boys and girls engage in close same-sex friendships (e.g. Way, 2004; Way *et al.*, 2005); and peer-groups begin to replace the family as a social and value-oriented context for the developing adolescent. Friends are less likely than parents to coerce or criticize, and more likely to provide personal validity and share interests.

In close friendships, and in peer-groups, young people can learn different social skills from those they practise in the family context, though it is interesting to note that relationships with parents and peers are not mutually exclusive but rather mutually enhancing. Social skills learned in one setting help young people to become more effective in others, and good relationships with family members are highly associated with good peer relationships (DeGoede et al., 2009; Hsiu-Chen & Lempers, 2004; Krappman, 1996). There is often an unequal distribution of power in friendship-cliques and larger peer-groupings (Furman, 2001), even though they can be seen as 'horizontal' (equal) relationships compared with the hierarchical nature of relations with adults.

Some young people have difficulty in establishing out-of-school friendships because they lack confidence, the necessary social skills, or transport, and many feel awkward about meeting and joining established groups (Vernberg, 1990). Since young people can join many groups – school-based, community-based, those based on leisure activities such as sports teams or dance groups, casual pursuits – it is difficult for some to 'penetrate' these as newcomers because different groups have different norms and demand different roles. Then some adolescents have difficulty in establishing and maintaining autonomy within the peer-group, making them more susceptible to peer-influence, participating in activities that they would not necessarily have chosen for themselves, in order to impress their friends (Allen et al., 2006). In the long run, such lack of autonomy leads to declining popularity in the peer-group, and ultimately, to loneliness and feelings of depression (Hartrup & Stevens, 1999).

While some adolescents have to accept the role of 'follower', others are more influential and assume leadership positions. Admired traits such as friendliness, athletic ability, intelligence and popularity qualify the young person as a dominant member of an adolescent group. Nevertheless, qualities that are admired (such as looks, sense of humour, physical skills) may change from one phase of adolescence to the next (Hendry et al., 1993). Those in leadership positions tend to initiate new ideas and activities. Hence, to some extent, high-status members are role models for their peers in their ongoing construction of a personal identity. Importantly however, each individual influences, and is influenced by, the others in a group.

Not surprisingly, being popular is highly valued during adolescence. Popular individuals typically are friendly, sensitive and have a sense of humour. Other attributes that are important to adolescent popularity can include being 'smart', wearing fashionable clothes, following particular 'popular' musical styles or having sporting abilities (Lerner *et al.*, 1991; Wentzel & Erdley, 1993).

Being physically attractive is important to popularity. Attractive individuals benefit from a 'halo effect': They are assumed to have pleasing personalities, matching their physical appearance. One disadvantage of this halo effect may be that popular adolescents, assumed to be competent and self-reliant, find it harder to receive peer-support when they do need help. Furthermore, jealousy of very popular peers sometimes leads to accusations of their being 'stuck up' and conceited, so that adolescents can be popular and lonely at the same time. Hence, frequent contact with peers does not necessarily guarantee satisfying relationships (Savin-Williams & Berndt, 1990).

As we have seen in Chapter 3, biological and psychosocial changes in adolescence influence the nature of interpersonal relationships. Advancing cognitive and verbal abilities, in combination with physical and emotional growth, change the way adolescents view and interact with their peers. The improving ability to empathize and see the other person's viewpoint can enhance young people's understanding of how relationships work. Friendship groups offer the opportunity to expand knowledge, to experiment with new identities and to 'rehearse' styles of behaviour within a relatively safe context and away from the watchful eyes of adults (Coleman & Hendry, 1999). They provide young people with support and a platform to negotiate their independence. Friendships empower the individual and provide opportunities to rehearse social skills, such as co-operation, sharing and conflict-management (Newcomb & Bagwell, 1996), while improving strategies for using and detecting deception (Taylor & Gozna, 2011).

Friends and peers become increasingly important across the teen years, often at the expense of family involvement, and the term 'peer-pressure' has been widely used in the media to explain why well-behaved children turn into 'teenage monsters'. However, apart from the fact that the majority of young people remain relatively well-behaved across teenage years (as we noted in Chapter 3), recent research shows that peer-pressure is a wildly over-estimated factor in young people's behaviour.

To start with, it would be wrong to assume that all young people are equally susceptible to peer-influence. Most are somewhat susceptible to certain peer influences at certain times, but only a small minority of socially inept young people try to make friends by simply responding to what they perceive as the expectations of their peers (Allen *et al.*, 2006). Rather, adolescents are more likely to experience subtle pressures to conform to group values and standards ('gentle persuasion') than overt attempts to control or manipulate them (Shucksmith & Hendry, 1998). Further, this 'pressure' is more often aimed towards encouraging acceptable behaviour rather than norm-breaking, since young people mostly share the norms and values of their parents (Smollar & Youniss, 1989). Thus, when a non-deviant teenager meets a deviant peer, the influence they exert over each other can make them both either more or less deviant (Allen *et al.*, 2006). Using 'peer-pressure' as an explanation for adolescent behaviour underestimates the self-agency of young people and their ability to choose the companions with whom they want to socialize.

Young people are capable of staying away from situations that invite problem behaviour, of turning from peers who engage in deviant behaviours, or to assert themselves as 'non-participants' within a 'delinquescent' peer-group (Michell & West, 1996). Equally, young people who belong to, and participate in, a deviant peer-group have chosen that particular group because of shared interests and behaviours (i.e. peer-selection). For delinquent teenagers, with few social choices, attachment to a group with a similar label can be a consciously employed strategy to avoid alienation, to secure companionship of a sort, and to enhance personal and social power (Ungar, 2000). Even more positively, psychologists, youth- and social-workers have employed the possibilities of peer-influence to support young people, instead of blaming their misbehaviour on 'following the crowd'. Adolescents have been successfully trained to tutor their peers in school (Ryan *et al.*, 2004) to assist in anti-bullying programmes (Cowie & Hutson, 2005), to facilitate the transition to high school (Ellis *et al.*, 2009), and aid immigrants with cultural adjustment (Yeh *et al.*, 2007).

Crowds: A network of peers

Another phenomenon of adolescent social relationships is the 'crowd'. While friends gather in cliques and identify closely with one another's music taste, fashion style, sports team or political ideas, members of 'crowds' do not necessarily know one another and do not always choose the attributes with which they are associated (Thurlow, 2001). Some crowds function as style trend setters, imposing attributes on individual followers, such as a distinctive style of dressing and hairstyle like the Goths (the crowd 'uniform') that indicates their 'separateness' from other crowds (Brown *et al.*, 1994) and, in some cases, from adult society. They provide adolescents with opportunities to experiment with an identity while maintaining a sense of social belonging. The price for all this is pressure to conform and identify with the crowd's lifestyle (to some degree) by dress, personal appearance, musical tastes and leisure pursuits. However, adolescents make these choices in the knowledge that participation in different crowds will involve them in different specific behaviours (Shucksmith & Hendry, 1998).

However, there are also groups, which are reputation-based where 'outsiders' assign their label. Sometimes, these labels are positive (the 'sporties') or neutral (the 'class 9 kids') but more often, they serve to describe despised out-groups (the 'bad', the 'sad' and the 'not-cools who think they are cool') (Hendry *et al.*, 2002a; Thurlow, 2001). Young people readily assign such labels to groups in school though hardly ever classify themselves as a member of these crowds, usually referring to themselves as 'normal'. This is a typical example of discrimination against out-groups to enhance self-image and identity.

Communication and the Internet

Information technology has revolutionized the world, and created a learning environment for young people that no other generation before has experienced. Furthermore, the Internet has made frequent and daily contact with hundreds of 'friends' across the whole world a possibility. For the first time in human history, there is a context where young people show more competence and have more experience than the older generation. This ability empowers and liberates them from adult influence. Few parents can monitor or prevent what their offspring do on their computers. In fact, more often, it is adults begging teenagers for assistance in using electronic devices.

The media have been quick to point out a number of negative effects on the adolescent generation (Turow, 1999), and researchers have followed the media's lead. Greenfield and Yan (2006), for example, warn that the Internet has caused various societal concerns about privacy, security, pornography, Internet crime, the virtual community and intellectual property rights. Nie and Hillygus (2002a, 2002b) predicted that time spent on computers would leave less time for face-to-face social contacts. As a result, parents are extremely worried and ambivalent about their young people's Internet use. What empirical evidence is there to justify this moral panic?

The first studies looking at the influence of Internet use on well-being presented contradictory results. This was due to a lack of clarification of the term 'Internet use' – originally, researchers simply measured how many hours young people spent at their computers. When Internet use was differently categorized (for example, distinguishing between chatting, looking for information and leisurely surfing), results became clearer (Subrahmanyam & Lin, 2007).

Usually, it is socially competent adolescents who use the Internet as another vehicle for contacting friends and maintaining existing friendships (Valkenburg & Peter, 2007b). Such usage is associated with increased well-being (Bessière et al., 2008; Kraut et al., 2002). In the relatively few cases where the Internet is used by shy adolescents to make new contacts and chat with strangers, it is associated with a decrease in well-being (Valkenburg & Peter, 2007a, 2009).

The frequent use of electronic communication leads to the enhancement of 'best' friendships (Blais et al., 2008), which might be due to greater ease of self-disclosure in electronic communications (Valkenburg & Peter, 2007a, 2009). This may be of special importance for young men, who have some problems engaging in self-disclosure when communicating face-to-face (McNelles & Connolly, 1999), finding it easier online (Schouten et al., 2009).

Contrary to adult expectations, teenagers use the Internet mainly to communicate with offline friends through e-mail and instant messaging (Gross, 2004), continuing the gossiping and chatting about daily issues that occurred earlier in person. They do not often lie about their identity, and if so, they usually pretend to be older in order to access age-restricted sites. Pretending to be someone completely different than themselves is usually motivated by the desire to play a joke on online friends – there is no indication of online identity exploration.

A small group of young people spends time in chatrooms, where they have the opportunity to talk to strangers, and where the chat is public – that means everybody who logs on can follow the online discussions. This virtual world of mostly anonymous chat may offer a safer environment for exploring sensitive topics, for example, aspects of emerging sexuality, than the real world. Subrahmanyam *et al.* (2006) examined the online construction of sexuality in a large selection of conversations from monitored and unmonitored teen chatrooms. More than half the participants provided information about themselves that would have been obvious in face-to-face communications, such as gender and age. Participants who identified themselves as 'female' sent more *implicit* sexual communications while those who self-identified as 'male' sent more *explicit* sexual communications. However, fewer than 5 per cent of the content of chat messages consisted of sex-related topics and less than a third of participants engaged in erotic chat.

Social networking sites, such as Facebook and Myspace, open up yet another area of socializing behaviour that has not existed before, such as the ability to rekindle contact with long-lost friends, to maintain connections with very little effort, and to build up immense international networks. Some young people have more than a thousand 'friends' in their virtual networks, and, though they might not have personally met them all, they constitute a vast base of social resources for gaining information, organizing groups and engaging support, thus increasing their 'social capital' (Ellison *et al.*, 2007).

However, Internet use does not only support social connections. Engaging in activities such as writing blogs helps younger participants to explore and try out new identities, while older ones shape and express their existing identities on their personal home pages (Schmitt *et al.*, 2008). Engaging in chatting and instant messaging also teaches teenagers new ways of linguistic interaction. Merchant (2001) observed how they develop sophisticated and marketable skills in their rapidly written conversations, which combine features of face-to-face talk with explorations in interactive writing and the exchange of additional digital information, such as image files and web addresses. Merchant also emphasized the creativity used in inventing new words and abbreviations in cyber talk. In a study of Internet use over 16 months by urban teenagers from low-income families, Jackson *et al.* (2003) showed that the more frequently teenagers used the Internet at home, the better was their academic attainment in school.

Elements of the Internet that attract young people, such as anonymity, interactivity and connectivity, also enable online harassment and cyberbullying (e. g. Cassidy *et al.*, 2009), and the risk of sexual harassment by adults (Mitchell *et al.*, 2001). The availability of web pages and chatrooms can also encourage pathological behaviours such as self-injury, suicide and anorexia. However, the educational and psychosocial benefits far outweigh the potential dangers (Tynes, 2007), and information technology has come to stay, whether the adult generation approves or not.

Gender differences in peer relationships

Golombok and Fivush (1994) described the development of peer relations of girls and boys as follows: During the first years of primary school, boys and girls play separately. Girls have a best friend with whom they talk a lot and share small secrets. They also play, but games as such are not of great importance to them. If conflict arises, they end the game in order to regain harmony in the relationship. Boys, on the other hand, play in groups and do not often have a single best friend. They play competitive games with clear rules. If conflicts arise, they are resolved in order to continue the game. Boys do not have long conversations with their peers. If they talk, they talk about the game and its rules.

Thus, boys learn to negotiate, to cooperate with a group and to compete. By comparison, girls learn to communicate, to listen and to keep a relationship going. What both boys and girls do *not* learn, or to a much lesser degree, is to communicate across the gender divide. This has led to researchers talking about 'separate gender cultures' (Underwood, 2007), and to point out that because of the different friendship styles during childhood, young men and women find it difficult to communicate with each other in courtship and in the work place (Maccoby, 1998).

These gendered friendship patterns can be observed over the rest of the life course. Males seem to form friendships based on mutual interests and competition, while females are more interested in forming deeper relationships, characterized by self-disclosure, empathy and nurturance as well as anxiety over fear of rejection (Galambos *et al.*, 2004; Shucksmith & Hendry, 1998; Thurlow, 2001). While friendships are emotionally fulfilling for young women, this deep emotional engagement and empathy, and a reliance on close relationships for emotional well-being, makes them vulnerable to interpersonal stress and depression (Joiner *et al.*, 1999; Rudolph *et al.*, 2007).

Intimacy, as expressed in self-disclosure of feelings, fears and inner thoughts, is important for the development of close friendships in both genders, but it is easier for females to engage in it (Bank & Hansford, 2000; Fehr, 2004). In a climate of competition, it is not appropriate for a young man to confess fears and shortcomings to other men, and admitting to anxieties and pains is considered as effeminate in male culture (Pollack, 1998). Male adolescents are aware of their emotions within interpersonal relationships, but also of the 'macho' and homophobic attitudes within their peer-groups. Hence, they face a dilemma between their relational needs and the risk of peer-ridicule (Chu, 2004, 2005). The perceived pressure to develop masculine identities prevents a seeking of support from male friends and deters offering such support. Actually, discouraging any displays of physical or emotional pain in friends is seen as the most valuable help males can offer (Oransky & Marecek, 2009). Fortunately, many male adolescents have female friends, and if they do, they see their relationships with them as more interpersonally rewarding than those with male pals (McDougall & Hymel, 2007; Thomas & Dauburan, 2001). Way (2011) argues that during early and middle adolescence, boys do display intimacy and shared feelings, but that they lose these friendships when they grow into men, preferring to become lonely and isolated than to be considered unmanly. Homophobia and the adoption of hyper-masculine values affects not only friendship groups, it has a profound impact on school achievement, too, as we will see in the next section.

School as a context for relationships

The University of Cambridge did not allow women full membership until 1947, and, until 1970, fewer than 20 per cent of all students enrolled were female. In the last decades, though, this has changed. Today, the majority of students – at Cambridge and elsewhere – are female. Formerly male-dominated professions in medicine, law and architecture are now over-populated by women; and girls outperform boys every year in most areas of education. A meta-analysis of data from 69 nations showed that, even in mathematics, there are no longer significant achievement differences between the genders (Lindberg *et al.*, 2010). Given that, only half a century ago, many parents thought that prolonged education was unnecessary for girls, this is a remarkable achievement.

We can propose that girls matching boys in school achievement and exam results is because of changing values in society and increasing gender equality – but why do they actually outperform them? One explanation for this phenomenon is the adherence of some male adolescents to hyper-masculine values. Academic success and *being seen* to make efforts to learn are not viewed as either 'manly' or 'cool'. In mid-adolescence, boys rate academically achieving men negatively (Green, 2005), find reading to be a 'girlish' activity (Millard, 1997), associate school work with being gay and give high status to peers who oppose teachers' rules and classroom learning (Frosh *et al.*, 2002). Consequently, they are by far more disruptive than girls in school (Esturgó-Deu & Sala-Roca, 2010). Indeed, it is the boys who give strongest support to traditional gender roles who are least successful in school, irrespective of how intelligent they are (Whitehead, 2003). Ironically, their 'macho' values allow many girls a head start towards future career achievements.

Being teased as 'a sissy', or for not being manly enough, is only one of the negative features of school peer-relationships. Peer-to-peer bullying occurs regularly, and most children will experience bullying at some time in their school career, either as bully, victim, both bully and victim, or witness. Large-scale international surveys record victimization rates of between 9 and 32 per cent (Stassen Berger, 2007). However, there are many more roles involved in bullying than being an active perpetrator: Co-conspirators, defenders, bystanders (Salmivalli *et al.*, 1996).

Broadly, two types of bullies exist: One with poor social skills, who finds it difficult to maintain normal friendships; and one with high social competence, using social skills to manipulate others (Sutton *et al.*, 1999; Vaillancourt *et al.*, 2003). Gender differences are apparent: Boys are more likely to be involved in physical bullying, and girls in verbal and relational bullying (James, 2010). Most often, bullies are older, stronger, tougher and more aggressive than their victims (Schäfer, 2004; Smith, 2004b).

The most common form of bullying is verbal abuse, name-calling and 'whisper-campaigns' aimed at destroying peer-relationships by exclusion and rumour (Tapper & Boulton, 2005). A new variant, 'cyber-bullying', involves using the Internet, e-mail and mobile phones to send round offensive images and defamations (Dehue *et al.*, 2008).

Victims often lack self-esteem, self-assertiveness and social skills (Scheithauer *et al.*, 2006; Wolke & Samara, 2004). Being bullied lowers their self-esteem further, and, as 'victim', their status in the peer-group is lowered, preventing them from gaining peer-support for protection (Goldbaum *et al.*, 2003; Schwartz *et al.*, 2000). Yet, peers can be a source of support in threatening social situations, and peer-based intervention strategies, now widely used in Britain, appear to be highly effective (e.g. Cowie & Hutson, 2005).

While adolescents enter school with differing needs and abilities, the teaching emphasis is on cognitive skills. Classroom groupings are usually arranged by chronological age together with some 'streaming' by ability in key subjects such as English and Maths. There is little evidence of individually devised learning programmes. Unfortunately, for those who miss the basics, this also means cumulative disadvantages. As Andersen (1995, p. 113) pointed out:

> School is good for many students, but school is also bad for too many students.

This has been echoed by Oldman (1994), who suggested that school is disliked so much by many children that they 'vote with their feet' and play truant. School truancy rates are at a record high, despite the Government's prosecuting 9500 parents and fining thousands more because their children regularly play truant from school. Some 67,290 pupils truanted every day in 2008, 2000 more than the previous year (Department for Children, 2008). It is possible that some pupils play truant because they are bored by what is on offer academically, some because of poor relations with teachers, and others because they, as we have seen earlier, absent themselves to avoid bullying.

To be fair to the secondary schooling system in the UK, authoritarian educational and teaching styles are limited, the social ethos has become friendlier and 'safer', and independence of pupils' learning is an emphasized goal. Teachers try to create learning situations which demand independent and individual decisions from pupils, such as weekly planning of their own learning programmes, project work, and a selection of optional courses. However, these adaptations do not fulfil, indeed may conflict with, the need to provide more pupils with learning experiences that realistically match their capabilities.

This can lead to clashes between schools' requirements, young people's values and resistance behaviours, parents' expectations and employers' demands. Furthermore, social behaviours learned in the family and in leisure time may not match that which is required by the school. Adolescents are not quiescent and do not obey authority figures, such as teachers, just because of their formal social position. Respect has to be earned, and motivation for learning has to be created, not enforced. A focus on reproduction of knowledge, testing and certification is encouraged by various macro-social forces, curbing the natural desire to seek information, reconstruct arguments and challenge ideas. Instead, the emphasis on adult-constructed incentives, such as grades, prestige, competition and national curriculum tests (SATS), leaves little room for the development of self-organizing skills (Bjørgen, 2001; Kohn, 2000). Young people themselves believe that skills gained through the experiences of living, even in difficult circumstances, are generally more relevant to growing up than formal academic learning (Barry, 2001).

Another factor that affects school achievement and feelings of well-being within the school environment is social background. Much of the contents of lessons and prevailing school values are build on a middle-class ethos, which often alienates and excludes working class teenagers. In Britain today, the postcode of a pupil's home address is still one of the best predictors of school success or failure (Webber & Butler, 2007).

Particularly for children from deprived areas, the desire 'to be good at something' can be extremely important in creating positive changes for their future lives (Kloep *et al.*, 2010). As adolescents themselves stated, the 'something' can be any talent, from academic skills to musical, artistic or sporting ability. The young person does not have to be outstandingly gifted – just able to demonstrate a degree of self-competence. This achievement can strengthen their self-efficacy by giving them enhanced self-perceptions, status in the peer-group, the attention of possible adult mentors, goals to aspire to, and convincing reasons for 'staying out of trouble'.

◉ Leisure transitions and transformations

The leisure sector of the teenager's life is a valuable setting for learning social skills and strategies and developing relational competencies in a variety of forms.

Adolescents have become high-level home consumers of media products and materials, such as television programmes and films, DVDs, music, computer games, comics, magazines and the Internet. These opportunities, together with a decrease of natural outdoor areas available for gatherings and games, has led to a transformation of young people's leisure over the last few decades. Much more of it is now taking place indoors (Zinnecker, 1990). 'At home' can mean solitary leisure, but not necessarily so. Often computer games are played with friends, and LAN parties, where large groups of young people meet to connect their computers to play games, are very popular. Even when alone, young people stay connected through e-mail, chatlines and mobile phones. For example, adolescents make and receive an average of 18 phone calls a day (Weisskirch, 2008), and that does not include text messages. Mobile phones are so important in young people's lives today that they have become status symbols, and for many, getting a phone is a 'rite of passage' into adolescence (Blair & Fletcher, 2011). This is not only because 'everyone else has got one' but because it allows young people to stay in touch regularly with friends and creates a way of increasing autonomy of which parents approve: Parents are more relaxed about curfew rules and the whereabouts of their children if they know that they can contact them. However, depending on parental mobile phone literacy, this sometimes comes at the cost of enhanced parental monitoring, as they can now check where their offspring are, whom they have called (seen on itemized bills), and even read their old incoming and outgoing text messages (Blair & Fletcher, 2011). In other words, young people exchange the softening of parental rules for potential intrusion into their lives in any context (Williams & Williams, 2005), at the same time adding a security net to their attempts for autonomy, as parents are now available wherever they go (Ling, 2003).

Home-based leisure occupies young people throughout adolescence. The European study by Flammer *et al.* (1999) showed that watching television and listening to music are the most common leisure activities for teenagers in all countries.

Regarding 'out-of-the-house' activities, a series of leisure transitions can be observed (Hendry *et al.*, 1998). In the early adolescent years, young people associate with a range of adult-led organizations and activities, such as Brownies, Scouts, choirs, dance groups and sports clubs. Dworkin *et al.* (2003) have shown that in organized youth activities, young people develop personal skills such as learning to set goals and manage time, and acquire strategies for the regulation of emotions. Their interpersonal experiences include acquiring new peer-relationships and knowledge, developing group social skills such as taking responsibility, working together as a team, and developing valuable relations with adults.

However, there are large individual differences regarding the relationship between leisure and social adjustment. In one American study, Metzger *et al.* (2009) examined patterns of involvement in organized activities and their associations with academic achievement, problem behaviours and perceived adult support in a sample of urban early adolescents. The outcomes suggested that, while some organized activities are generally associated with more positive outcomes, those involved in a school-based or sports-related group had the highest levels of delinquency, drug use and school exclusions – once again showing that there are no simple recipes for success in fostering young people's development. Moreover, there is a general feeling among many young people, as they progress across the teenage years, that organized activities and clubs become too adult-dominated to appeal to them.

Between 13 and 15 years, many young people, especially girls, drop out of organized activities (Flammer *et al.*, 1999) and move more exclusively towards the peer group and informal leisure pursuits. Generally, many urban venues serve as popular meeting points for adolescent groups: Shopping malls, amusement arcades, street corners or public parks may serve as convenient assembly points (Fisher, 1995). In such settings, adolescents spend more time simply talking to peers than in pursuing any other leisure pursuit. 'Fooling around' and laughing may seem aimless and pointless to an outsider, yet are perceived as very fulfilling pastime (Williams & Thurlow, 2005). Typically, adults are not present except as peripheral background figures, and the purpose is to begin discussing and rehearsing some of the behaviours and social skills and strategies necessary for young people's transitions to various adult leisure contexts.

Having left youth clubs where adults had organized leisure activities, but not being allowed into many adult leisure venues, adolescents feel at a loss, not knowing what to do in their free time. This is partly because they have never learned to organize their own leisure time. After years of adult guidance, they lack initiative, creativity and courage to arrange group activities for themselves, leading to the widespread complaint that there is 'nothing to do' (Kloep & Hendry, 2003). This feeling is even more exacerbated for those who live in rural areas, as the following quote from a 15-year-old girl illustrates (Hendry *et al.*, 2002b):

> I think of all these weekends that have been spent doing absolutely nothing . . . What is there to do? The weekends have all the same pattern. Go down to the youth club, talk some shit, go up and down the main road. Is that what life is about? I understand exactly why more and more get drunk during the weekend!

This expression of 'leisure boredom' is so common that Caldwell and her colleagues (Caldwell *et al.*, 1999) suggest that it has become a 'resistance response' to adult influence and, as such, a routine aspect of adolescent culture. This is of some concern, as experiences of boredom seem to impede growth (Hunter & Csikszentmihalyi, 2003), while engagement in their own lives and the development of leisure interests facilitate young people's positive development (Caldwell *et al.*, 2004; Sharp *et al.*, 2006).

Finally, towards the end of adolescence, young people enter the commercial world of adult leisure, including cinemas, theatres, discos, pubs and fitness clubs. Available cash and employment opportunities, family commitments, young people's general links with adult society and cultural values all play their part in this. For example, young women appear to make earlier transitions to commercial leisure settings, perhaps in concert with older boy friends, while working-class boys are more likely to exit from adult-led activities earlier than their middle-class peers are, perhaps because of a clash of values and interests (Coleman & Hendry, 1999). In the last two decades there has been a trend towards engaging in commercial activities at a much younger age than previously (Hendry & Kloep, 2006).

Thus, in this section we have seen that the leisure sphere provides a series of learning contexts to enhance the developing adolescent's social competencies. Nevertheless, as we have suggested, leisure activities may have greater learning potential than has been realized. There can be opportunities to help young people to 'be good at something', and to aid them to become effective self-agents in extending their leisure skills in ways that have both present and future advantages.

Civic participation and citizenship

Research reveals a declining interest in politics among young people, a high rate of abstentions from voting in elections in the UK (Stewart & Vaitilingam, 2004) and general political disengagement (Snell, 2010). In a study by social scientists from the Universities of Cambridge and London (Anonymous, 2004), almost half of the teenagers questioned knew little about the workings of democracy. Comparing results with similar surveys undertaken in 1976, a worrying lack of knowledge and apathy towards the basic facts of parliamentary democracy and the European Union was shown. More than half said they were 'not much interested in politics'.

Nevertheless, in spite of an obvious lack of interest in party politics, how involved are young people in community activities? Youniss and Yakes' (1997) answer to this question was an unequivocally positive one. If given the chance, youths are involved in all kinds of community service, though there are large individual differences: Some young people are heavily involved, other do not care at all. Roker *et al.* (1999) looked at those who are volunteers and campaigners. Regular members of voluntary groups, such as first aiders for the Red Cross, volunteer youth workers, working for Oxfam or the National Trust, often joined because of friends or family, or because they perceived the experiences gained as being useful for their planned future careers. They are active campaigners, give to charities and are positive in their views of politics and their ability to create societal change through political action. Factors perceived as discouraging involvement include the lack of payment and the poor public image of such organizations; while campaigners for pressure groups such as Greenpeace or Amnesty International mention their fear of getting into trouble with the police as discouraging factors.

Adolescents whose parents are engaged in politics or community affairs are more likely to become involved, and Glanville (1999) showed that extracurricular activities, such as school government by pupils, positively predict political involvement in early adulthood. Metzger (2007) found that adolescents from more-educated households are more involved in activities than those from less-educated families, and young women more often involved than young men, though sometimes females are prevented by their parents from translating their political ideals into action (Gordon, 2008).

Thus, it seems as if young people are not unwilling to contribute to their community. But are adults willing to allow them? There are some possible 'barriers' young people face in being accepted as equal participating partners in community affairs. One consequence of adult restrictions on young people's independence and initiative is that they are deprived of many rights of citizenship. As Qvortrup and Christoffersen (1991) wrote:

> First of all, the law of majority not only gives rights to those who have reached the age of 18: it also obviously deprives those under 18 of the same rights... Children are explicitly excluded from participating in democracy by having no right to vote. They may exert freedom of speech; but their access to all types of written and spoken expression is limited, since censorship is practised towards them in a number of cases. Children's freedom to organise is nowhere directly prohibited, but is limited in the sense that they cannot as minors provide the necessary signatures.... We must, of course, acknowledge the protectionist background for the exclusion of children from

a number of rights. Yet it is not always clear whether it is children or adult society, which is the primary object of protection.

The situation does not allow young people to exercise much self-agency or to participate in decision-making even at the local community level. Sixteen-year-olds in Britain, regarded as old enough to work, marry, pay taxes and die as soldiers, cannot vote. Yet there is no evidence to prove that they are less informed about political matters than older citizens. Hooghe and Wilkenfeld (2008) examined and compared political attitudes in people aged 14, 18, and 19–30 in eight European countries. Their analysis suggests that national patterns in political trust and attitudes are already well established by the age of 14 years. Moreover, Morrissey and Werner-Wilson (2005) showed that pro-social behaviour is highly associated with being given opportunities to participate socially and politically. In other words, the lack of adolescent social participation is not so much due to a lack of interest from their side, but by the unwillingness of adult society. At least, that was the conviction of one 15-year-old young woman (Kloep, 1998):

> Our generation will be a good generation that will be able to rule this country. We care for the environment, and we have experienced an economic crisis, so we know how difficult it can be to be without a job. We are an international generation that knows how to behave in other countries and to be good representatives for our country . . . There are many young people who are active in political organisations and today's youth is engaged in many activities. I just think it is a pity that adults do not listen to us, because we have many good opinions.

Summary

In this chapter, we looked at young people's relationships within the family, before turning our attention to their relationships with close friends and with the various peer-networks they encounter. We reflected on the qualities necessary for acceptance to the peer group and the social skills and strategies acquired within peer activities. Then, we considered the use of the Internet by teenagers in communicating with one another, and the benefits and risks of Internet usage.

We examined gender differences in peer relationships and noted that different gender-styles have their genesis in childhood play-patterns.

We then viewed school as a context for friendships, and outlined aspects of various perspectives on bullying. We also commented briefly on ways the curriculum might become more relevant to young people's needs.

We analysed leisure transitions and transformations, offering general reasons why young people progress from adult-organized activities through casual peer-centred pursuits to commercial adult leisure. Finally, we looked at young people's political community participation and citizenship.

◉ Further reading

Coleman, J. C. (2010) *The nature of adolescence*. 4th Edition. Hove: Psychology Press. This provides comprehensive, up-to-date coverage of European and North American research on adolescence.

Chapter 5

From Teenagers to Early Adults

Summary

In this chapter on the transition to early adulthood we describe:
- De-standardization of the life course
- Emerging adulthood: A new stage in the life course?
- A critical view: Do we need stages?
- Adult children, parents and leaving home
- Dating, romance and sexual relationships
- Young adults, changing society and social and economic uncertainties.

Introduction: Disappearing age-boundaries

We have seen in the previous chapter that postmodern society, with its rapid changes in norms and values, is making it difficult for young people to identify with adult role models and to adapt to differing, sometimes conflicting, societal values. No longer are there age-bound signposts or clear developmental tasks for young people to achieve, as Havighurst (1953) postulated many years ago. Now it is possible to be a mother at 16 or 60, hold down a responsible job in one's teens, become a university student at 30 or be a middle-aged bachelor of 40 living in the parental home. Which one of these has, in fact, reached full adult status? It is clear that transitions and transformations, rather than chronological age, now determine how we progress developmentally across the lifespan.

Sociologists have called this phenomenon the 'de-standardization of the life course', meaning that there are no expectations as to when or whether individuals should do certain things at certain times in their life. Hence, there are no longer clear boundaries between different phases of the life course. Once the few legal markers, such as the right to vote, smoke, drink alcohol, have sexual relations or enter military service, are reached, there are no markers left to distinguish 'adulthood'. Unlike the teenage years, after the very obvious and significant maturational changes, early adulthood is a relatively quiet time biologically, though the individual continues to grow in strength and power until full physical maturation is reached.

Certain social changes are noteworthy. Only some decades ago, the average age for entering marriage was late teens or early twenties. Now, in Western industrialized cultures, the average age for marriage is closer to 30 years (Douglass, 2005, 2007). The age of entering parenthood has increased in parallel to the rising age for marriage. Premarital sex is now widely accepted, as is cohabitation before marriage in the countries of northern Europe and North America. Fifty-years ago, young women were somewhat restricted to future roles as wives and mothers, struggling for education and for significant positions within the workforce, but now, internationally, young women exceed young men in educational attainment (Coleman & Brooks, 2009). Education has become more important than ever as the economy has shifted from a manufacturing base to a focus on information, technology and client services.

There is some evidence that early adults are less happy nowadays than they were generations ago. Data from birth cohort studies in the UK (Stewart & Vaitilingam, 2004) and the USA (Kasen et al., 2000) show that symptoms of depression and anxiety at age 24 have doubled from the cohort born in 1958 to the cohort born in 1970. There is also a huge increase in reported unhappy relationships from one cohort to the other, as well as a decline in social attachments to the community and interest in politics, with a doubling of abstention from voting in elections.

While the pathways to adulthood were relatively predictable for young people in earlier times, dependent on their gender and social class, young people today have many more options. Modern society offers them flexibility and variety: To marry or not marry, to live in a partnership with a same-sex or opposite-sex partner, to have children as a teenager, in mid-life or not at all, to have a job first and a higher education later or the other way round, to live in a town or in the countryside or abroad. Clearly, none of the stage theories described in Chapter 1 can effectively account for the life transitions of those between 18 and 30 years in modern societies. There is a need for a new approach, and we will now explore two such attempts, one stemming from traditional stage theories and one using an ecological approach.

Emerging adulthood: A new stage?

Even though he was not the first to observe the changing face of young adulthood, Jeffrey Arnett has been the most influential researcher in drawing attention to this developmental stage. In 2000 he introduced the concept of '*emerging adulthood*', arguing that there is a new age-stage between adolescence and adulthood in response to recent societal shifts.

Prior to Arnett's work, several developmental stage theories identified the age period of emerging adulthood and distinguished it from both adolescence and adulthood. For instance, Erikson's theory (1950) posited adjoining stages, adolescence (stage 5) and young adulthood (stage 6), during which individuals encountered related tasks: identity vs identity confusion and intimacy vs isolation. In this developmental framework, individuals between 19 and 34 years are universally oriented to the resolution of self in relation to others (intimacy) and society. Also, Levinson's work highlights the transitional nature of the young adult years, noting that, for some, the twenties involved a tension that was resolved by making commitments to adult roles. However, Arnett argues, none of these researchers pinpointed clearly – and actually, could not do so, because the phenomenon did not exist at the time they published their theories – that the age-stage between 18 and 29 years of age has now distinctive characteristics that make it clearly different from adolescence and adulthood, though there may be some overlap at both ends of the stage.

Based mainly on interviews with young people in this age-range, he concluded that there are five principles that distinguish this period:

It is the age of '*feeling inbetween*'. Young people themselves cannot determine whether they have reached adulthood or not. In both interviews and surveys, the most prominent answer is 'in some ways yes, in some ways no' (Arnett, 2001, 2004). This means identity development is not completed, because the young person has yet to experience some of the events that define the sense of 'who am I', such as employment or leaving home, and has no commitment in terms of career, family or values. In Marcia's terms (see Chapter 3), in many aspects, emerging adults are still in the period of moratorium. To illustrate this, Arnett in his case studies relates that many young people tell him that they chose temporary work (so-called Mc-jobs), alternating with long trips abroad, and had a strong desire to delay the commitments of starting a family into the not-too-distant future.

Not knowing who one is and who one will become is somewhat stressful, and demands psychological energy for attempts to try out and evaluate different identities. This seems to be one of the most important tasks of this age phase, and, according to Arnett, young people try hard to solve it. So hard, that they do not have much energy left for other responsibilities and concerns. Thus, it is a *time of self-focus*, devoted to introspection and reflection.

As we have outlined above, the life course is now de-standardized, and there are no clearcut pathways through it. According to Arnett, this allows young people to choose between a whole variety of life options. They can select priorities, such as education, career or family, and within these they can opt for many variations. Furthermore, most of the choices they make are reversible: University subjects can be changed or abandoned, romantic partners are inter-changeable, and careers can be started and left at any time. Therefore, this is *the age of possibilities*, where the world is open and promising, and the young person, free from parental tutelage and societal expectations, has the freedom to choose, experiment and defer decisions and commitments. In Arnett's terms, this variety of choices leads to 'many different emerging adulthoods' (Arnett *et al.*, 2011). This description deviates somewhat from basic ideas inherent in previous stage theories, where lifestyle is much the same for all individuals in a certain age-group.

Box 5.1: Averaging the rainbow?

Many descriptive quantitative statistics use 'means' (i.e. averages) in presenting results. This is fine as far as it goes. We get a picture of the group's average. But is this good enough? Might this mask information we really need to know? The simple answer to the first questions is: 'No', and to the second: 'Yes'!

Let us present an example, which is so good we wish we had thought of it first, but we did not. So, here goes: Think of a rainbow and guess what its average colour is. You are right, you are a genius; the answer is 'Grey'! Does that colour truly represent what a rainbow *is*? How can we somehow show the myriad of colours and shade that makes up what we see when a rainbow appears? Maybe it is better to leave the rainbow alone and not average it?

If we now consider an example from developmental psychology, we might want to know possible differences between men and women in driving a golf ball for distance. Okay, let us test them and calculate means for both genders. Well, we will find the obvious – that, on average, men do better.

But wait a minute: Remember the rainbow. Well done, do we not need more information: Maybe golf handicap has an influence? Being a professional or amateur player? Playing experience? Being a club member? If we do that, we will find that there are actually many women who outdrive men by many, many metres.

To use another example: You want to measure how happy people are with a training programme in which they recently participated. You let them rate their degree of satisfaction on a scale of 1–5, and you calculate an average rating of 3. Does that mean that they all were moderately happy? It might. But it might also mean that half of the group absolutely loved the programme (and gave a rating of 5), while the other half hated it (and gave a rating of 1). In this example, nobody was moderately happy!

Most statistical procedures used in research are based on averages, which means, that often the results do not apply to all participants in the study. These individual variations are usually ignored, or treated as 'error variance' in the data. Hence, it is easy to see that this affects the interpretation of results quite substantially.

The key point is: What we should do more often is to disaggregate data-sets, have a more person-oriented perspective, and sometimes direct our attention to the exceptions rather than to the averages. Or, to really grasp the nuances of the colours of the rainbow, try not to capture them in numbers at all! (see Box 6.1 on Qualitative research).

While having many options to choose from, the sparcity of guidelines or role models to steer the young person through the postmodern jungle of ever-changing opportunities might be a liberating experience, but it can also be a frightening one. Any choice made might be the wrong choice; any commitment chosen might exclude other possibilities. So the greater freedom and choice available to today's young people, compared with any previous generation, brings with it a loss of security, certainty and guidance. So, Arnett further describes this age-stage as the *time of insecurity*. For example, Galambos *et al.* (2006) found that 'being married' and 'having fewer months in unemployment' are powerful predictors of well-being in young adults. This data implies that those who have already made their choices and have commitments are more contented than their age-peers who are still exploring and experimenting. In addition, regarding oneself as an adult as opposed to an *emerging* adult is related to a healthier lifestyle (Blinn–Pike *et al.*, 2008), a lower incidence of depression and a higher sense of identity (Nelson & McNamara Barry, 2005) and coherence (Luyckx *et al.*, 2008). Twenge (2006, p. 216) describes the reasons for·these feelings of insecurity as follows:

> One of the strangest things about modern life is the expectation that we will stand alone, negotiating breakups, moves, divorces, and all manner of heartbreak that previous generations were careful to avoid. This may be the key to the low rate of depression among older generations: despite all the deprivations and war they experienced, they could always count on each other. People had strong feelings of community; they knew the same people all their lives; and they married young and stayed married. It may not have been exciting, and it stymied the dreams of many, but it was a stable life that avoided the melancholy that is so common now.

To summarize what has been presented so far: There is no doubt that life for the age-group between 18 and 29 years of age looks very different today than it did just a few decades ago. It is equally obvious that the stage theories described in Chapter 1 are no longer sufficiently accurate for describing this phase of the life course because of ever-changing social conditions. As a solution to this, Arnett has proposed inserting a new life stage, 'emerging adulthood', into the existing theories. This stage is characterized by feelings of being 'in-between', having high self-focus, a range of life options, and high insecurity.

The critics: Do we need stages?

While nobody denies that the descriptions that Arnett offers about 18–29-year-olds is largely accurate for a number of young people, some theorists dispute that it is necessary to invent a new stage in the lifespan to explain young adulthood. They argue that emerging adulthood, as other stages, is not universal: It does not occur for *all* young people in *all* cultures. Furthermore, they insist that development depends upon the cultural contexts in which young people live, the social institutions they encounter, and the normative and non-normative shifts they experience (Bynner, 2005; Côté, 2000; Ford & Lerner, 1992; Heinz & Marshall, 2003; Hendry & Kloep, 2002). Cross-cultural studies and studies of ethnic minority groups suggest that a stage theory of emerging adulthood does not adequately cater for intra-individual and cross-cultural differences (Lloyd *et al.*, 2006). In many countries, young people, particularly women in rural areas, are granted no moratorium for identity exploration, but glide quickly from childhood into adulthood. Human beings develop by meeting and coping with a myriad of life challenges – and not by moving through age-bound stages.

To illustrate this, we interviewed a group of young people between 16 and 20 years from the Welsh valleys about their daily life, and their future plans (Hendry & Kloep, 2010). Deliberately, none of these young people selected were university students, since Arnett has been criticized for formulating his theory mainly on the basis of data collected from students. We identified at least three different transitional pathways for these young people, with significant individual differences within these broad groupings.

There were those who still live at home: they can afford to seek new opportunities, delay in choosing a career, 'have fun' and not feel fully adult. Though some of them complain about too much parental interference, they are clearly happy to stay at home and enjoy the advantages of dependent living and parental support. This group most closely resembles Arnett's description of early adults.

Another group also *seems* to fit into the description of emerging adults, as they also continue to live at home and work in temporary jobs, if they work at all. However, unlike the first group, they do not *choose* this lifestyle; rather they are forced into it through a lack of personal resources, skills and opportunities. As a consequence, for them the world does not offer an array of choices, and they feel bitter and hopeless about this. Rather than being in 'emerging adulthood', they are in a state of 'prevented adulthood'! It is not an abundance of options, but rather a complete lack of them, which describes this group's lifestyle and their state of 'developmental stagnation'. As Côté and Bynner (2008) have reasoned, exclusion processes in education and the workplace exist which prevent young people in certain socio-economic and geographic situations from enabling developmental transitions.

Very different from both these groups is one containing individuals who display adult maturity at an early age. They perceive that they have matured through experiences such as caring for ill parents, divorce, having to look after younger siblings or their own children, holding down a responsible job or being forced to become financially independent because their parents cannot afford to support them. The majority of these young people mention that leaving school and entering full-time employment was a major turning point in their transition to adulthood. None describes themselves as 'feeling in-between' or 'shying away from responsibilities', and they have all made definite commitments in their lives, though all of them, being under 20 years of age, are only moving into the age-range Arnett has denoted as emerging adulthood.

If one combines all the young people in Western industrialized societies whose transition to adulthood varies from Arnett's 'emerging adults' with the near 1.5 billion young people from developing countries living under completely different social and economic conditions (Lloyd et al., 2005), then there remain relatively few for whom this new life stage is actually available, viable and relevant. Describing all others as 'off-track' and 'non-normative' as Arnett does (Arnett et al., 2011, p. 173) is a stigmatization, not an explanation. For this reason, researchers who support the ecological approaches outlined in Chapter 2 prefer to investigate the individual life circumstances of young people to find out what obstructs and what facilitates the transitions to adulthood, trying to explain developmental variability instead of ignoring it by only concentrating on those who are perceived to be 'normal' (Fischer & Bidell, 1998).

◉ The push for independence

Leaving the nest

As many researchers have pointed out, one of the most important tasks on the route to adulthood is gaining independence from one's parents. Most of the theories discussed in Chapter 1 see this as a task to be accomplished during the late teens and early twenties. Nowadays, for many, due to prolonged education, rising house prices and youth unemployment, the decision about leaving the parental home occurs at a much later age

(Goldscheider & Goldscheider, 1999). Depending on traditions, national policies and socio-economic status, there are great variations in this transition across Europe. In Denmark, for example, half the young men leave home before they are 22, and they do so mainly to live alone. By contrast, in Italy, half are still living with their parents when they are 30, and will not leave unless moving in with a partner (Iacovou, 2001). In the UK, the number of young people under the age of 34 still living at home has been increasing over the last three decades (Office for National Statistics, 2010).

It is not particularly unusual that socio-economic factors have a strong influence on family patterns. In agricultural societies, for example, it has always made sense for children to remain at home after reaching adulthood, as they did in pre-industrialized Britain (Ruggles, 2010) and in rural areas of contemporary India (Ram & Wong, 1994) and Africa (Silverstein, 1984). However, while the average age of leaving home was 28 years for males and 25 for females in the early nineteenth century, more than half of the children under 19 (some being under ten) were working in service away from home (Schürer, 2003). This illustrates that there was never a time or a place where an exact age could be allocated as 'the right time' for leaving home. The task of becoming independent from parents has been, and is, tackled by young people anywhere between 14 and 30 years of age depending on personal circumstances.

Autonomy

Becoming independent from parents has many dimensions. First of all, there is the process of reaching emotional autonomy (Steinberg & Silverberg, 1986), often an issue in early to middle adolescence. Then, there is the ongoing conflict of gaining more and more behavioural autonomy, which, in turn, is closely related to the possibilities of gaining economic independence. We will examine these issues and related topics in this section.

From a psychoanalytic perspective, Blos (1962) described the development of emotional autonomy as a 'second individuation process' towards adult independence. He called this the 'second' individuation process because he assumed that the first one occurs when babies make the transition towards becoming self-reliant toddlers and discover that they exist as individuals independently from their care-giver. Later, in adolescence, they come to understand that they are also emotionally separate from their parents, and that they can possess their own feelings that do not necessarily coincide with their parents' emotions. Both transitions contain common elements: Psychological changes that enable maturation, increased vulnerability of personality, and, should the transition be fraught with difficulties, then it can be followed by a period of psychopathology. For psychoanalysts, 'disengagement' is a key aspect of the process. In childhood this 'separation' from dependency requires the child to internalize the loved one (i.e. the mother), whereas, in adolescence, the individual needs to loosen earlier childhood ties, give up the internalized figure and search for love objects outside the family.

Another important component is 'regression' – a manifestation of behaviour more appropriate to earlier developmental stages. Hence, a breaking of childhood emotional attachments can only be achieved by a re-activation of child-like emotions and patterns of behaviour:

> The adolescent has to come into emotional contact with passions of his infancy and early childhood . . . only then can the past fade into conscious and unconscious memories. . . . '
>
> (Blos, 1967, p. 178).

According to psychoanalysts, ambivalence accounts for much that is misunderstood about teenage behaviour: There is emotional instability in relationships, contradictions in thoughts and feelings, fluctuations between loving and hating, acceptance and rejection, illogical shifts in reactions, uncertainty and self-doubt, the demand for freedom coupled with retreats to almost child-like dependence. These swings of mood and behaviour lead to demonstrations of rebellion and non-conformity; some caused by ambivalent ways of relating, others as part of an extended disengagement process. Blos has conceptualized the idea of 'object and affect hunger' – a need for intense emotional states including delinquency, drug use, mystical experiences and short-lived but intense relationships – to explain the adolescent's way of coping with inner emptiness (compare this view with the discussion of 'storm and stress' in Chapter 3!). There is a need to behave 'just for kicks' to combat depression and loneliness during the separation process. Blos believes that 'object' and 'affect' hunger can to some extent be alleviated within the teenage peer-group, where all the essential feelings for individual growth can be experienced – stimulation, empathy, belongingness, role-playing, identification, and sharing anxieties and guilt.

Scholars who research human development more from an ecological perspective see the emergence of emotional autonomy as a process evolving from changing interactions with parents. By arguing with parents and testing ideas learned in other micro-systems (such as from peers or at school), both young people and their parents develop a new image of themselves and of each other, and thus a changed, more symmetrical and reciprocal relationship is created (Collins & Steinberg, 2006). Conflicts such as these provide the challenge for both parents and adolescents to trigger change and development (Kunnen, 2006). Tanner (2006) calls this process 're-centring', describing it as a shift from parent regulation to self-regulation.

Adolescents have to accept that their parents are not as omnipotent as they once thought, but that they have their faults and weaknesses, which can be disappointing to the teenager. At times parents can be seen as 'embarrassing', and others fulfil the role of idealized 'hero-figure' – celebrities, peers and romantic partners. Eventually, parents are 'forgiven for not being perfect' and accepted as 'normal' (Smollar & Youniss, 1989). Parents have also to adapt to changing roles and power-shifts, and to '... come to grips with the fact that adolescents are not always wrong, and actually can make mature, reasonable decisions' (Williams & Nussbaum, 2001, p. 188), and they are often unprepared for these changes in family roles. Steinberg (2001) found that, while this long process of reaching emotional autonomy is not associated with psychological upheaval for young people, it does cause mild distress for parents, particularly mothers.

While the process of individuation and the consequent construction of a self-identity were once expected to take place in adolescence, nowadays there are indications that this process tends to be delayed into early adulthood. For example, continued co-residence with parents seems to delay individuation (Kins & Beyers, 2010; White, 2002), while many young people in their early twenties feel that they are still treated as children and not given enough behavioural autonomy (Flanagan et al., 1993). In interviews, both parents and young people expected disagreements about autonomy matters (with young people wanting more than parents are willing to give, particularly regarding financial matters) during young people's transitions to college (Kenyon & Koerner, 2009).

Indeed, gaining adult status predicts well-being, so delayed home-leaving can be a problem for some (Flanagan et al., 1993; Kins & Beyers, 2010). However, this depends on the degree of choice young people have in the decision about whether to stay or leave the parental home: Those who stay because of economic necessity seem to be more adversely affected (Kins *et al.*, 2009). This also depends on parenting styles. Autonomy-enhancing parenting facilitates the individuation process, while over-protective parenting reduces autonomy (Seiffge-Krenke, 2006). Only two decades ago, it was the norm that children left home in their early twenties, and parents were not only happy to let them go (Adelman *et al.*, 1989; Fiske & Chiriboga, 1991; Ryff & Seltzer, 1996), but also felt ashamed if they did not succeed in launching them successfully at that age (Clemens & Axelson, 1985; Schnaiberg & Goldenberg, 1989). These attitudes seem to be changing in the current climate. From a series of interviews with parents of young adults (Kloep & Hendry, 2010), it became clear that in the present day they have certain difficulties in allowing adult children to seek and gain autonomy. Though some parents reluctantly accepted that they will have to 'let go' their adult children, many employed various strategies, ranging from bribery (such as continuing to do their laundry or meals) to coercion (such as threats of withdrawing total support), to obstruct their offspring's gaining autonomy and independence. Descriptions of adult children as 'he is my only child, my blue-eyed beauty' or 'I just feel that he is my baby' clearly show parental problems in accepting their children's adult independence.

Individuation, like so many other developmental processes, is co-constructed between parents and their children (Buhl, 2007) and greatly influenced by macro–systemic circumstances such as length of education, availability of housing and jobs, traditions and societal norms. Eventually, most young people move away from their parents, and reduce the frequency of face-to-face contact with them – at least until they have children of their own (Bucx & van Wel, 2008).

◉ Romance, dating and sexual relationships

While sexual exploration nowadays starts at an earlier age than before, fewer people get married, and if they do so, it happens later in their life. However, these figures are based on averages. We get a clearer view of reality, revealing wide variations, when we take a more detailed look at the overall statistics:

- While there are some adolescents under 13 years of age engaging in full sexual intercourse, there are also some young people at the age of 18, who have never done so (Centre for Disease Control and Prevention, 2010)

- About 1 per cent of the whole UK population classify themselves as asexual, which means not being sexually attracted to any gender (Bogaert, 2004).
- While the average age at first marriage has increased by five years to 30 years in the last decade in England and Wales, 3 per cent of males between 20 and 24 years, and 14 per cent of males between 25 and 29 years of age, are married.
- For females, the figures are even higher: 6 per cent of young women between 20 and 24, and 25 per cent of those between 25 and 29 years, are married (Office for National Statistics, 2010).

There are many reasons both for this demographic change and for the individual variations in lifestyle. For example, many more women are now self-supporting, so that a husband's economic security is no longer a necessity. Many prefer to invest in their own careers and education, which also delays the search for a marital partner. Further, many young people in modern societies wish for greater 'space' for individual interests and freedom, and no longer see marriage as a necessary 'marker' of adulthood.

Another reason is that marriage as a legally binding contract does not have the same status as before. Given the high divorce rate and the high costs of both marriage and divorce, increasingly higher numbers of people opt out of this form of partnership.

Do these data mean that a majority of young people are not willing or not able to commit to a serious relationship? The answer seems to be both 'yes' and 'no'. To stay with statistics for a while, though young people are reluctant to marry, they still make relational commitments. If we add the number of young people who co-habit to the number who marry, we find that nearly a third of the 20–24-year-olds, and half of the 25–29-year-olds have opted to commit to a serious, relatively long-standing relationship.

We have emphasized several times that there is a great variability in lifestyle choices in modern societies. Dhariwal et al. (2009) illustrate this clearly, after following a cohort of Italian adolescents from their teenage years until they were 25 and observing their commitment patterns. They identify two different romantic styles used by these young people. One, which they call 'consolidated romantic style', is characterized by striving for the formation of committed relationships. The other one, labelled 'exploratory style', consists of experimentation with different partners and romantic activities. However, this does not mean that there exist two groups of people, those who want to commit and those who do not:

Young people switch between these styles, depending on circumstances. For example, after the break-up of a serious relationship, they might for a while go back to exploring and experimenting, until they settle down with a steady partner again. And, interestingly, there are no gender differences in employing these strategies.

Further, given the pressures of education and career, young people complain that it is increasingly difficult to find the time to meet eligible partners, particularly as relationship ideals have changed: in addition to attractiveness, intellectual and social compatibility have become more important, decreasing the choice of suitable partners (Sperry et al., 2005). This problem has led to a significant change in dating patterns. As there is a great variability as to when and how young people find partners and decide whether to to commit to serious relationships, there is also variation in the choice of their partners' gender. While the predominant pattern in our society is to have romantic relationships with the opposite gender, there are a variety of other choices. Until quite recently, researchers believed that sexual preferences other than heterosexuality were not a matter of choice, but of biology. Nowadays, we are not so certain.

The reason is that, though some lesbian, gay or bi-sexual individuals say that they have had their sexual preferences from childhood on, there are others who change from their original sexual orientation across their lifespan. This is true for both genders, but particularly women report that they did not experience any same-sex attractions until adulthood (Diamond, 1998, 2007). Diamond followed a sample of non-heterosexual women over the course of ten years and found both variability and discontinuity. For example, 60 per cent had a sexual encounter with a man during this period, and 10 per cent had settled into long-term heterosexual relationships. Moreover, two-thirds of the women changed the initial label that they had assigned to themselves – 'lesbian', 'bi-sexual', 'heterosexual' or 'unlabeled' – at least once over the period of the study. Particularly interesting is that many women described such changes as happening quite abruptly, often instigated by circumstances such as seeing a TV programme or talking to a friend. Some women even reported that their desires were not so much directed towards a specific gender, but towards a specific person, who just happened to be of a certain gender. Similarly, Cassingham and O'Neil (1993) and Kitzinger and Wilkinson (1995) report that women after decades of satisfactory heterosexual experience 'suddenly' fell in love with another woman.

Though it seems as if it is more common for women than men to change their sexual preferences in adulthood, it does happen with males. Furthermore, certain circumstances, such as incarceration in prison, might change sexual behaviour temporarily, but not sexual preference. Additionally, Bell and Weinberg (1978) report a difference between actual sexual behaviour, sexual feelings and romantic feelings, and find all possible combinations of these three aspects of sexual preference in their sample. Diamond (2007, p. 142) concludes that the development of sexual attraction is not a linear process with one certain outcome, but 'a multi-factorial phenomenon, characterized by multiple causal factors, multiple developmental pathways, and multiple manifestations.'

These findings on sexual behaviours illustrate interesting examples of both transitions and transformations.

In sum, there is much diversity in the way human beings in our society conduct romantic partnerships. Some decide already in their teens to commit to a serious relationship, others take their time to explore, and some are still single by the end of early adulthood and may stay so forever. Some adapt a homosexual identity, some a heterosexual or bi-sexual one, some change their sexual preferences over their lifespan, and some refuse to label themselves at all in such terms.

◉ Summary

In this chapter we considered the effects which social and economic changes over the last few decades have had in de-standardizing the life course and in making traditional norms and values redundant; thus leaving young people growing towards early adulthood without clear, authoritative adult guidance, since adults themselves have become somewhat uncertain about social values with recent rapid societal changes. This led Arnett to suggest that a new stage needed to be implanted into the life course, which he called 'emerging adulthood'. He proposed that this new stage allowed those from late teens to late twenties to explore aspects of living and to delay career and relational decisions.

Arnett's theory has its critics, and to be honest, we rank amongst them, essentially arguing that the idea is merely descriptive, not universal, and non-explanatory. His stage of 'emerging adulthood' provides a very general, and perhaps partial, picture, because it only appears to be significant for a number of young people. Evidence suggests that several trajectories are available from adolescence, and earlier transitions, rather than delayed transitions, seem more beneficial to both the young individual and to society.

From this academic debate, we moved on to discuss the implications of adult children living with parents and the tensions (or joys) when young people plan to leave home and live independent lives. We then explored some aspects of dating, romance and sexual relationships, concluding that young adults follow a variety of paths towards styles of dating, selecting partners and determining sexual orientation. Overall, it seems as if the long-term consequences of emerging adulthood are more advantageous to those who do *not* spend lengthy years in identity exploration or in an over-extended moratorium.

⟨◉⟩ Further reading

Arnett, J. J., Kloep, M., Hendry, L. B. & Tanner, J. (2011) *Emerging adulthood: Stage or Process? A Debate*. New York: Oxford University Press.
This book presents opposing views on the value of understanding transitions to early adulthood as a number of successive stages or, alternatively, as a developmental process. The book demonstrates how conflicting theoretical ideas can be debated in an academic yet friendly manner.
Berzin, S. C. and De Marco, A. C. (2010) Understanding the impact of poverty on critical events in emerging adulthood. *Youth and Society*, *42*(2) 278–285.
This article shows how transitions to adulthood can vary enormously and how poverty can determine negative trajectories for some young people throughout adulthood and may not allow less wealthy young adults the same opportunity for an extended period of emerging adulthood as Arnett's university graduates.

Chapter 6

From Early Adults to Mid-Lifers

Summary

In this chapter on middle adulthood we will focus on:

- Choices
- Career
- Leisure activities
- Romantic partners, marriage and co-habitation
- Disharmony and divorce
- Parenting and the 'empty nest'
- Parents and siblings
- Physical changes and the menopause
- Is there a 'mid-life crisis'?

Introduction

In the previous chapter, we considered young people's transitions to early adulthood and the social and personal transformations involved. Here we look at the processes of transition from early adulthood to mid-life: What is life like, advancing through the thirties, forties and fifties?

The range of choices available is created by a relatively de-standardized life course, a fluctuating and uncertain job market, demands for higher qualifications, a greater need for qualified women in the workforce and burgeoning leisure industries. If they wish, adults can choose a new partner, start a new family, begin a new career, drop out, go back to education, have exciting leisure activities, or copy youth fashions. Fiske and Chiriboga (1991, p. 286) described these new cultural variations in relation to families and lifestyle in the following way:

> Next time you visit the supermarket, you may encounter ... newborn infants with their mothers who are aged fifteen and sixteen and newborn infants with mothers aged thirty-five to forty ... You may encounter, in fact, grandparents in their early forties as well as parents in their sixties and seventies.

In the earlier phases of the transition to mid-life, people may be at a peak of their attractiveness, vitality and enthusiasm. But then, after the relative freedom accorded to young adults in Western cultures, various expectations and pressures in the occupational and relational spheres of their lives begin, which, over time, direct them towards a lifestyle of either conventionality or exploration. Further, for the individual, gradual physical and biological changes begin to occur. So the key to understanding the most important aspects of mid-life is to view them as a series of extremely individualized transitional trajectories: Uniquely varied pathways differentiated by historical, cultural, social, biological and psychological forces and factors (Lachman, 2004).

Defining mid-life is just as difficult as it was conceptualizing adolescence or early adulthood: It is not a clearly demarcated age-stage but rather more closely tied to a series of life events, ranging from a zenith of optimism and vitality to slowly declining physical prowess, the 'ticking biological clock' of women's fertility, partnerships and 'life after divorce', and eventually, the menopause and adult children leaving home, with these events dealt with differently by each person encountering them.

Therefore, in this chapter we will describe the more usual events and changes, whilst being aware that not everyone will experience all of them. As Brim (1992, p. 171) has said: 'Mid-life is the last, uncharted territory of the life course', because it is so varied and individually diverse.

◉ Choices?

Middle adulthood, then, sees the beginnings of some reduction in choices. It is already too late to develop certain physical abilities to a high level – for example, most sporting records are achieved by young adults. In business, whilst not impossible, in mid-life it can be difficult to gain further qualifications or promotion or to pursue a quite different career. Some life choices will no longer be reversible. For instance, it is impossible to send back your children once you have them!

By mid-life, adults are often settled and have already made many of their important life choices. Only occasionally do events, like job loss, the birth of a child or a partner's death, create significant changes. In the main, those in mid-adulthood have to create their *own* transformations. In other words, further development is now very much in the hands of the individual.

All this makes middle adulthood a time for looking, Janus-like, both backward and forward, evaluating what has been achieved so far and assessing what is yet to be. People can decide whether they want to remain with their current choices or if they want – and are able – to change. Generally, if and when they have found a job or a source of income, a place to live, a partner with whom to share their life or a chosen solitary existence, if they have made the choice whether or not to have children, nothing pressurizes people to make any additional life decisions *right now*.

So, many respond by accepting a comfortable and conventional lifestyle, having little interest in seeking new challenges. Yet, there are others who actively change the parts of their life they are dissatisfied with, adding new experiences and competencies. Thus, there are decisions to be made concerning 'challenge' or 'consolidation' in middle-age.

Though evaluating one's life is not confined to mid-adulthood, it attains a certain importance in the middle years. There is still time to reconsider one's life decisions and initiate possible new beginnings. People are still young enough to take on further education, start a new career or family, and develop a different lifestyle or to move to another place.

This developmental opportunity to 'take stock' in mid-life is closely related to the resources and challenges in a person's life, as we have discussed in Chapter 2. The evaluation whether or not current life is satisfying is influenced by experiences of non-normative shifts such as unresolved grief, unsatisfying relationships, identity issues and the number and kinds of resources the individual possesses, such as health, income, self-esteem and social support (McQuide, 1998).

◉ Career and unemployment

An important aspect of middle adulthood is the role which work fulfils. Again, we observe large individual variations, with some adults not embarking on a career until their thirties, while others are approaching their personal zenith at about the same time. For men, and increasingly for women, work plays a significant role in their identity formation and existential meaningfulness. Striving to better one's occupational position and trying to maintain it, often means a considerable workload and feelings of stress.

Karasek and Theorell (1990) suggested that there are mainly two characteristics that in combination dramatically affect stress, namely, how much control one has over one's work in terms of autonomy and skills level, and how high the demands of the work tasks are. They claim that tasks that put high demands on a worker with high skills lead to learning and growth, to a more active leisure time and to fewer stress symptoms. Jobs with few demands on highly skilled workers cause least psychophysical symptoms, but do not enable further development. Passive jobs, where low control and low demands are experienced, lead to a gradual loss of skills and abilities, a more passive leisure time and signs of depression. Most significantly, high demands combined with low skills and low autonomy lead to most stress-related illnesses: Depression, exhaustion, pill consumption, coronary heart disease and job dissatisfaction.

However, their research mainly focussed on groups with low control/high demands, while the implications on well-being and physical symptoms in high demand/high skills jobs are less well researched. Over the years, attempts to find empirical support for their model have yielded inconsistent results, mainly because researchers use different methods of measuring 'control and demand', and because few of the studies are longitudinal to allow for genuine causal explanations (Kain & Jex, 2010).

In one of the few longitudinal studies, which also controlled for occupational status and pre-existing mental symptoms (Melchior et al., 2007), it was found that the most important predictors for development of anxiety in men and women are experiences of hectic work days, pressure and work overload. Age and gender are factors that interact with the effects of work on stress-related outcomes. The current cohort of middle-aged employees, for example, is particularly affected by control issues created by the swift increase in demands for high skills and by organizational restructuring (Wickrama et al., 2008). For women, household duties exacerbate the effects of stress at work (Krantz et al., 2005), suggesting that the work situation with its stresses, challenges, opportunities and rewards affects not only individuals, but their children, spouses and friends – and vice versa.

Mid-life is often seen as a period when one reflects on the realization of earlier aspirations. Not surprisingly, those who deem themselves success-ful in achieving their aims show higher life satisfaction than others (Carr, 1997). Those who judge themselves as not having achieved their goals have two possibilities for coping, either to lower their goals or to attempt a career change. The latter option is not easy. Middle-aged people them-selves perceive several obstacles, such as worries about age discrimination and not possessing appropriate skills to cope with the demands of a new job (Bailey & Hansson, 1995). The number and quality of the resources they possess determines whether they embark on a career change, rec-oncile themselves to their current job, or continue reluctantly in spite of ongoing disaffections (Cooper & Davey, 2011). Job insecurity increases with age and is associated with depression (Meltzer *et al.*, 2009).

However, more often than not, it is not the employee who makes the decision about career change but rather the employer who dismisses them against their will. With unemployment rates around 8 per cent in the UK, an increasing number of people of all age-groups experience periods of unemployment and have to face growing competition for jobs. Those in work are constantly threatened by the possibility of losing it, and those already unemployed have to cope with the stigma of not being 'a worker'.

Present day societies are characterized by a shrinking manufactur-ing sector and a growing service sector, and a dramatic decline in the demand for unskilled labour. So, younger people who are less educated and experienced are at higher risk of not finding a job. Yet, for the middle-aged, whose self-identity is strongly linked to their occupational role, job loss might be harder psychologically than it is for young people seeking employment. Furthermore, re-entry into the labour force is less proba-ble for the over-forties, particularly if no new job is found within the first year after redundancy. This leaves the older, long-term unemployed with feelings of resignation and uselessness (Henkens *et al.*, 1996).

Similar to other challenges, the effects of unemployment on the indi-vidual vary with circumstances and the support of significant others. For instance, unemployment for one partner can lead to increased arguments between a couple, reduced satisfaction with the quality of the partnership and even to the risk of divorce – but only in marriages already distressed before the onset of unemployment (Liem & Liem, 1990).

In this section, we discussed the role of employment and career in mid-life. The aim of mid-life employees to establish and maintain a career position is coupled with a sense of meaningfulness but also considerable stress. Some have to concede that they have not – and will not – attain the goals they envisaged earlier, while some experience a high workload that impinges on their health and family relationships. A few decide on career change, after realizing that their present occupation does not match their expectations. Increasingly, the threat of unemployment overshadows working life, and particularly affects older workers. However, as in all other life domains, there is no 'one size fits all' description of mid-life work and career since there are tremendous individual differences because of other life-events and individual circumstances.

Box 6.1: Qualitative research

Much of the research conducted in developmental psychology is of a quantitative nature, which means, it tries to quantify results, expressing them in numbers. Attitudes, intelligence, well-being, depression and so on are measured in scores. That makes it easy to compare results. The use of statistical tests to estimate the probability that the results are significant means that they are not the products of chance or coincidence.

However, sometimes we are not so interested in numbers and measurements, but are more eager to understand a particular phenomenon. For instance, we can measure the average age when the menopause is normally experienced, the amount of hormones in the blood of a peri-menopausal woman or the number of hot flushes she experiences in a normal day. Yet that does not tell us very much about how it feels to experience these body changes, and what they mean for her daily life. If that is what we want to know, we should use a qualitative method.

Qualitative methods have a completely different purpose from quantitative studies. They do not want to test a hypothesis (most of the time, it would even be impossible to try to do that), they do not aim to find results that can be generalized to a whole population, and, of course, they are not especially interested in numbers. Qualitative methods are most often used in the following types of situation:

1. We want to explore a completely new topic. How can we devise a theory or construct a questionnaire if we know very little about a certain aspect of developmental psychology? Let's say researchers want investigate what it means for teenagers to have to stay even longer at school because the government has

raised the school leaving age. Researchers are not teenagers anymore, and most of them went to school under very different conditions. To construct a questionnaire about young people's feelings would be difficult, since they would be uncertain of what questions to ask. Obviously, you can't get more out of a questionnaire than you put in, and thus, some very important questions might be omitted. So, it would be clever to conduct some interviews with young people themselves, and let them talk freely about their experiences of raising the school leaving age, before constructing a questionnaire to find out how many share this opinion.

2. We want to understand how people themselves make sense of their life experiences. 'Objective' data, for instance, can measure what kind of attachment grown-ups have to their parents, how often they have contact, how often they argue, how close they rate the parent–child relationship. Nevertheless, these measures cannot show us the intricate interpretations people construct for themselves about their relationships. They may see childhood events in a completely different light, based on their relationship with their elderly parents in the present, and they might forget events and embellish others from the past. So, they construct a narrative. This personal narrative is more influential in their present-day life and in their ongoing relationship with their parents than whatever 'really happened' earlier in their life. These narratives are much easier to capture using qualitative methods.

3. As explained in Box 3.1, quantitative methods often provide only means, telling us what the 'average' person is like. We might want to find out the opposite, and gauge individual variations. What does it mean if people rate their life quality as high? How do different people define life quality, and how is it expressed in their individual lives? Again, a qualitative method might extract much more colourful and diverse data than a quantitative method could.

4. Sometimes, we find that results from quantitative studies contradict each other. For example, in Chapter 4 we discussed the fact that the vast majority of teenagers complain that they have nothing to do. At the same time, looking at leisure surveys, we find that many adolescents are actually extremely busy

during their leisure time. In a case like this, it helps to go back to the teenagers themselves and ask them for clarification of the apparent contradiction (which, in our study, led to the conclusion that it was not the quantity but the quality of activities they moaned about!).

Sociology and Anthropology have used interviews, diaries, observations, drawings and photographs in their research for some time now, while, more recently, developmental psychology is also beginning to embrace these styles of research. Particularly popular and useful are mixed-methods approaches, where qualitative and quantitative data are combined to complement each other.

◉ The mid-life moratorium and the importance of leisure

As we have seen, many people invest a great deal of time and effort to maintain a career position, or indeed, to advance it. Therefore, one area that can offer a compensatory development-zone is leisure, where individuals can try out new skills, form new relationships and break out of 'expected' social roles to follow new adventurous activities.

As a preparation for future living, mid-life is as important to the life course as is the 'moratorium' in adolescence. This is because there are few totally new skills that *have to be* learned. However, in modern societies, the speed of technological advance demands that individuals constantly adapt and enhance their skills in order to keep abreast of social change. Consider, for example, that in many European countries one now requires basic computer skills in order to buy a railway ticket! There is a risk in mid-life that the individual ceases to be alert to the possibilities and properties of change. Then, if societal shifts *do* occur and become part of the social fabric, this will leave the individual 'suddenly' de-skilled, feeling a loss of security because of opting out of any future consideration of adapting to these innovations.

Furthermore, as a preparation for the next transition, mid-life can be used to create a basis for successful ageing. Health behaviours and leisure participation in mid-life prepare the individual for the challenges of a life after retirement, and help to create a network of social support (Mancini & Sandifer, 1995). Research tells us that leisure activities in mid-life are highly predictive of leisure participation in old age (Agahi *et al.*, 2006).

However, not everyone has the same opportunities to engage in leisure activities. For example, having a long history of exposure to physical work and a high current job-strain contributes to class differences in leisure activities, where lower-skilled workers do not have the residual energy to participate (Mäkinen *et al.*, 2010). An increasing number of leisure activities are costly and/or need expensive equipment, thus excluding all those who cannot afford them. Additionally, urban and rural areas differ widely in the range of leisure activities on offer, and in available transport services to reach them.

To summarize: Leisure is a context for improving social networks, providing rich opportunities to learn new skills for a meaningful post-retirement life, and to counter-balance existing work stress.

◉ Romantic partners, marriage and co-habitation

After the 'serial' romantic relationships of early adulthood, people begin to settle into lengthier, more stable partnerships of co-habitation and marriage in the transition to mid-life. However, the number of marriages in England and Wales in 2008 was the lowest recorded since 1895 and the mean age at first marriage is now on average 6.5 years later than 50 years ago.

Today, co-habitation is a common pattern among people in the western world. Although marriage may be the preferred form of relationship, co-habitation is more and more seen as a prelude to marriage or an alternative to it. People may live together for a number of reasons. These can include wanting to test compatibility or to establish financial security before marrying. It may also be because they are unable to marry legally for reasons such as being of the same sex. Other reasons include: Living together as a way of avoiding higher income taxes paid by two-income married couples or seeing little difference between the commitment to live together and the commitment to marriage. Some individuals may choose co-habitation because they see their relationships as being a private matter, not to be controlled by political or religious institutions.

Some couples may prefer co-habitation because it does not commit them legally for an extended period, and because it is easier to establish and dissolve without the legal costs often associated with divorce. There were around 2.2 million co-habiting couples in England and Wales in 2007, a figure projected to rise to 3.7 million by 2031.

Postponing marriage, relationship break-ups and high divorce rates have extended the amount of time individuals search for romance (Sassler, 2010). As a person grows older, choices become increasingly limited with regard to finding a romantic partner. Once settled into a job and living in a particular geographic area, it becomes difficult to meet a range of appropriate partners. Especially among people in high-skilled positions, long working hours put a constraint on available leisure time. There are few opportunities for just 'bumping into' possible romantic partners (Burt et al., 2010).

This is one reason why considerable numbers of not-so-young people turn to Internet dating, shown by the massive explosion of advertised over-fifties dating sites. They offer a much larger number of available partners than could be met face-to-face, and the availability of matching facilities to filter out completely unsuitable partners from the start. The Internet also reduces the role of physical attributes in contacting possible partners, so that other factors such as similar interests, mutual self-disclosure and rapport become more important, 'thus prompting erotic connections that stem from emotional intimacy rather than lustful attraction' (Cooper & Sportolari, 1997, p. 7). Particularly people with concerns about body-esteem are given an opportunity to present themselves attractively, at least initially (Clark, 1998). Furthermore, the Internet is regarded as a safer place to meet unknown people, as it gives greater control over how much contact information is revealed, and it seems as if shy people feel less handicapped when expressing themselves in written form than face-to-face (Lawson & Leck, 2006). Dating sites are not only used to actually find a partner for a long-term relationship, but may serve several different functions: Companionship, comfort after a life crisis, freedom of commitment, adventure and living out romantic fantasies.

Though Internet dating might be perceived as easier than meeting people in real life, it also creates the necessity of learning completely new skills. Apart from obvious computer skills, such as uploading a photo and creating a profile, there is sometimes a special language to learn, such as the abbreviations only used in chat rooms and text messages: lol (laugh out loudly), s/l/a? (what sex, language, age are you?), brb (be right back).

More importantly, there are issues of finding the right balance between trust and caution, disclosure and secretiveness, given that deception and exaggeration are common on the Internet (Lawson & Leck, 2006).

There is also the issue of overlap between the virtual and the real world. Couples are not too pleased when finding out that their real-world partner has intimate relationships with other people they have never actually met. The fact that some people disclose more intimate details to their online partner than to their live-in lover (Underwood & Findlay, 2004) might be a reason for jealousy and distress. Graff (2007) reports that people are more likely to classify an online relationship as 'cyber-cheating' and infidelity if there is a high rate of disclosure, and when the interactions happen late at night as compared to daytime hours.

Of the many things affecting happiness in a stable relationship, intimacy between partners seems to be one of the most important (Harper et al., 2000). This includes trust, shared interests, being friends, honesty and mutual respect – qualities that are more valued than physical attractiveness in mid-life (Watson & Bell, 2005). These characteristics are also closely associated with a satisfying sexual relationship (Fraser et al., 2004). However, as individuals develop a loving partnership and grow older together, changes may begin to appear in their sexual response cycle.

Responding sexually is a complex physiological, psychological and sociological process. Mid-life women of today have been socialized by a mixture of traditional information about female sexuality and by views emergent from the women's movement and the post-contraceptive pill era. Mansfield et al. (1998) were surprised to find that one-fifth of their sample reported an increased desire for non-genital expressions of emotion (hugging, kissing and embracing). The researchers interpreted this finding as either a step towards having more fulfilling intercourse or as wanting to enhance feelings of intimacy.

These changes may be attributable to psychological and/or physical effects of ageing, their partners' physical or psychological difficulties, and possible changes associated with the menopause (Leiblum, 1990). However, psychological influences seem to have the strongest impact on women's sexual functioning, for example, their sexual responsiveness is affected by thinking that their partner might not find them attractive anymore now that they show signs of ageing (Trudel et al., 2000). Similarly, changes in sexual functioning in males can leave them feeling anxious and concerned about their virility (Notman, 1990). However, with age, men gain also more control over their sexual responses, which can make sexual relations more satisfying for their partner (Carpenter *et al.*, 2009). As Leiblum (1990) noted, alterations to the love-making 'script' can ensure pleasurable encounters in middle-age, and accordingly, the majority of middle-aged people still engage in frequent sexual activities (Fraser *et al.*, 2004).

We can conclude that courtship, love and sexual encounters occur throughout the middle years. Social changes such as the emergence of online-dating, maturational changes in sexual responsiveness and gender differences have a large impact on interpersonal behaviours and are responsible for creating many different and varied experiences amongst this age-group.

⊙ Disharmony and divorce

Though most fairy tales and Hollywood films end with a promise that 'they lived happily ever-after', we know from everyday life that it is not easy to sustain a blissful, long-term relationship. Even the happiest couples have arguments and have to face problems that put stress on their relationship. There are, for example, the difficulties of parenting: lack of sleep, re-negotiation of roles, worries about children, and the division of domestic tasks that lead to irritability and the need to discuss solutions. Many marriages deteriorate after the birth of children, and again when the firstborn child reaches puberty (Crawford & Unger, 2000; Whiteman *et al.*, 2007).

Later in life, when children leave the home, the couple needs to find new tasks to fill the day, new topics to talk to each other about, and cope with worries about their children's adjustments to their new independent lives. Additionally, for some parents, their children's leaving is finally the chance to develop their own lives, and to pursue adventures which they have been waiting for years to commence. Some might want to do so together, but others may wish to try this independently, free from marital restraints.

Conflicts arise when partners perceive an inequality in power or rewards gained from the relationship, and suspect that the other does not care about them. The two most common topics for arguments are disagreements about money and children, particularly step-children, but issues such as career pressures, infidelity and alcohol abuse also cause conflicts (Stanley *et al.*, 2002). Having arguments *per se* is not a danger for a relationship, but the way they are handled does have long-term effects. Negative interactions including hostility, escalation and particularly withdrawal reduce marital satisfaction and predict divorce. The outlook is bleak for couples who rely on destructive problem-solving strategies (Birditt *et al.*, 2010).

In the last decades, training programmes for constructive problem-solving have been developed to prevent marital break-down, and they have proven to be effective (e.g. Hahlweg & Richter, 2010). The goal of these programmes is to train couples in positive communication skills, such as listening to each other, keeping to one topic at a time when solving a conflict, describing one's own problem instead of accusing the partner, and aiming for constructive solutions.

The number of divorces in England and Wales fell by 5 per cent in 2008, constituting the lowest number since 1975, meaning that out of 1000 married people, 11.5 got divorced. It is possible to suggest that divorce rates are falling because, with fewer people marrying, those who do so, and those marrying later, are more committed to staying together. Yet, the number of divorces is highest amongst men and women aged 40–44 years (Office for National Statistics, 2010).

Thus, divorce and relationship break-ups constitute a major challenge to adult development in mid-life. Apart from having to deal with conflict and emotions, there are repercussions on the children, finances and friendship networks, and often other practical issues such as moving house or career changes are involved. How individuals cope with this situation depends on many interacting factors. For example, those who initiated the divorce, or who arranged it in mutual agreement with their partner, more often see it as a new start in life and as a chance for personal growth than those who are unprepared and surprised by their partner's decision (Sakraida, 2008). Marital loss through divorce or widowhood is associated with an increased risk of cardiovascular disease (Zhang, 2006). In the long term, the consequences of a divorce for former partners and the children are largely dependent on how the break-up is handled. If partners remain bitter and engage in continuing conflict, their psychological well-being is reduced, their friendship networks diminish, and worst of all, children suffer (Hetherington, 2003; Terhell *et al.*, 2004).

Children feeling caught in the middle between parents exhibit lowered psychological well-being, and are more likely to engage in failed relationships when they are grown up (Amato & Afifi, 2006). However, this is also true for children from high-conflict marriages where parents do not divorce and children cannot escape the constant conflict situation at home. Overall, it is the complex interaction between factors such as gender, age at separation, quality of relationship with both parents, extent of conflict, pre- and post-divorce parenting skills, personality, parental re-marriage and economic situation that determine how much, and how negatively, parental divorce affects children.

However, the majority of them adjust well over time, despite the gloomy picture presented in the media (Kelly & Emery, 2003). Moreover, there is a general lack of research investigating possible *positive* outcomes of divorce for children, as the majority of researchers have been guided by problem-focused hypotheses, thereby overlooking any potential benefits (Boney, 2003).

It is equally difficult to predict outcome and adjustment for the adults involved in a divorce, because there are too many factors that interact before, during and after the divorce process. Hetherington (2003, p. 318) concluded from her longitudinal study of divorcees' personal adjustment that:

> It was the diversity rather than the inevitability of outcomes following divorce that was striking, with most people able to adapt constructively to their new life situation within 2-3 years following divorce, a minority being defeated by the marital breakup, and a substantial group of women being enhanced.

To summarize, mid-life is the time for most to establish a long-term relationship, but this is not easy. Conflict-solving and communication skills are needed to retain the relationship and a large proportion of couples experience its dissolution. Divorce has many and varied consequences, both for the couple involved and for their children. Not all of these are negative, and outcomes depend to a large extent on the process of divorce and the amount of conflict involved both before and after.

◉ Parenting and the 'empty nest'

In post-modern society, there is no particular age when it is 'appropriate' to become a parent. The average age for having a first child in the UK is 29 years, though women frequently have children earlier and later than that. Men, who are not biologically confined to certain reproductive ages, can start a second or third family and become a father and a grandfather at the same time. As a consequence of medical advances in fertility treatment, there is also a growing number of women who decide to become mothers at an unconventionally high age – we all remember the headlines about the world's oldest mother, giving birth to twins at the age of 67.

Yet, after an early adulthood of exploring and experimenting with relationships (Arnett, 2004), infertility may come as a shock to some 'emergent' mid-lifers. One important consequence of delaying childbirth till the early thirties is the possibility that conception might no longer be possible, as happens to about one out of five couples. About half of the couples seek medical help, which is often successful, but can be stressful and costly, affecting the quality of the partnership and self-esteem.

This is particularly true for women and for couples whose treatment is not successful (Miles *et al.*, 2009; Schmidt, 2006). Anticipating such problems, and completely in line with the culture of choice and freedom of present-day society, an increasing number of young women decide to freeze some of their eggs in order to circumvent biological restrictions on their fertility later in life (Martin, 2010).

Those who do become parents in early adulthood are faced with a variety of life-changing challenges. Acquiring effective parenting skills is only one of them. We have already indicated that happiness in marriage tends to decrease after the birth of a child. Within the marriage, young parents are required to work on their relationship because they will have to adjust to a different lifestyle, often with one of them giving up work, reducing meetings with friends and usual leisure activities, re-negotiating the division of labour and drawing up more considered budgets for living expenses. Cox *et al.* (1999) studied couples before the birth of their first child, and 3, 12 and 24 months after, and found that, due to the additional challenges and stresses, young parents often experienced increased depression and a decrease in marital satisfaction. Young parents also report that they are often too tired to have sex (Ahlborg *et al.*, 2005).

Once there are children around, parents find themselves having to adapt to ever-changing situations and having to constantly learn new skills. The style of their parenting needs change over the years. New contacts have to be made with various organizations, such as schools, medical centres and leisure clubs, and with new social networks involving other parents, teachers, doctors and leisure leaders. Parents have to become familiar with children- and youth-cultures, fashions, music tastes and literature. They have to try to follow the newest technological developments, because their children will. They need to find a balance between supervision and the granting of relative autonomy, between wanting to spoil their child and being consistent, and they have to do all this while trying to meet the demands of their own lives and careers. Given this overload of challenges, it is no wonder that childless couples have lower levels of depression than parents (Bures, 2009).

In the last few decades, psychologists have developed parent-training programmes based on behavioural principles, to teach parents some of the skills that might make parenting easier. Meta-analyses of the outcome of such parent and child behaviour training show that programmes designed to increase positive parent–child communication and to teach parents to react consistently over their child's behaviour proved to be particularly effective (Kaminski *et al.*, 2008; Maughan *et al.*, 2005).

The dynamics of family living mean that both parents and children affect and influence parenting styles. Inter-dependent forces such as emotions, perceptions and behaviours consolidate over time, leading to a fairly stable style of interacting (Granic, 2000). The emerging relational patterns might not always create an outcome that is desirable for all participants in the long run. Hendry *et al.* (1993) have demonstrated how disagreements between parents and their *adolescent* offspring often revolve around daily issues such as the tidiness of teenage bedrooms, the volume of pop music and times of coming home, whereas the main arguments between parents and *early adult* children centre on issues of mutual respect and partnership (e.g. who decides what TV programmes to watch or arguments over sharing household tasks).

Once the child-rearing years are over, parents are still not freed from responsibilities. Family life has altered over the years with young adults remaining longer at home. The Office for National Statistics (2010) presented figures showing that 29 per cent of men and 18 per cent of women aged between 20 and 34 still live together with their parents.

Potentially depressive reactions of parents when children leave home have been labelled as the 'empty nest syndrome'. Fiske and Chiriboga (1991) described mothers' reactions as ranging from initial sadness and feelings of loss to experiencing opportunities for increased activities, and finally to a decrease in depression and an increase in happiness and pride. No such changes were found in men. Further, Dennerstein *et al.* (2002) found in their longitudinal study that for the majority of women, the departure of the last child from the household leads to positive changes in their moods and a reduced number of daily hassles.

However, there are large variations between parents and how they react to their children growing up and leaving home. In our own study (Kloep & Hendry, 2010), we interviewed parents whose adult children were still living at home. Only one group of parents gives the impression of being fairly happy with their children's developing autonomy. Another group shows some ambivalence, indicating that they accept their children's independence but regret having less power to intervene in their children's life choices, that they cannot 'ground them anymore', and have too little information about what they are doing in their lives. They seem to wish to retain their parental role and appear quite surprised that their children can already organize their lives effectively. However, they do try to come to terms with their new roles, working hard to keep interference to a minimum and admitting that to behave otherwise would be irrational.

This attempt to cope with role change distinguishes them from a third, apparently unhappy, group. These parents also talk about role loss and missing their children, but reveal the use of quite different strategies to come to terms with this situation: Consciously or unconsciously, they try to delay their children's independence and continue to interfere in their lives. The most frequent strategy was providing services and continuing to spoil adult children in order to keep them at home longer or to encourage them to visit oftener.

Finally, there is a small group for whom their adult children's independence is a matter of high conflict. The most obvious forms of continuing power struggles, found in the narratives of the few parents who completely disagree with their children's lifestyle choices, are non-compassionate, even triumphant descriptions of some failed attempts to achieve independence.

Hence, it is not only young people leaving home who are tackling a major turning point in their lives: parents, too, have to come to terms with this challenge profoundly affecting their lifestyle. Actually, as parents across the whole lifespan tend to be more emotionally involved in the relationship than are their adult children, changes might have a stronger impact on their development than on that of their offspring (Shapiro, 2004).

In this section, we discussed the increasing risk of infertility as women progressively postpone parenthood. Further, we showed that parenthood comprises of many different challenges, not all of them related to actual parenting skills, which can lead to a considerable amount of stress, particularly when parenting adolescents. In spite of these stresses, we illustrated how difficult it is for many parents to let go of their adult children when they actually want to leave the family home.

◉ The sandwich generation, parents and siblings

Nowadays, it is likely that the parents of many middle-aged couples are still active and relatively healthy. There are many signs of inter-generational solidarity, with parents helping their offspring economically, with childcare or in career development, and with children providing support when parents need care or advice.

However, there are also many incidents of inter-generational conflict, for example, when children perceive their parents as being intrusive and not treating them as adults (Fingerman, 2001); when parents complain that their children take too long to grow up and take on adult responsibilities (Fingerman et al., 2007); or when both sides cannot come to terms with problems from their past relationship (Shapiro, 2004). In most parent–adult child relationships, a certain degree of ambivalence can be detected, with love and conflict both being present (Pillemer & Lüscher, 2004).

Then, there seems to be a time when middle-aged individuals begin to accept their parents' weaknesses, which leads to positive changes in the relationship. Researchers call this 'filial maturity' (Birditt et al., 2008), indicating that parent–child relationships change further after the 'second individuation' occurring during the transition to adulthood (see Chapter 5).

Maybe, after having children of their own, individuals develop a deeper understanding of the challenges and difficulties their own parents had to face, and can forget old grudges and overlook weaknesses. Some new tensions might arise though, when parents develop serious health problems and need to be looked after. This role-reversal, where children start to monitor their parents' behaviour, manage their finances and make contact with caring institutions, can once more lead to ambivalent feelings as both parties try to find a new balance between support and independence (Spitze & Gallant, 2004).

With children leaving home later and parents living longer, middle-aged individuals might find themselves in a position where they have to care for both an adult child and a parent at the same time: They are 'sandwiched' between the needs of two generations. This can cause considerable strain, particularly as they might also have to fulfil the demands of a full-time job. In Britain, about 11 per cent of men and 18 per cent of women have held all three roles simultaneously at some stage in their lifespan, and this figure is expected to increase as more women are in full-time employment (Evandrou & Glaser, 2004).

The role of caring for elderly parents is considerably eased if it is shared between siblings (Wolf *et al.*, 1997). This is not the only instance where sibling support is crucial. Cicirelli (2004) showed that siblings felt closer to each other than they did to parents or friends. After all, in most people's lives, it is the longest relationship they will ever enjoy, and siblings are the only people who know them intimately from when they were very young. Siblings act as companions and confidantes and as a source of emotional and instrumental support, particularly in the absence of other core family members, which is frequently the situation in very old age (Bedford, 1998). Pairs of sisters, singles and childless individuals tend to have the most active and intimate sibling ties, and feelings about one's siblings enhance life satisfaction more strongly than how often one actually meets them (McMamish-Svensson *et al.*, 1999). Sometimes, though, siblings have to resolve issues stemming from their childhood, such as sibling rivalry, before they can form a helpful adult relationship.

To summarize, middle-aged individuals can find themselves in a position where they may have to care for a dependent child and for an ageing parent at the same time. This is why they are called the 'sandwich generation'. The relationship to their parents is characterized by ambiguity, involving both conflict and mutually affectionate solidarity. Finally, the important role of siblings for emotional and instrumental support was presented, demonstrating again the inter-connectedness of relational events across the lifespan.

◉ Physical changes

There is one significant change for all individuals – perhaps the most obvious one across the transitions from early adulthood to mid-life. Yet, because bodily changes occur over a relatively lengthy number of years, individuals are not necessarily aware of them. Occasionally, one briefly notices, for example, when it is just *a little more* difficult to fasten a belt, or by overhearing other people's critical comments on our looks.

Put simply, people are not as strong, fast and powerful, or blessed with physical endurance, as they were in their youthful days.

As progress towards mid-life continues, a receding hairline, greying hair, a paunch, sagging skin or wrinkles cannot just be overlooked. Mid-life for many is a busy period that does not leave much time for leisure, and much less for exercise. At the same time, as many still feel relatively strong and fit, they are not especially susceptible to their GP's health warnings, leading a lifestyle that intensifies the ageing process. Ziebland *et al.*'s (2002) interview study showed that weight is perceived as hard to control by middle-aged people, and perceptions of weight gains are related to sedentary lifestyles and hormonal changes. Few report engaging in an active lifestyle and sensible eating. Some feel it is impossible to include physical activity in their daily life. Most have limited awareness of health-related concerns, but are worried about their body-shape.

Women may be more vulnerable than men to expectations of ideal body shape, and are acutely aware of body changes, perceiving themselves as not matching up to society's standards of beauty (Saucier, 2004). Another important aspect of this is the 'cult of youthfulness' in society, which impinges on those in mid-life (Featherstone & Hepworth, 1991). Messages and photographs in the mass media portray success in business and in personal relations as highly correlated with vitality, health, attractiveness and youthfulness.

Given that people in mid-life seem susceptible to societal pressures, there are several strategies that they can adopt: Rigorous exercise regimes can be adopted to fight changes in body shape. However, we know from physiological research that in mid-life, with a slower metabolism, we have to put in more effort for fewer fitness gains. Those who are wealthy enough can turn to cosmetic surgery and Botox to lift sagging muscles and skin, to remove adipose tissue or replace a head of hair. A worldwide industry has been created on the basis of the search for youth. But change cannot be resisted, only slowed down and delayed. A different strategy is to enjoy the freedom of not having to be beautiful anymore, and exchange high heels for a comfortable tracksuit and trainers. Age brings seniority and more acceptance and respect from others, illustrating once more that any change consists of gains and losses.

In sum, we can say that though there are age-related changes in the body during mid-life, the social impact and symbolic value of the ageing corpus may have more influence on us than the effects of the actual bodily changes during this maturational shift. It seems as if we can 'get by' with a less efficient body in middle-age, but not without the approbation of our friends and peers.

◁◉▷ Evidence about the menopause

Perhaps more significant than a chronological milestone, the shift into mid-life for women is marked by the beginnings of the 'menopause'. What is the menopause? Firstly, it is a maturational change in the endocrine system, causing the ovaries to gradually stop producing the hormones that control the menstrual cycle. This leads to the cessation of menstruation, sometimes quite abruptly, sometimes over the course of several years. Often, this change in hormones is accompanied by bodily symptoms, such as 'hot flushes', night sweats, vaginal dryness, irregular menstrual cycles, fatigue, general irritability, sleep disturbances and depression (Nelson, 2008). Women also report decreased productivity at work, difficulties in meeting work and family demands, and an inability to control migraine effects (Moloney *et al.*, 2006). However, despite a large body of research, only 'hot flushes' and vaginal dryness can be directly linked to hormonal changes, all other symptoms seem to be secondary or unrelated (Nelson, 2008).

Furthermore, the individual's experience of the menopause can be affected by many factors. Lifestyle issues such as obesity, smoking and marital conflicts have an impact on the severity and frequency of symptoms, as has the timing. While menopause occurs normally between the late forties and late fifties, in a minority of women it happens comparatively early. As is the case with 'off-time' puberty (see Chapter 3), such a non-normative shift can affect women negatively, for example in terms of lowered self-esteem, emotional fluctuations of shock, denial, anger, feelings of loss and dashed hopes for parenthood (Singer & Hunter, 1999).

Cultural expectations, such as the attitudes of members of her social networks, the roles ascribed to older women in a given culture and the support she can activate, are also influential. Thus, there can be different quantities of symptoms, and different degrees of severity of these. Porter *et al.* (1996), for example, have shown that only 57 per cent of the women in their Scottish sample had experienced one or more of 15 usual menopausal symptoms, and only 22 per cent found such symptoms to be a problem. Wilbur *et al.* (1995) reported that the majority of women had neutral feelings towards menopause. Other researchers (see Robinson, 1996, for a review) comment on the enormous differences among women in how they experience the menopause, in the same society and across different ones.

In some cultures, menopause is seen as a kind of embarrassing female sickness that should be treated with medicines and hormone replacement therapy. For example, Defey et al. (1996) found that, while gynaecologists perceived menopausal women as depressed, striving for a better sex life, lacking a future perspective, and worrying about their health, women themselves stressed they saw the menopause as a turning point with opportunities for self-achievement and positive changes in autonomy and independence.

Women in non-Western societies often enjoy enhanced status, political power and psychological well-being in conjunction with the menopause, because they are accorded greater decision-making authority after having fulfilled the social duty of bearing children, as data from 15 different socio-cultural groups showed (Kaiser, 1990). Similar views were expressed by Korean women (Lee et al., 2010). Not surprisingly, given the positive social values of the menopause in many non-western countries, Chinese and Japanese women report fewer menopausal symptoms than women in the USA and Canada (Lock, 1998; Nelson, 2008). Moreover, lesbian women in Western societies also report fewer problems at the menopause than heterosexual women (Cole & Rothblum, 1990).

Palmlund (1997) describes how the menopause is socially constructed as a risk in popular culture and in the medical field, resulting in the medicalization of mid-life women's lives. Hepworth (1995) even suggests that it is mainly an invention of the pharmaceutical industry, convincing women they all suffer from an illness that has to be dealt with medically, notwithstanding the substantial risks associated with hormonal therapy (Senior, 2001).

Overall, women seem to regard menopause as a natural, inconsequential or even positive event, freeing them from contraceptive worries (Dillaway, 2005), and as a time-limited experience, signalling the beginning of a search for new meaning in their lives (Jones, 1997). In Svenson's (2005) study, women describe the onset of their menopause as a trigger to re-evaluate their lives and partnerships and as a reminder that time was running out. This led to changes in their approach to life. While for some, acceptance and resignation was the outcome of their life evaluation, others described a new sense of self, deciding that it was now time to put more emphasis on themselves as individuals.

Nevertheless, as always when individuals adjust to changes in life, it is easier to do so if they can concentrate on one issue at a time (Coleman & Hendry, 1999). Coping with menopause may be more difficult if, at the same time, the woman is confronted with other challenges, such as troublesome teenage kids, new obligations at work, or health problems.

Recently, researchers have begun to suggest the existence of a male equivalent to the menopause, labelled 'andropause'. Symptoms such as hot flushes, erectile dysfunction and mood changes are attributed to age-related decreases in testosterone. However, there is a lack of consensus as to whether these symptoms are due to hormone changes, lifestyle issues, or propaganda by the pharmaceutical industry (Charlton, 2004; Hollander & Samons, 2003; Vainionpaa & Topo, 2005).

To sum up, the menopause causes physical symptoms that vary in strength and impact between individual women. Clearly, it is a challenge that can be disruptive to the sense of self, and, dependent on various factors, the outcome can be either positive or negative.

⊙ Mid-life crisis?

It is common to describe the teenage years as a time of storm and stress. Similarly, a large number of popular publications exist discussing the problems of the 'mid-life crisis'. Might this crisis also be a myth?

Quantitative studies with large samples report conflicting results with regard to well-being and depression in mid-life. This is partly due to differing definitions of when in the life course 'mid-life' is experienced.

Yang (2008) reports a linear increase in happiness over the life course until the mid seventies, and Baird et al. (2010) found there was a large increase in life-satisfaction from the forties until the early seventies in the British population. However, Easterlin (2006) reported that life satisfaction peaks at around 50 years and declines thereafter. Blanchflower and Oswald (2008) claimed that subjective well-being is lowest in the mid- to late forties, while Mroczek and Kolarz (1998) said the same for the years between 30 and 40. Depression, on the other hand, has been shown to peak between 45 and 55 years (Lewinsohn et al., 1986).

The contradictions in these findings are partly due to the ways 'happiness', 'well-being', 'life satisfaction' and 'depression' are defined and measured, and partly to large sample variations based on gender, race, education, marital and health status, culture and cohort, thus, making overall average scores quite meaningless. For example, people with higher education tend to be happier than people with little education. If the sample consists of equal numbers from both educational groups, and scores are *averaged* across the whole sample, the result will be 'neither happy nor unhappy'.

Qualitative studies, on the other hand, reveal that mid-lifers are often not pre-occupied with a general crisis, but talk about various difficulties they had to overcome at different ages. Research from countries as diverse as the USA (Chiriboga, 1997), India (Tikoo, 1996) and Hong Kong (Shek, 1996), gives no indication whatsoever of the existence of a common crisis or dissatisfaction with mid-life. On the contrary, the most frequently mentioned 'turning point in life' experienced by American women between the ages of 20 and 40 years was 'growth' due to 'experiences in personal development', often as a response to some kind of loss (Leonard & Burns, 1999). In a further US study, participants of all ages saw mid-life as a time of increased stress and with little time for leisure. At the same time, however, they considered it to be a peak of competence, control and high productivity (Lachman *et al.*, 1994), indicating that, while it is a time of many challenges, individuals are well equipped to meet them.

As the period of 'mid-life' encompasses several decades, there is time for many events to occur with opportunities for development and growth, but also for many risks and negative events impacting on the individual's state of happiness. For example, Luhmann and Eid (2009) showed that repeated periods of unemployment tend to be associated with more negative outcomes, which can be explained by the cumulative draining effects on the individual's finances, self-esteem and social relationships. Furthermore, the effect is bi-directional: Those who feel less satisfied with life are 'at risk' of being unemployed more frequently. On the other hand, results are quite different for repeated divorce, as the second divorce is no more or less stressful than the first. Of course, there are large individual differences because divorce can ease difficulties for some, yet have devastating results for others.

So, it is fairly obvious that being happy or unhappy has nothing to do with age, but much more with the number and kind of life-events experienced, what coping resources are available, and how these events are linked to other earlier or concurrent life experiences. Obviously, there is the probability of crisis, but that is not confined to middle-age. Crises and stresses can occur anywhere in the life course, whenever there are too many concurrent challenges to deal with or when they exceed the individual's resources.

⊙ Summary

In this chapter, we have looked at the longest period of the life course, the middle years. In this transition, we found that little that happens across these decades has to do with age *per se*, but with life events and life circumstances that enable individual transformations to unfold. With life course de-standardization, most of these events can occur in one's twenties as easily as one's sixties, namely, romance, divorce, parenthood, career changes and unemployment. Accordingly, how people tackle these challenges depends more on the circumstances under which they occur, and on the resources they possess. Even seemingly biological changes such the menopause and biological alterations in the ageing body are strongly influenced by culture and individual coping styles. Development does not end in mid-life: Transitions and turning points encountered during any phase of the life course have the potential to create a mixture of gains and losses, that can lead to stagnation or growth.

⊙ Further reading

Dermick, I., & Andreolotti, C. (Eds.). (2003) *Handbook of adult development*. New York: Springer.
This is a compilation of articles written by scholars of adult development from an ecological and positive developmental perspective. Many aspects of adult development are presented, ranging from discussions on bio-cognitive and social development in mid- to later-adulthood to descriptions of appropriate research methods.
Triple P Positive Parenting Program http://www10.triplep.net/?pid=58
If we have frightened you by discussing the difficulties and stresses of parenting, have a look at the web page of Triple P, which offers a description of their parenting programme and has a selection of self-help manuals and contact details to practitioners.

Chapter 7

Old Age and Development: Towards Successful Ageing

Summary

This chapter on late adulthood discusses:

- Biological factors in ageing
- The impact of ageism
- Health issues
- Family and friends
- Bereavement
- Dating and sexuality
- Retirement
- Successful ageing.

Introduction

In this chapter we consider old age and ageing, and, after the problems we have had in finding clearcut definitions for any life phase in earlier chapters, it will come as no surprise that 'old age' is also a rather vague concept to explain. Previously, retirement from work has been seen as the psychosocial marker for entry into old age, an upper age limit by which people could be excluded from paid employment based solely on years and not on performance or capacity, with its subsequent impact on lifestyle. However, the age of mandatory retirement varies somewhat in different kinds of employment, and the UK government has recently scrapped it altogether, while increasing the age for receiving a state pension for both men and women.

Today, the growing number of retired people (and the decreasing sums in the treasuries of national pension schemes) has seen discussions in various European parliaments about encouraging individuals to delay retirement or to devise a more flexible retirement strategy, perhaps with part-time employment. On the other hand, some individuals are offered the possibility of retiring early and encouraged to take out personal pension schemes to offset a reduced state or business pension. So, once again, we can see that, like other phases of the life course, in a de-standardized society there is no clearcut age when old age begins. It does not occur 'overnight' and is further complicated by researchers talking about both 'a third age' – referring to those who are active and independent in later life – and a 'fourth age' – the period in old age when one is dependent on others.

One of the great freedoms of old age is in releasing individuals from the obligations of continuing to fulfil certain social roles and expectations (for example, one no longer *needs to be* beautiful or fashionable or to compete with others in business). On the other hand, not all individuals want to be free from social obligations. This is why retirement has very different implications for different people. Furthermore, people do not stop to be social beings just by getting older, but do have to face changes in their relationships: Losing friends, accepting a role-reversal from their previous family-care functions and defying age stereotypes affecting their social life.

◉ What is ageing and why do we age?

Though all living being eventually age and die, we do not know for sure why this is so. There are a range of theories trying to explain this inevitable fate, but none of them has been completely proven (for a comprehensive overview, see Stuart-Hamilton, 2006). One view is that we are born with an inbuilt programme to age and die to make room for the next generation. The fact that each species seems to have a maximum possible lifespan that cannot be prolonged seems to offer some evidence for this. Yet an argument against this idea is that in nature there are hardly any members of a species which actually reach extreme old age because life is dangerous and life-threatening enough to reduce numbers.

Another explanation proposes that, as individuals pass their genes on to the next generation generally in early- to mid-adulthood, the 'faults' that cause ageing are not apparent yet. They occur when time for procreation is over, and thus have no influence on natural selection. Put differently, extreme longevity or immortality never had a chance to be bred into any species (perhaps with the exclusion of a certain pine tree and a certain jellyfish). There are further suggestions that those particular characteristics which increase our chances of survival and procreation (for example, the amount of male testosterone) also accelerate the processes of ageing and decline, meaning that individuals with these characteristics pass them on to their offspring.

Several processes at a cellular level seem to be responsible for manifestations of the ageing process. Body cells are capable of renewal by duplication. However, the number of times they can duplicate is finite, and having reached their maximum number of duplications, they die. Furthermore, sometimes they duplicate incorrectly, so that after some time there is a range of damaged DNA cells in the body. As by-products of normal cell activity, the body fabricates toxins, the so-called free radicals, which accumulate over the years. Naturally, there are further 'wear-and-tear' effects and environmental influences that cause bodily ageing.

In sum, there are many processes that interact to cause the ageing process, and the last scientific word has not yet been pronounced to explain why they occur and if they can ever be prevented.

◉ Ageism and society's values

We saw in the previous chapter that some mid-lifers fight to hold back the ageing process by using cosmetic surgery. Where does this glorification of eternal youth and the fear of old age come from? Why should there be a stigma associated with old age? The answer seems to be that there is a socialization process whereby the dominant prejudices of society are presented to the developing individual, who over time internalizes them. Where societal values emphasize productivity, a somewhat pessimistic picture of age after retirement is offered, as if life loses its meaning after work. This has its consequences in social policies, and in stereotypical views of old age being equated with decline, weakness and dependency:

> Ageism legitimates the use of chronological age to mark out classes of people who are systematically denied resources and opportunities that others enjoy, and who suffer the consequence of such denigration, ranging from well-meaning patronage to unambiguous vilification.
>
> (Bytheway, 1995, p. 14)

Consequently, what senior citizens fear most is increased dependency, loss of autonomy, and becoming a burden, particularly to their own children (Dittman-Kohli, 1990). The use of chronological age to judge people's abilities and performance has led to biased decision-making about retirement and old age, and creates age-related stereotypes that guide the ways older people are approached and talked to (Williams & Nussbaum, 2001). Ageism affects the quality of treatment offered to older patients in hospitals (Helmes & Gee, 2003; Peake & Thompson, 2003), and even research scholars concentrate their investigations on ageing *problems*, with few interested in studying *growth*. Hardly any investigations attempt to explore whether there are activities or mental tasks where older people might perform better than younger people. It seems even researchers expect nothing but deterioration and decline. Betty Friedan (1994, p. 75) summarizes the effects of ageism as follows:

> The public policies of compassionate ageism and the scientific parameters of gerontology, no less than outright age discrimination in industry and professions and the social exclusion of older people from the mainstream of the community, have reinforced the terror of age: the weak, catastrophic, victim face of age.

Not surprisingly, prejudices about ageing negatively affect older people's self-esteem (Robins *et al.*, 2002). However, Binstock (2010) argues that over the last five decades, while the political behaviour of older individuals has remained largely the same, societal views on ageing policies have changed considerably. Now, in the context of the ageing of the large generation of 'baby boomers' together with governmental concerns about reducing large financial deficits, he wonders if ageing policies may change and asks whether there might be possible future inter-generational conflicts over taxes and costs of old-age benefits. Since 2010, the Equality Act makes age discrimination in employment, training and adult education unlawful, and in April 2011, the default retirement age has been abolished. However, the law still allows loopholes for compulsorily retiring people at a fixed age, and only covers age discrimination in the workplace. In our culture, a look at birthday cards for people over 50 is enough to confirm that ageist jokes and comments do not have the same stigma attached to them as sexist or racist ones.

To summarize, ageism can still be found in wide sectors of society, even though its negative effects on older citizens have been clearly documented.

👁 Health

> When you are over 70 and you wake up in the morning without pain, you know you are dead!

This was said by the American comedienne, Joan Rivers, being over 70 years herself. Ageism is widespread and has for a long time haunted even research. Thus, research themes emphasize the identification of risk factors and factors explaining diseases in old age, rather than exploring development and growth. The good news, according to Vaupel (2010), is that age-deteriorations have been delayed by at least a decade and people are reaching old age in better health. With future scientific advances, healthy survival to even greater ages seems possible. Further, the proportion of severe disability in the elderly has declined (Gorin & Lewis, 2004). Such a demographic shift is having, and will have, profound implications for individuals, society and the economy.

According to Draper and Anderson (2010), the baby-boomer generation is now in the 65-years-and-over age-group. They argue that this growth in the older population between 2011 and 2030 will challenge healthcare systems worldwide. For instance, mental health services for older people will need to prepare for a near doubling of demand. Larson (2010) reports that, as the lifespan is lengthening, there will be the possibility of increases in later-life dementia, particularly Alzheimer's disease. He claims that after age 65, rates of dementia tend to double every five years in developed countries and concludes that if the onset of dementia could be delayed, more fulfilling lives could be led for longer.

In this context, it is important to stress that cognitive decline in older age is vastly exaggerated in the public mind and often confused with symptoms of diseases such as Alzheimer's. Despite numerous attempts to show such a decline, no research findings exist proving that it is a natural part of ageing. With regard to mental health, there are actually improvements in old age, apart from illnesses related to cognitive impairment (Stuart-Hamilton, 2006).

However, symptoms of depression seem to be different, and perhaps underestimated, in old age compared to younger ages. For example, Bergdahl et al. (2007) showed that symptoms of depression in old age include increased loss of interest and motivation, sleep disturbances, anorexia and fatigue, chronic diseases, declining health, taking inappropriate medication and poor eating habits. Further, though clinical depression might not increase, incidents of reactive depression might, as there could now be a personal fear of death, which, alongside relationship issues and family bereavement, might affect symptoms of depression (Cicirelli, 2009).

Further, health generally might decline. As an example, in the Berlin Ageing study, Mayer and Baltes (1996) pointed out that, by age seventy, 33 per cent of the sample suffered from at least one serious disease, while 98 per cent experienced some kind of illness. So, by this age, a large number of people will have faced coping with some health problems. Up to middle-age most people have to deal mainly with episodic stresses such as work problems or family issues, influenza and industrial injuries. In old age, health problems tend to become continuous and chronic (Aldwin et al., 1996).

The ability to perform the necessary activities of daily life is clearly important for independent living. Seidel et al. (2010) looked at the difficulties older people have in relation to different household tasks and found that most problems are attributable to movement limitations, particularly bending/stooping, whereas actions and hand functions create fewer difficulties.

Normal ageing processes lead to reduced functions in the body system, affecting, for example, the lungs and heart, the gastro-intestinal and the urinary tract. This makes the ageing person more prone to cardiovascular disease, potentially leading to strokes and heart attacks, osteoporosis, Alzheimer's, dementia and eye diseases. Further, just by living longer, the probability increases of developing illnesses not necessarily age-related, such as cancer. Because of prolonged life expectancy, people now experience more years of living with a disease than earlier generations.

However, health and life expectancy vary widely according to different geographical regions, and are strongly associated with socioeconomic status. A longitudinal study (House *et al.*, 1994) showed that, at lower socioeconomic levels, morbidity and functional limitations increase steadily throughout middle- and old-age, and this is further mediated by differential exposure to risk factors. The higher socioeconomic groups exhibit better health behaviours, lower levels of stress and greater self-efficacy across the lifespan.

Some ailments can be prevented or alleviated by lifestyle factors, though there are no easy formulae of recommendations because there are complicated interactions among diet, exercise, substance use, genetic factors and social support that influence health and life expectancy (Stuart-Hamilton, 2006).

Box 7.1: Studying human change

Looking at lifespan development means we want to learn how human beings change over time. For example, in what ways do older people differ from younger ones in several aspects of their lives? How do we go about finding out answers to this question?

First, that seems to be easy. We take a group of adolescents, young adults and older people and measure their behaviours, their values and attitudes, and see if we find differences (this is called a cross-sectional design). Let's say, we are interested in finding out if music taste changes over time. So we play some samples of music to our three groups, and let them rate how much they like each of them. Most probably, we will find that the youngest group gives the highest ratings to Lady Gaga, while the middle-aged group rates the Beatles highest, and the oldest ones give the highest scores to Frank Sinatra or Ella Fitzgerald. Can we now draw the conclusion that with increasing age, music taste will change, and that the teenagers of today will be the Beatles fans of tomorrow?

No way, Jose! What we observe here is *not* an effect of ageing; it is a so-called cohort effect. Members of one age-group grew up under certain societal conditions, which included certain fashions, tastes, values and living conditions, and they are still influenced by these shared experiences. So, what we are measuring is more the effects of their socialization process, not the changes affected by their increasing age. That is fairly easy to see when we are examining music tastes, but it also affects everything else: Results on intelligence tests (affected by different educational experiences), attitudes towards money and savings (affected by different economic situations in adolescence), relationships with family (affected by family values as they grew up), work commitment, and so on. For this reason, it is impossible to know whether a difference that we find between age-groups in a cross-sectional design is due to increasing age, or due to the fact that the different age-groups had different experiences throughout their lives.

What, then, if we take a large group of babies, take our measurements, and then measure them again every fifth year until they are old? Surely, that should give us more information about the effects of ageing, since they all grow up under the same societal conditions? (This is called a longitudinal design). One of the difficulties with longitudinal research is that it takes a very long time. Actually, it is very likely that the researchers who first examined the babies are no longer alive when their research participants reach retirement age. But that is not the only problem. Though we have now eliminated the cohort-effect for this group, we cannot be sure whether we can generalize our findings to other generations that will be born under different societal conditions. For example, we might find that as our group gets older, they become less active in sports and more interested in family life, grandchildren and sedentary hobbies and we might draw the conclusion that this is caused by ageing. However, the picture could be very different for future generations when medical inventions might have eradicated immobilizing diseases, retirement age has been raised to 70 years, and very few people have grandchildren.

The best current solution for researchers is to carry out studies that combine both approaches. Not only one cohort is selected and followed longitudinally, but every few years or so, a new, younger cohort is added to the design. That is, there might be a sample of 15-year-olds, 20-year-olds, 25-year-olds and so on, who all will be examined every fifth year. This is called a sequential longitudinal design, and it evades most of the pitfalls of the other two designs – but it is very expensive and time-consuming to set up, and so it is not often possible to carry out. So, you will find many cross-sectional and longitudinal studies in the research literature – just be aware that their results need to be interpreted carefully and with caution.

In some cases, a factor that is protective for one aspect of health might be harmful for another. For example, exercise is advantageous in preventing cardiovascular disease, but might contribute to osteoarthritis; exposure to sunlight can cause skin cancer, but is necessary to produce vitamin D; cod-liver oil eases the effects of arthritis, but increases the risk of cranial bleeding.

As we have stated above, psychological and medical research tends to concentrate on the gloomy aspects of life and investigates problems more often than opportunities.

However, older people themselves do not necessarily share this view. In many studies, older people report that their subjective health is good (often despite medical evidence revealing the opposite), or that their health condition does not limit their daily activities (Herzog *et al.*, 1991). In the above-mentioned Berlin study, almost 30 per cent judged their health as good or very good, though objectively, the vast majority suffered from at least one illness. A woman in one of our own studies described her attitude to objective health problems as follows:

> Health is good. I have, well, I have diabetes, too high blood pressure, a little bit of angina, but I am not thinking a lot about all that usually. I take pills (laughs) and I think if one is occupied with, if one has a nice hobby, a lovely family, good friends, then it is nonsense to go and think so much about these small hassles. I mean, to lay down like 'Oooh, I have high blood pressure', 'Oooh, I have angina', I think that embitters one's life.
>
> (71 years, Kloep & Hendry, 2006, p. 587).

Most importantly, subjective health is a better predictor for how long a person will live than medical diagnoses (McMamish-Svensson *et al.*, 1999). Subjective health is strongly associated with feelings of well-being, which in turn are influenced by many factors. For example, the conviction of having a purpose in life is a powerful element in well-being. Among community-based older persons, greater purpose in life was found to be associated with being able to function effectively, to carry out the basic and instrumental activities of daily living and retaining mobility (Boyle *et al.*, 2010). Of course, it facilitates continuing physical activity if people have a history of being active, but it is still possible to engage former sedentary individuals in physical activities other than housework by offering supportive environmental conditions (Del Castillo *et al.*, 2010). Such conditions are often provided by family and friends, who have a major influence on well-being and health, to the degree that they can offset the consequences of decreasing capacities (Merz & Huxhold, 2010; Prieto-Flores *et al.*, 2010).

To sum up, it seems inevitable that health declines with increasing age, even though medical advances can ease many of the effects of age-related diseases. However, for the well-being and even the longevity of older people, subjective health is much more important than their actual medical conditions, and this, in turn, is influenced by factors such as maintaining a meaningful role in life and the availability of social support.

◉ Family and friends

As if writing a children's story like Cinderella where the 'wicked' stepmother was cruel to poor Cinders, we want to suggest that this is the time in the life course when adult children can 'get back' at their parents for all the miseries they have endured as they grew up! More seriously, now is the time when adult children may be required to look after ageing parents as one of their roles as members of the 'sandwich' generation. Whitbeck *et al.* (1994) have pointed out that the quality of parent–child relationships during early childhood is a determining factor in whether middle-aged children want to support their ageing parents. Perceptions of past unfairness on the part of parents have a significant impact on the current feelings of affection or animosity in adult children (Allen *et al.*, 2000). Family tensions occur when parents cannot allow their children to demonstrate that they are now truly adult and continue to intervene in their domestic and daily affairs (Fingerman, 2001; Fingerman & Pitzer, 2007). On the other hand, ambivalence about autonomy and independence in the family circle also emerge, when parents need their children's support (Pillemer & Lüscher, 2004; Spitze & Gallant, 2004). From the perspective of parents, they fear a loss of independence, and often refuse to be cared for, not wanting to be a burden on their children nor ask them for help (Ikkink *et al.*, 1999; Martini *et al.*, 2001). Adult children, on the other hand, worry about their elderly parents. Many families negotiate these changes in domestic and caring roles and relationships successfully over time, but it is nonetheless a crucial shift for both parents and adult children.

Looking at another aspect of change in family relationships, this is also the time when many parents are transformed into grandparents. With the de-standardization of the life course, becoming a grandparent can happen at almost any time from early adulthood on. Giarrusso *et al.* (1996), for instance, found the range of grandparents' ages in their sample to run from 30 to 110 years.

In a study of more than 150 first-time grandparents, Somary and Stricker (1998) looked at their expectations of grandparenthood before their first grandchild was born, and again, in the first two years after birth. Grandmothers report greater satisfaction and overall meaning in grandparenthood than grandfathers, who feel more able to offer child-rearing advice to the parents. Then, maternal grandparents rather than paternal grandparents are more satisfied in grandparenthood than they expected to be.

Being occupied with travel, hobbies, friends and other interests, many choose a part-time role as grandparents, preferring not to have too intense or sustained contact with the new generation and to focus on other aspects of their daily lives (Hansen & Jacob, 1992). On the other hand, while they face retirement, health problems, and transitional age concerns and need their children's support, their adult children are, in turn, more concerned with their new-born and requesting help with baby-sitting.

Nevertheless, links to grandchildren appear to be warm, helpful and rewarding. Grandparents have multiple roles to fulfil, ranging from sur-rogate parents to playmates for their grandchildren, to counsellors, inter-fering know-alls and even the source for marital disharmony (Pruchno & Johnson, 1996). If parents get along well with their adult children, and show a high level of involvement and responsibility towards their grandchildren, all three generations can derive much satisfaction out of the relationship (Bates, 2009). With the growing needs of young peo-ple in present-day society, the proportion of grandparents supporting their grandchildren economically has been increasing lately (Hoff, 2007).

The presence of close family members seems to provide a particu-larly strong support in dealing with daily life in old age. The quality, rather than the quantity of support, is *the* characteristic that enhances the older person's well-being (Merz & Huxhold, 2010). In particular older people without a spouse or children appear to gain from emotional sup-port and care they receive from their siblings. Simply perceiving that sibling support *would* be available *if needed* promotes their well-being, and presumably ensures greater resources for older persons (Connidis & Campbell, 1995).

Victor and colleagues (2002) raised the intriguing question of whether loneliness is increasing because of the decline in multi-generation house-holds and changes in family structure since the Second World War. Through a comparative analysis of historical and more recent data, they discovered that reported severe loneliness in old age ranged from 5 to

9 per cent of the participants and showed no increase over the years of the survey. Five sets of factors have been shown to be consistently associated with loneliness: socio-demographic attributes (living alone, being female, not having any surviving children); material circumstances (poverty, limited education, low income); health resources (disability, self-assessed health, mental health, cognitive function, anxiety and depression); social resources (size of social network, isolation, time alone and presence of a confidante); and life events (recent bereavement and admission of a relative into care; [Victor *et al.*, 2005]). The researchers proposed three 'loneliness pathways' in later life, namely, a continuation of a long-established lifestyle, the late onset of loneliness, or decreasing loneliness. In a study of over four thousand community-dwelling older citizens, more than one-third suffered from loneliness, though feelings of loneliness were not connected with the frequency of contacts with children and friends, but rather with the expectations of and satisfactions with these contacts. The most powerful predictors of loneliness were living alone, depression, not being understood by closest relatives and unfulfilled expectations of contacts with friends (Routasalo *et al.*, 2006).

Loneliness can have different meanings. It can mean being physically separated from others (social disconnectedness), not participating in social life, or the feeling of not having social support. Social disconnectedness seems not to vary across age-groups, but the oldest old feel more isolated than the young old, and both social disconnectedness and perceived isolation are greater among those who have poorer health (Cornwell & Waite, 2009). These results remind us of how inter-connected coping resources are: Poor health, financial problems and lack of education all increase feelings of loneliness, and these, in turn, influence health and well-being. Many older people, however, can escape this downward spiral, and, in general, age has been shown to be positively related to frequency of socializing with neighbours, religious participation and civic volunteering (Cornwell *et al.*, 2008).

Though the size of social networks tends to decrease in very old age, the number of really close friends does not, thus guaranteeing a continuity of support (Lang & Carstensen, 1994). Further Field (1999), in her US sample of 74–93-year-olds, could not find any changes in their perceived ability of making new friends, of keeping old friends and in the amount of contact with friends over a period of 14 years. Some time ago, Hendry and Kloep (2002) theorized that in old age many people return to organized social and leisure activities as venues for making new friends, extending social networks, meeting new partners and developing new interests in the wake of possible partner and friendship losses. For example, the University of the Third Age is a self-help and teaching organization offering a wide range of activities and interests for retired people. In many ways this is a successful model of both local, national and international proportions that could be copied on a smaller scale in rural and urban communities. In such a form, the legitimate wishes of older people for activity, engagement and social interaction could be resolved by themselves, with support from others, on a local basis.

One significant alteration for older people in our increasingly technological society has been the need to adopt and adapt to new ways of communicating and finding new friends and romantic partners. The use of Twitter, Facebook, chatlines and online dating agencies has opened new possibilities for the so-called silver surfers. The Internet has proved to be a valuable resource for information and emotional support for people suffering from cancer (Fogel *et al.*, 2002), caring for someone with Alzheimer's Disease (White & Dorman, 2000) and in life crises and bereavement (Vanderwerker & Prigerson, 2004).

To summarize, as in all other spheres of life, inter-individual variability in social relations is high in older people. Many become grandparents, but their engagement in this role depends very much on individual factors. Relationships with their own children are often somewhat ambivalent, particularly if a form of role-reversal is perceived. Siblings and friends continue to play an important role as sources of social support, and the use of information technology for networking is spreading among senior citizens.

Bereavement

> Then one had more of a social life and that has become gradually less. It is relatively thin now. It is like, in my circle, one is 80 and the other soon will be, there is no one who has a car and a licence ... (After retirement), we had more time to be together, we in the girls' gang. They were four. Three died 8 years ago, my best friend died then. The other, she lost her husband when I lost mine, and then she married again, and so she disappeared more and more. And then she became ill, and cut herself off.
>
> (woman, 79, from Kloep & Hendry, 2006, p. 586)

The above quote offers clear support for Greenbaum's (2000) comments that the medical profession has become very competent in holding back death for years, or even decades, but that they are not so clever in preventing loneliness or the other problems of advanced old age. One life change that is likely with increasing age is that old friends and relatives die and bereavement becomes a normative event. It is particularly older women who bear the burden of bereavement because they live longer, have more friends, and are more involved in comforting others (Williams *et al.*, 2006). It is also mainly women who experience the loss of their marriage partner. Those whose self-identity consisted mainly of being a wife and a mother have greater difficulties in finding a new role in widowhood than those who had a variety of social roles throughout life. This may explain why women over 65 years of age, who have been single all their lives, are healthier and more satisfied than divorcees or widows (Newton & Keith, 1997).

For men, coping with widowhood seems to be more difficult, particularly if they are little involved in social activities and have few close friends (Bures *et al.*, 2009), and this is true even when variables like income, education and health (of which men have more) and the number of social networks (of which women have more) are taken into consideration (Stevens, 1995). If partners had held gender-stereotyped roles during their marriage, adaptation to widowhood is complicated by the lack of skills in daily living (household activities for men; house repairs, financial and legal issues for women [Lund *et al.*, 1993]).

Another issue is coping with the expectations of others, such as adult children disapproving of a new marriage or removal to another place. Not all feelings are instantly understandable to other people. Even the adequacy of expressions of grief might be questioned by others (Doka, 2005, 2007), since some experience a range of contradictory feelings in bereavement: anger, guilt, loneliness, relief, personal pride in coping.

The experience of grief is influenced by many different factors including previous loss, attachment style, and relationship to the deceased, the circumstances of death, whether or not it was expected, if there was time to say good-bye and the availability of social support (Lobb *et al.*, 2010). Yet even an event as sad as the loss of a beloved does not have to be unbearable forever. Some show resilience immediately, others achieve it gradually, and for some there is a turning point, an event that 'brings them round' (Bennett, 2010). Adaptation to life alone does not mean *not* missing or grieving. Feelings of loss have been reported for up to two decades after a death (Wortman *et al.*, 1993). As with all major life events, in time even widowhood can lead to positive growth experiences such as creating a new social network or learning new skills (Lieberman, 1992).

In sum, the death of a beloved, particularly a spouse, is often initially devastating for the survivor. Nevertheless, in time there are positive adjustments in many individuals, enabling them to recover psychologically and re-establish friendships and social contacts, and even to experience personal growth.

◉ Dating and sex

After the death of a spouse and a period of mourning, older people often consider dating, even if it is not intended to lead to marriage, but as a source of companionship or possibly as a sexual relationship (Bulcroft & Bulcroft, 1991). A relatively large number of people enter into new partner-relationships after bereavement or divorce, and cohabitation and 'living-apart-together' arrangements are frequent in new partnerships.

De-Jong-Gierveld (2004) argues that age at partnership dissolution, the number of dissolutions, working during and after the most recent dissolution, together with social class and education are important elements in weighing up different types of living arrangements to choose in later life. As we have mentioned before, widows cope better than widowers. Perhaps because of this, many widowers in old age often seek new brides after a relatively short period of mourning, whereas widows generally seem less interested in seeking new live-in partners. In line with these ideas, research in Sweden revealed that more and more elderly widows choose to have a 'living-apart-together' relationships with new partners, insisting in keeping their own flat for themselves – and refusing to act as a cleaning lady for their partners (Borell & Karlsson, 2000). Pickard (1994) reported that elderly widows in Wales are reluctant to re-marry, not wanting to give up the freedom they finally gained through widowhood, and not daring to risk their good relations with other family members by introducing a new man into the household.

More recently, Dickson *et al.* (2009) carried out an interview study of older women's views on dating and discovered that they have quite different views on relationships compared with men of the same age. Women complain that their new male partners have been spoiled in an earlier marriage and are now looking for somebody to provide these services again, an idea which is not shared by the women:

> They want someone to be a nurse and I want someone to date.
>
> (69 years, woman, p. 74)

Consequently, they are not keen on marriage, but are looking for friendship, companionship and some excitement, not for any disadvantages marriage would bring them. This nearly looks like a late-life reversal of gender roles, mirroring the reluctance of males to commit to marriage in young adulthood. This is also reflected in the choice of partners:

> I almost prefer to date younger guys because they have more energy and I don't want to hear how his back hurts.
>
> (72 years, woman, p. 74).

This wish to date younger men has also been observed by Levesque and Caron (2004). Further interview data reveal the desire of older women for intimate hugging and kissing rather than explicit sexual activity. However, sexual contact is not excluded (Bulcroft & Bulcroft, 1991).

There has been relatively little research on sexuality in later life, particularly among those over 60 years of age, and current findings stem mainly from a biomedical perspective. DeLamater and Sill (2005) suggest that age, hormone levels, illnesses and various medications all negatively affect sexual functioning in older persons, while factors such as having a partner, the value put on sexuality and level of education can be positive influences. This shows that attitudes are more significant forces for sexual desire than biomedical factors.

As evidence that older people are sexually active, Beckman *et al.*'s (2008) statistics show that the prevalence of sexual activity among married men aged 70 years is 69 per cent, and among married women 57 per cent. There is evidence of increasing sexual activity and satisfactory relationships in the over-70-year-old cohorts from 1971 to 2001. A US investigation (Lindau *et al.*, 2007) with a national sample between 57 and 85 years of age indicates that sexual activity declines somewhat with age. The most prevalent sexual problems among older women are low desire, difficulty with vaginal lubrication and inability to climax. Among men, the most prevalent sexual problems are erectile difficulties. Another study (Cornwell *et al.*, 2009) concludes that older men are more likely than women to have a partner, more likely to be sexually active with that partner, and to have more positive and permissive attitudes toward sex. Though showing some decrease in sexual activity, and considerable gender differences, research results contradict typical ageist stereotypes in later life:

> There is a belief, in the general public and even among professionals, according to which sexuality is among the first functions to diminish with age. This belief is a myth because sexuality is rather one of the last faculties to decline.
>
> (Trudel *et al.*, 2000, p. 382)

Health workers have recently become alerted to sexually-related health risks in old age, for example the prevalence of unprotected sex within a generation that did not receive targeted health education on condom use when they were young (Jacobs & Thomlison, 2009). So, without doubt, in the absence of chronic illness, both men and women have sex until very old age. Sexual functioning is often psychologically influenced, for example, fears of not being attractive enough can interfere with performance. However, sexual capability lives on until death, even if it may be altered by physiological changes (Trudel *et al.*, 2000). In the light of this, it is appalling that older people's needs for privacy, intimacy and sexual expression do not receive sufficient attention in residential care homes (Bauer *et al.*, 2009).

In general, we have seen that older women like to date but do not want to marry, though men do. To conclude our review of sexuality in older age, we noted that biological factors that began to impinge on mid-lifers continue to cause some decrease in sexual activity in later life, but it is equally clear that many older people continue to enjoy intimacy, sexuality and sexual encounters.

◉ Retirement from work

One of the main adjustments as the individual enters old age is retirement from paid work. Denton and Spencer (2009) summarize the various definitions of retirement: From non-participation or reduced participation in the labour force, receipt of pension income, end-of-career employment, self-assessed retirement, or combinations of those characteristics. They conclude that no one measure is especially effective as a conceptualization of retirement. They suggest a more positive approach would be to focus on what people actually do, including their involvement in socially productive, non-market activities even though these do not contribute to national income as conventionally measured.

Winston and Barnes (2007) conducted interviews with academic women who were born between 1946 and 1964, asking what they expected from retirement. The women reject traditional definitions, determining their age of retirement according to personal needs and envisaging retirement as an active period involving a mixture of work and leisure activities. Decisions regarding retirement are influenced by social and family factors as well as health status and personal wishes regarding future life (Smith, 2004a).

One of the main issues affecting the decision to retire is health. Not only does existing poor health play a role in employees' decisions to retire, but also the wish to protect one's health and, before health deteriorates, to dedicate more time to other life goals (Pond et al., 2010).

But retirement is not necessarily a voluntary choice. Rather, it is a realistic adjustment of goals to objective possibilities. Accepting their own limitations, older people can regard re-adjustments in their life as challenges and find ways to deal with them. Van Solinge and Henkens (2010) found that older employees who believe that they still have a long time to live show a preference for later retirement, even if they do not succeed in carrying out their intentions. To date, there are few signs that a sizeable number of older people – particularly in the middle classes – necessarily want to disappear entirely from the workforce.

Being forced into retirement is negatively associated with personal satisfaction (Herzog et al., 1991). However, this is compounded by other variables. For instance, people who are forced to leave work because of redundancy, ill-health or care responsibilities are more likely to experience financial problems and have more constraints on their social and leisure pursuits (Barnes et al., 2002). Nevertheless, in the UK the number of pensioners living in poverty has decreased over the years, and is now smaller than the percentage of working-aged adults and children living in low income households. However, even a figure of 16 per cent means that apart from health problems, economic hardship is one of the largest obstacles to well-being in old age.

What are some of the tasks retired individuals need to achieve? In the first place, retirement means having to learn to re-structure the day and find hobbies and pursuits. Losing contact with former work colleagues might mean having to build up a new social network. It might also mean adjustments to a new economic situation, which could imply moving to a smaller flat or giving up more expensive hobbies.

It can have implications for marital relations. Suddenly, a couple who might have rarely seen each other during the day for the whole of their working lives will have to interact 24 hours-a-day, find topics (other than work) to talk about and re-allocate household tasks. Or at least *discuss* the re-allocation of household tasks! As a German study has shown, these negotiations often end with men having fewer, and women having more, household tasks to do than before retirement (Klumb & Baltes, 1999). Retirement is also positively related to having a hobby and pursuing leisure activities, if health allows it (Scherger *et al.*, 2011).

In one of our own interview studies with over 60 retired men and women (Kloep & Hendry, 2006), it became clear that, like other life events, retirement has different meanings for different people. We identified four groups among our sample:

The first, and by far the biggest group, consists of active individuals, for whom retirement is a growth experience. They liked their job but were also happy to give it up to make time for other activities. They have an intensive social network and cope easily with some perceived health problems.

They are very different from the second group, whose members refuse to retire, or, when forced to do so, develop major adaptation problems. Their whole identity is closely linked to their work position – they have few other interests. In our sample, all individuals belonging to this group are males in relatively senior work positions.

The third group consists of recently retired people who have not quite adjusted to the new demands of retired life, and complain about the loss of status and meaning. However, there are signs that at least some of them will eventually mobilize sufficient resources to move on, find a turning point and develop.

Finally, the smallest group consists of individuals suffering from a range of co-occurring problems. They disliked their work, they dislike retirement, too.

These results highlight the many different pathways into retirement, and the many interacting factors influencing them. Interestingly, Crosnoe and Elder (2002), using a quantitative person-centred approach, classified their sample of older men into four clusters that are similar to those we found: The 'well-rounded' group, consisting of individuals who excelled in all life domains, the 'family-focussed', the 'career-focussed, socially disengaged' and the 'less adjusted'.

To summarize, retirement is one of the major shifts in old age. As in other periods of life, it depends on when, how and under what circumstances people retire, how well they adjust to this major change consisting of many different social and economic tasks. Some people choose to retire, others do not, some adapt to retired life, others find new employment, and some despair. As with other challenges, retirement brings losses and gains, can be devastating for some, yet a chance for psychological growth in others.

◉ Successful ageing

Earlier in this chapter, we discussed how societal prejudices and socially constructed stereotypes of ageing influence social policy and provision for senior citizens and direct research towards the more negative aspects of old age. Such coverage offers an extremely pessimistic and uninspiring view.

However, it is possible to paint an altogether rosier picture of lifestyles in old age and to present a much more positive perspective of life as a senior citizen. In reality, for most people, a steady plateau of life satisfaction is maintained for a fair span of years. The most dreaded event, total loss of independence and institutionalization, only happens to a small percentage of very old people – around 4 per cent of the over 65s in the UK (OECD, 2009). Over the last decades, cultural and social forces together with medical advances have been able to offset many of the deficiencies inherent in the biological make-up of old people (Smith & Baltes, 1999), and increasing amenities such as ambulatory nursing and Meals on Wheels services allow a growing number to remain in their own home if they so wish. This has rekindled a growing interest in the concept of 'successful ageing'.

However, as with other concepts, what constitutes successful ageing is ill-defined. Much medical research literature equates it with good health, or at least the absence of disability or deficits in physical performance. Studies using this definition find that around a third of people over the age of 65 could be classified as ageing successfully (Depp & Jeste, 2006). When successful ageing is defined as having 'exceptional good health', this percentage shrinks to 8 per cent (Kaplan *et al.*, 2008). This seems to be a very narrow conceptualization, given that the World Health Organisation (1946) describes health as 'a state of complete physical, mental and social well-being and not merely the absence of disease or infirmity'. Consequently, most researchers use wider criteria. For example, Rowe and Kahn (1998) include absence of disease, disability and risk factors, maintaining physical and mental functioning and active engagement with life.

In our health section, we discussed how people do not always share medical views about their health and well-being. Those studies using a self-assessment of successful ageing show different and more optimistic results than those using researcher-defined medical criteria. Strawbridge *et al.* (2002) found that in their sample of 65–99-year-olds, more than half assessed themselves as ageing successfully, but, using Rowe and Kahn's criteria, they classified only about one-fifth as belonging to this category. The reason for the discrepancy was that many participants with chronic conditions and with functional difficulties still rated themselves as ageing successfully. Furthermore, self-classifications correlated much higher with well-being than objective criteria used. An even more optimistic result was achieved in another study (Montross *et al.*, 2006), in which 92 per cent of the over 60s rated themselves as ageing successfully, though their self-ratings were not associated with their objective health, age or socioeconomic status. Obviously, successful ageing is a multi-dimensional construct, consisting of both objective and subjective elements, and accordingly, it is associated with a variety of factors ranging from earlier lifestyle elements, such as level of education and activity-involvement, to current health behaviours and social support (Pruchno *et al.*, 2010).

These findings show that individual experiences of ageing and coping with age-related challenges tell a different story from those using criteria defined by young or middle-aged researchers. Reichstadt and her colleagues (2008, 2010) decided that instead of using researcher-defined questions, they would simply ask older people to talk about their experiences of ageing. They conducted focus group and individual interviews around the topic 'successful ageing' with individuals between 64 and 96 years of age, and identified two primary themes: Self-knowledge and continuing growth. Their interviewees are aware of the activities they can no longer do, acknowledge the fact and then adjust lifestyle to their capacities. The key is to emphasize what is still possible, to enjoy that and live in the here-and-now. Further, they find it important to remain socially engaged, follow novel pursuits, cherish friendship, retain a positive attitude and not abandon opportunities for personal growth. One significant point old people make – which casts doubt on many research attempts to measure successful ageing – is that they perceive these factors not as outcomes but as an ongoing, developmental process beginning in the present not the past.

The most amazing aspect of Reichstadt *et al.*'s results is that what these older persons mention in their interviews as the important components of successful ageing closely parallel the theoretical view offered by Smith and Baltes (1999, see Chapter 2), who state that growth is still possible in advanced age, if individuals use the coping strategy of selective optimization with compensation. To reiterate: Their recommendation is that when some resources are depleted, the optimal way of dealing with a particular challenge is to reassess what is still possible and adjust one's goals to the level of resources one still has. This might imply disengaging from some lower level priorities in one's life and accepting that it might be necessary to rely on compensatory means to continue developing. For instance, if I break my leg, I may have to walk with a stick, play golf instead of squash, and so on. This is not easy for some, and we have to accept that life is unjust. Nevertheless, we would like to cite one of the women from our studies, who summarizes what is needed to age successfully:

> There is a lot to it that one keeps oneself active. I do not want to go to the nursing home, so I try to prepare my own meals and care for myself. The only thing is that I have to keep the house in order, and old things really need to be cared for. But I have to say, I do not receive free help. The only thing I say is, you cannot sit down and wait for help. That is the silliest thing to do. You better try and fix it yourself. I've tried up till now. Now I do not manage any more to go down to the cellar with the laundry machines. I can't look after these new machines, so now I do the washing myself. I keep myself in order, with clothes and everything. I like to be decently dressed and to keep myself beautiful. I am very conceited (laughs). Do not allow yourself to be left behind. You have to manage yourself; there is no one who asks about you. It is up to yourself, and you have to activate yourself and keep track of the daily events and of politics and everything, as much as one can. One cannot give up and say that I am old. No, one has to stand up for oneself and make sure that one keeps track.

(woman, 94, Kloep & Hendry, 2006, p. 588)

For those who have been concerned by the bleak outlook that both researchers and the media paint of old age, we would like to present two successful examples of what is still possible – given, of course, some necessary resources. Sawchuk (2009) investigated a group called 'the raging grannies', who are older women using their outfit as a protective identity and alter the words of traditional songs to send out political messages. They see their age status as empowering and as something to be embraced and moreover, they are still in the process of identity exploration – something that younger researchers try to confine to the adolescent years.

The other example, showing that there is no age limit to education and learning, determination, enthusiasm and future-orientation of older citizens, is not a research finding at all, but a magazine report. This is a feature about a dustman who retired in 1983 and then went back to university in 2002, first completing a BSc and then a Masters in Waste Management from the University of Northampton in 2007, when he was 88 years old (Times Higher Education, 2010, 19–25 August, 24).

Thus, the message of this section is that successful ageing (however defined) is possible. In objective, health-related terms, about one-third of the population over 65 years can be regarded in these terms. However, when old people self-report, a much higher proportion regard themselves as ageing successfully, and this includes those with a disability or chronic health condition. There is no evidence that getting older reduces happiness and self-perceived health, provided that there are sufficient positive factors in one's lives to maintain morale. Given an adequately satisfying emotional and social life, it is possible to adapt to adverse conditions, such as stiffening arthritic joints, and still continue to lead a full life. However, it seems as if the number and nature of challenges confronting very old people eventually drains even the most resourceful, though it may take many years to do so (Crimmins et al., 1996).

Conclusions

In this chapter we have examined certain aspects of growing old. First, we discussed the effects of 'ageism' in society on transitions to old age. Then, we focussed on the increasing health problems people encounter as they age. Resources for coping, such as high quality of social contacts, a satisfying family life, ongoing activities and good health all interrelate, so that a serious loss in one life domain often has a serious impact on others, however temporarily (Kloep & Hendry, 2006).

Notwithstanding objective medical diagnosis, people tend to rate their subjective health as fairly satisfactory in old age. Retirement is one of the major transitions during this period, and, depending on work and family circumstances, health and finances, it is a challenge that can lead to growth or cause despair. Though older people do experience the loss of loved ones and friends, only a minority encounter severe loneliness. Despite common prejudices, many re-engage in dating after widowhood or divorce and have an active sex life.

Old age presents some individuals with an array of difficult tasks, while not all older citizens have sufficient resources to cope with them all. Nevertheless, a considerable percentage use their difficulties as opportunities for further growth. Perhaps even more than in other phases of life, we see great variability in lifestyle, attitudes and subjective well-being, due to the different experiences and circumstances the individual has encountered across the life course. Crosnoe and Elder (2002, p. 322) summarize the results of years of research into ageing with the following words:

> Some individuals experience this time of life as a period of decline and frustration, while others experience it as a time of renewal and activity. The factors that help to determine which of these broad patterns will characterize a man's later life are related, as expected, not only to specific aspects of his life during this time but also to his experiences – physical, psychological, interpersonal, social – across his adult years. These lifelong experiences influence aging style in their own right by capturing the nature of the individual pathways throughout life, not simply by establishing current circumstances. In other words, knowledge of the journey supplements knowledge about the destination in explaining patterns of adjustment in the later years.

At any point of our life course, we carry the consequences of our former selves with us – but also the germs of the person we are going to be.

👁 Further reading

Stuart-Hamilton, I. (2006) *The psychology of ageing: An introduction*. 4th edition. London: Jessica Kingsley Publishers.

This book is a comprehensive overview of theories and research regarding ageing, particularly covering health and cognitive functioning. At the time of writing, we know that a completely updated edition is in preparation, so watch this space!

Friedan, B. (1994) *The fountain of age*. New York: Touchstone.

This is a biographical account of how the author, Betty Friedan, an American activist and feminist, mastered her own prejudices about old age and discovered through her own experiences and by chartering the life of other age-peers, how life after 60 can be a time of growth and a source of novel discoveries. The book's ideas are supported by a wide ranging of research findings.

Chapter 8

Towards a New Positive Theory of Human Development

Summary

This chapter considers how transitions and transformations occur and how growth and development can be enhanced.
In detail, we look at:

- Shifts and challenges
- Transitions and transformations
- Positive psychology
- Resources for growth
- Future research and interventions.

Shifts and challenges

When we examine and analyse human development, we see that it is a response to the shifts and challenges individuals encounter across the lifespan. We described in Chapter 2 that there are maturational, normative and non-normative shifts. Though they all press the individual towards adapting to changed circumstances, adaptation is easier when the challenges are fairly predictable, maturational or normative shifts, because individuals can prepare to cope with these changes. Certain cultures even organize and arrange learning programmes to help people to prepare for these transitions. For example, nursery school children are inducted in preparation for the start of primary schooling; there are pre-marriage counselling seminars and pregnancy classes for couples; and many businesses have pre-retirement courses for older employees to offer them pension and investment advice and ideas on how to gain most from retirement.

Because these shifts are common and expected, they allow individuals to prepare for them by observing how their peers cope, finding role models and seeking out possible support groups. Experiencing the same shifts as other people also involves less stigma. For example, it is not too catastrophic to start losing your hair and getting wrinkles in mid-life when this process is also occurring to your age-mates, while hair loss during the late-teens or early-twenties creates some social embarrassment.

By contrast, the most difficult challenges are the non–normative shifts that often hit us unexpectedly, unprepared or alone, and put us 'at odds' with a particular societal norm. Non-normative transitions present a powerful challenge to the individual, much greater than the more predictable normative ones and – as a consequence – they offer a greater potential for development and change. Fiske and Chiriboga (1991, p. 285) came to a rather similar conclusion after a 20-year longitudinal study of US adults:

> Curiously, we found that the normative transitions defining the study did not themselves provide much in the way of a catalyst for change. Normative transitions, by their very nature, can be anticipated long before they occur and thus give people ample time to prepare. Moreover, most normative transitions are either ambiguous or positive. Thus it was the unanticipated events that most often brought upheaval and change.

One difficult challenge to overcome is being somehow different from physical norms, whether due to birth-damage or lifestyle or an injury later in life. Societies, with their social structures and buildings designed for the comfort and convenience of healthy, mobile people, often present an extra challenge for those with impairments. As with all other non-normative events, physical handicaps pose a challenge that lead to depression and resignation or encourage aspirations for achievement and development. Daniel James was a rugby player, paralysed after injury who decided he was unable to deal with this condition and took his own life. But we also know of people like Stephen Hawking who fights an increasingly incapacitating disease that does not stop him – maybe inspires him – to be a world leading scientist, or the amazing athletes who train and compete at the Paralympic Games.

Transitions and transformations, processes and mechanisms

These are a few examples of normative and non-normative shifts that can lead to turning points in our lives. But what exactly happens, when an individual goes through a turning point? Transitions may take some time to be accomplished and completed – few occur overnight! Transitions are triggered by changes in the environment or in the individual and require adaptations to occur. These are often periods of some upheaval, as the individual tries to adjust to the changed conditions, and solutions do not always come easily. One of the first signs of change and an indicator of increasing instability in the system is behavioural and emotional variability (Van der Maas & Molenaar, 1992). There might be a time of trial and error, of success and failure, but in the end, the individual is transformed.

Transformations can happen in the individual's perceptions of self and others, in their behaviours, attitudes and lifestyles, and in their status within groups at both the micro- and macro-levels of society. As we have pointed out repeatedly, on the surface, transitions at particular points in the life course appear radically different for different individuals, yet the underlying processes remain the same. What exactly happens during a transition? One of the values of an ecologic approach is that it can offer explanations of how long-term psychological development emerges from ongoing day-to-day events and interactions.

What triggers a minor change or a major transition is always a change in the actual situation, an event that stops the individual from achieving his or her goals. This always creates confusion or even anxieties within the individual – here, dynamic systems theorists would say that equilibrium has become disturbed. What happens next is a process of adaptation, which sometimes takes a few minutes and sometimes needs years, but eventually the balance is restored, and a new state of stability returns. The transition process is over and a transformation has occurred.

Brandtstädter and Rothermund (2002) suggest that there are essentially two strategies individuals employ during a transition. One consists of 'assimilative strategies'. If one notices that a goal is blocked and unattainable under existing circumstances, one can counteract this by trying to change the situation. Depending on what the obstacle and what the goal is, one could try to get rid of the obstacle (e.g. divorcing a partner who obstructs one's life plans), one could intensify one's own efforts (e.g. go on a diet or exercise more if unhappy with one's body shape), find help to achieve the original goal (e.g. ask a mentor for guidance and support, undergo fertility treatment), or change one's circumstances (e.g. transfer to another university). All these are active interventions to pursue one's chosen goals in spite of adversity. These strategies can be very adaptive in the long run. We all know of the success stories told about persevering people who 'never gave up' and succeeded 'in the end'. However, whether this is the optimal strategy to select depends on how important these goals really are, and how high the probability is of actually attaining them. In extreme cases, stubbornly futile attempts to continue on a chosen path pursuing impossible goals can lead to hopelessness and depression.

Particularly with 'hopeless case' scenarios, a viable second option is available: An 'accommodative' strategy. This kind of strategy consists of giving up the original aim in the face of difficulties, and refocusing one's ambitions (e.g. giving up ideas of becoming an X-Factor pop star but joining a choir), of disengaging from personal ideals (e.g. admitting that one cannot single-handedly change the world), giving up activities (e.g. discontinuing a sporting pursuit), letting go of a beloved (e.g. adjusting to divorce or death) or re-defining priorities (e.g. changing one's work-life balance). Hence, this too can be a highly effective strategy, reflecting the individual's ability to correctly self-assess their own capacities in the light of difficulties and have energy to attempt other (perhaps less arduous) goals. However, if employed too easily or too often, the individual might find that they give up so many aims there are not many achievable goals left! Such a state could have a serious impact on self-esteem.

Most people experience a period of uncertainty in deciding which of the strategies to employ. They waver between the two, contributing to feelings of stress and insecurity. In other words, it is part of the crisis, which nearly all theorists describe as being an essential component of developmental change. Eventually, people settle for one of these two strategies or a mixture of both. An example of the latter is given by Baltes *et al.* (1999): Arthur Rubinstein, one of the world's most famous pianists, gave performances until he was in his late 80s. Asked in an interview how he was able to do that, he said that he concentrated on fewer pieces (an accommodative strategy), and practised these pieces more often (an assimilative strategy). And when, finally, his performing commitments reduced, he wrote a two volume biography (accommodative strategy).

To summarize: Whatever happens in one's lifespan – whatever events and challenges one encounters, whatever individual outcomes might be – is all rather unpredictable. This is because of the tremendous individual variations in the combination of resources, current and former challenges, time and place in history, our interlinked lives, time in the life course when an event occurs, and the form and importance the change may have for us.

So, it is impossible to create anything like a normative description of the life course which gives a basically true picture and conveys how it feels to be 16-, 36-, 66- or 96-years-old. However, we can get some grasp of the underlying mechanisms and processes of change. In other words, we can offer general descriptions of what exactly happens in the here-and-now when a transition occurs.

This is a new field of research and there are not too many insights yet available. However, Brandtstädter and Rothermund's (2002) attempt to describe adaptive strategies to changing environments is one promising step towards this. When people like Greg Mortensen (Mortensen & Relin, 2007) encounter a myriad of complications in their attempts to build schools for girls in Afghanistan; or a grandfather finds it hard to make his daughter accept that he has fallen in love again; a teenage girl does not fit into a size 8 dress; a young adult cannot get on to the property ladder; or a Haitian girl tries to leave her hometown slum – they will all eventually use assimilative and accommodative strategies in trying to solve the challenge So, though contexts and challenges vary enormously, the engines of transitions and transformations – the processes and mechanisms – remain the same.

⊙ A positive perspective on development

Another important point we have made throughout this book is that development always consists of losses and gains (see Paul Baltes, Chapter 2). Losses are inevitable, but they open up opportunities for gains and change. Perhaps now is the time to concentrate on positive aspects of lifespan development, which, in our opinion, have been rather neglected by social sciences, media and the general public. There has been an over-emphasis on problem-based topics, particularly around adolescence and old age, giving a somewhat distorted image of the qualities and potential of young people and senior citizens and what they may add to society. Similarly, major shifts occurring throughout the lifespan, such as divorce, health problems or risk-taking, are frequently treated as inevitably problematic, with a range of negative consequences for everyone involved. A more optimistic outlook on lifespan development would be to look at all life events as challenges and potential triggers towards development and growth.

This perspective has been recommended by, among others, Seligman and Csikszentmihalyi (2000). They proposed the term 'Positive Psychology' as the name for the scientific pursuit of optimal human functioning, focusing on human strengths and qualities. They note that there is a set of human qualities that can act as crucial 'buffers' against mental conditions, such as depression. These qualities include: courage, optimism, inter-personal skills, hope, honesty and perseverance. These two academics believe that a great part of the task of prevention is to create a science of human strength that can foster such virtues. Based on the life histories of people who were resilient in situations most likely to cause helplessness and anxiety, Seligman (2008) suggests that the best antidote against personal helplessness and other mental health conditions is to gain early experiences of mastery. According to him, people wish to achieve feelings of well-being, above and beyond relief from their suffering.

As Seligman and Csikszentmihalyi (2000) discuss in greater detail, the emphasis should be on positive individual characteristics, including: a capacity for love and vocation, originality, courage, future-orientation yet enjoying the *here-and-now*, inter-personal skills, spirituality, aesthetic sensibility, high talent, perseverance, wisdom and forgiveness. At the group level, there is a need to create institutions promoting positive growth, that move individuals toward civic virtues and better citizenship, including characteristics such as responsibility, nurturance, altruism, civility, moderation, tolerance and work ethic. Thus, these empowering institutions – healthy families, work environments, schools and whole communities – will develop and sustain qualities that enrich such human potential.

Resources for growth

Now, we want to have a closer look at some of the resources that repeatedly emerge as facilitating growth across the whole lifespan. The first is the importance of education. It has been shown in a vast array of studies, that a higher level of education is strongly associated with a higher quality of life, well-being, health and cognitive capabilities (Feinstein & Hammond, 2004). This is not only true for formal schooling during childhood and adolescence, but also for all kinds of formal and informal education in adult life (Hatch *et al.*, 2007). Discussions about the benefits of education in present-day media tend to concentrate on whether or not a degree leads to employment and higher income, but the benefits of education are broader than that. Lifelong learning provides many important abilities that are helpful in meeting everyday challenges and coping with major transitions. For example, it endows the individual with skills such as attaining and using information, understanding and following instructions, communicating in oral and written form, questioning facts and information, and being able to appraise one's own capabilities in relation to present tasks and future-oriented goals. People with these skills are not easily manipulated or deceived, they are more likely to have control over their finances and social life, and participate more effectively in political and community actions. As we have seen throughout this book, across the lifespan, these are powerful resources to enhance well-being and quality of life.

It does not have to be formal education or an education with a high emphasis on academic skills to achieve these advantageous outcomes. Forcing people into a curriculum that does not correspond to their needs and interests can have the opposite effect. Not only teenagers 'vote with their feet' and play truant, retired people also prefer to arrange their own courses than to attend accredited university modules with the associated formal assessments.

For instance, the University of the Third Age, which has as an essential principle to promote learning for pleasure, and which neither requires nor awards any qualifications, has over a quarter of a million members in the UK alone. Furthermore, in the UK the percentage of 16-years-old who opt to leave formal education is about 30 per cent, while the corresponding figure for Sweden is less than 10 per cent. One reason for this difference is that Sweden offers a wide choice of vocational secondary schools. There is, for example, the option to attend a sixth-form course for truck drivers. Apart from learning to drive and repair heavy lorries, pupils learn enough Swedish, mathematics and social sciences to fulfil the demands of a job. They gain a vocational qualification and the opportunity to continue their education if they so wish. This makes it more attractive to many young people than the alternative of 'hanging about' in the streets. Similar schools exist for hairdressers, shop assistants, gardeners and so on.

Apart from providing vocational qualifications, these programmes have the capacity to bestow on young people another key resource for successful living, namely, self-efficacy or the belief of being able to attain one's goals. Self-efficacy appears as a strong protective factor in both quantitative and qualitative studies investigating health, well-being and successful ageing, as we have shown in the various chapters of this book. Individuals who have faith in their own abilities are more likely to accept challenges and persist in the face of initial failure. Whether one is 'good at something' or not – be it school subjects, sports, music, computer games or truck driving – can be one of the major distinguishing factors between people who persist or who perish in the face of adversity (Kloep *et al.*, 2010; Masten, 2007).

The third significant resource associated with psychosocial well-being is subjective health. Naturally, this resource is inter-twined with self-efficacy, as it depends on personal assessments of how incapacitating certain physical deficits are and how strongly one believes they can be overcome in daily functioning. Self-efficacy is also highly associated with the capacity to change one's lifestyle in order to improve one's health. This applies to behaviours as divergent as stopping smoking, exercising, dieting, condom use or seat-belt use (Conner & Norman, 2005). Although, objectively, health outcomes depend on many varied and different factors, the ways we have learned to adopt optimal health behaviours can also have a powerful impact. We enhance this resource not only by our behaviours but also by our self-agency, by our self-knowledge and by becoming generally informed through formal and informal educational experiences.

Finally, one of the most powerful resources for attaining developmental growth is the existence of social support. Emotional, informational and instrumental help provided by others has been shown to enhance well-being, buffer the effects of stress and add to quality of life. However, social support does not appear at the wave of the good fairy's wand, it requires the existence of a network of family and friends, again highly dependent on the individual's social skills in acquiring, nurturing and retaining friendships.

Adolescents and adults with social skill deficiencies – displaying aggressive behaviour, lacking emotional regulation, shyness and social withdrawal (Blandon *et al.*, 2010; Bohlin *et al.*, 2005; Bongers *et al.*, 2008; Rubin *et al.*, 2009) – often appear to have had social difficulties from pre-school years. The good news is that social skills can be learned, improved and trained. Such training programmes have been conducted success-fully with children and adults and with those with mental disabilities. Training usually consists of establishing skills for making contact, solving conflicts, regulating angry feelings, active listening and asserting oneself (Durlak *et al.*, 2010; Gresham *et al.*, 2004), and there is a large poten-tial for enhancing personal well-being by helping people to access social support.

In contrast to what many people believe, money does not play an especially significant resource role for personal development and growth. Of course, poverty may well affect the individual's psychosocial progress and goal attainment, but once basic needs are met, an increase in income is only weakly associated with feelings of happiness and well-being (Kahneman *et al.*, 2006). This is partly due to the heightened stress and reduction of leisure time often associated with high-income occupations.

These few examples show very clearly how resources are intertwined and can act to enhance one other. Further, they illustrate that they can be strengthened both by individuals themselves and with the help of others – within the school system, in the community, at the work place, in leisure or in therapy.

A view of future possibilities

The effort to enhance individual well-being and create a higher quality of life should extend beyond the individual level. An over-narrow focus on individuals and their personal development might deprive us of opportu-nities to bring about real change. As we have repeated over and over again, people are part of larger social systems, and there are many elements in a system that can be changed in order to enhance life quality.

New insights into the ecological nature of lifespan development call for a different approach to research and intervention. Richard Lerner has long since claimed that laboratory-based research is of little value if we want to understand real-life change (e.g. Lerner *et al.*, 2000). He has pro-posed the concept of 'applied developmental science' for a new approach to research that consists of interventions in real-life contexts. This would mean that scientists and scholars would participate within communities in promoting life-chances. Such involvement would be multi-disciplinary, based on scientific criteria, evidence and the experiences and needs of the participating individuals, and be continuously evaluated. In other words, he suggests planning 'natural experiments', whose results would be specific to the context in which they are created. There might also be the need to introduce new research methods to match this innovative approach.

This is easier said than done. There are old research traditions which are difficult to change. Research councils prefer to fund projects that are based on established research approaches, academic journals apply review criteria unlikely to include pioneering initiatives, and researchers (having been trained to use certain research techniques) are unlikely to experiment in the face of such orthodoxy.

However, some attempts have been made. A group of Swedish researchers (Stafström *et al.*, 2006), for example, successfully designed an intervention to reduce harmful under-age drinking in a Swedish community. The intervention, under the guidance of scientists, consisted of intensified police inspections of venues where alcohol was likely to be sold illegally, an anti-drinking curriculum introduced to all the community's schools, a parents' training course and a campaign in the local media.

However, the best examples of ecological, community intervention are *not* to be found in the academic literature, but in real life: The Welsh Assembly Government has started a ten-year project for enhancing well-being in the most deprived communities in Wales. Actions begin with an audit of each community to find out the most pressing needs of people living there. Communities then receive encouragement towards self-help in the form of advice and small grants. As an example, in one village, residents voiced concerns about their health, and in particular, healthy eating. Over time, this led to the founding of a food co-operative, run by local volunteers, who aim to increase their employability skills and their confidence. Once a week, they provide bags of fruit and vegetables at cost-price to residents. Within a few weeks, the number of bags sold increased from 30 to 180. Further, the action had an immediate spin-off effect: Where the bags are sold became a community meeting-place and residents decided to open a small cafe where customers could enjoy refreshments while picking up their weekly shopping. This led to the establishment of a gardening club, whose members exchange advice on how to cultivate their own fruit and vegetables, and to the opening of a book-swap club. Moreover, governmental agencies offer informal advice and courses on job-related skills. As a result of these grass-root initiatives, residents now have access to affordable, healthy food, meeting places to access social support and advice – and, in the meantime, the volunteers have gained catering-related qualifications (Communities First Information Centre, 2010). Amongst others, projects within this initiative include: A community radio station, hot meal deliveries to senior citizens, a credit union to lend money at reasonable rates to residents in debt, arranging for young people to help older residents to become computer literate – a fine example of empowering and enhancing growth in individuals while establishing inter-generational contacts and friendships.

While these examples clearly fulfil the requirements of promoting positive development, particularly through the community responses, they do not effectively contribute to the scientific need of advancing theories about the factors and forces that influence human development, and as such they are non-scientific interventions. So, we are faced with the dilemma of having theories and corresponding research that lack relevance for changing lives in a 'real world' context, while we have a set of practical interventions that have the potential to have a positive impact on lives, but do not really help our understanding of how and why they work, or how their results could be generalized.

The task for the future is to develop more collaborative research between scholars and communities, which can result both in effective interventions and in theoretical contributions to an understanding of human change. In other words, there are still significant tasks to be solved for the next generation of researchers of human development.

◉ Summary

We have now come to the end of our journey through the life course. To summarize, we have shown how lifespan development is best described as an ongoing process of transitions and transformations, interspersed with periods of stability. Transitions are triggered by events that demand an adaptation by the individual, which will ultimately lead to transformations. There is a vast variety of such events, some of which happen to nearly everybody in their life, and others that occur only to a few. However, the processes and mechanisms of adaptation are the same. We described associative and accommodative strategies that people use to adjust to change, and pointed out that development always implies losses *and* gains. We stressed the need of substituting problem-oriented perspectives with an emphasis on positive development and well-being. We examined how education, health, self-efficacy and social support can act as resources to meet life's challenges and encourage change. Finally, we presented ideas for possible future directions for research and interventions based on a new understanding of lifespan development within a framework of dynamic, inter-dependent systems.

Further reading

Compton, W. C. (2004) *An introduction to positive psychology*. Wardsworth Publishing: Stamford, Connecticut.
This is a brief coverage of the aims and intentions of positive psychology, with examples of how it can be applied in developmental, clinical, personality, motivational, social and behavioural psychology.
Hutchings, S., Comins, J., & Offiler, J. (1997) *The social skills handbook: Practical activities for social communication*. Speechmark: Milton Kaynes.
This is a guide for practitioners who want to set up social skills training groups. Apart from a theoretical overview, it offers many ideas for activities to enhance basic and complex social skills, from correct eye contact to conflict-solving.

Glossary

Accommodative strategy adaptive approach, whereby one adapts oneself, one's goals and expectations to achieve a better 'goodness of fit' with the environment.

Alzheimer's disease degeneration of the brain leading to loss of cognitive ability.

Ambivalence mixed feelings.

Assimilative strategy adaptive approach, whereby one adapts the environment, or one's perceptions thereof, to achieve a better 'goodness of fit' to the environment.

Bi-directional mutual influence.

Blog part of a website designed and updated by an individual, delivering regularly updated information and opinions about a topic.

Cardiovascular linked to heart and blood vessels.

Cognitive mental activities of thinking and reasoning.

Cyber-bullying bullying through the medium of information technology, such as Internet or mobile phones.

Delinquescent potentially delinquent or anti-social.

Demographic change population shifts (e.g. the fact that the group of people aged over 65 years is increasing compared with younger age groups).

De-standardization the process being observed, mostly in industrial countries, that there is no longer a standard or normal life course; rather that people's lives become increasingly diverse and individualized.

Developmental shift an event in one's life that leads to a change in development.

Domain specific restricted to a particular area.

Ecological taking into account the inter-dependency (dependency on each other) of several parts in a complex whole.

Endocrine system all the hormone-secreting glands that function together to regulate the body's physiology.

Equilibrium balance, harmony.

Generativity a term used by Erikson to describe the willingness of the older generation to provide nurture and care for the next generation.

Halo effect the perception of how one observed characteristic (e.g. attractiveness) influences the judgement of other unknown characteristics (e.g. personality).

Homophobic hostile attitude towards homosexuals.

Identity perception of the self, of who one is in comparison to others.

Individuation social process through which children become independent and separate from their parents.

Longitudinal research studies that observe individuals or groups over a period of time, often used to establish factors of cause and effect.

Magnetic resonance imaging (MRI) a special technique designed to image internal structures of the body, using magnetism and radio waves to create computer pictures of 'body slices'.

Menarche the first menstruation a girl experiences.

Multi-directionality the same event having different outcomes.

Multi-finality the same outcome possibly caused by different events.

Neuropsychology the study of how brain structure and brain functions influence behaviour, cognition and emotions.

Osteoporosis a medical condition in which the bones become brittle and fragile.

Peripheral distal, being distant from the centre, on the side; the opposite of proximal.

Plasticity the ability to be shaped and adapted to changes.

Respiratory related to breathing.

Role-confusion uncertainty about one's place in society and one's role in it.

Secular trend Long-term population trend; here, that nowadays the occurrence of menarche is earlier than previous decades.

Self-disclosure revealing private information to other people.

Self-fulfilling prophecy an expectation about a future occurrence, which then, because of the expectation, comes to pass.

Self-organization the creation of order within a system of interacting elements that is at first chaotic, but eventually and spontaneously leads to all elements finding their place in a coherent form.

System a set of elements that interact with one another.

Trajectory here, the pathway an individual follows through the life course.

Transformation change that occurs as the result of a transition.

Transition the process of adaptation to a change; leading to a transformation.

Turning point a decisive moment which instigates a change, leading to transition and then to transformation.

References

Adams, G. R., & Marshall, S. (1996). A developmental social psychology of identity: Understanding the person in context. *Journal of Adolescence, 19*, 1–14.

Adelman, P. K., Antonucci, T. C., Crohan, S. E., & Coleman, L. M. (1989). Empty nest, cohort, and employment in the well-being of midlife women. *Sex Roles, 20*, 173–188.

Adolph, K. E. (2008). Learning to move. *Current Directions in Psychological Science, 17*(3), 213–218.

Agahi, N., Ahacic, K., & Parker, M. G. (2006). Continuity of leisure participation from middle age to old age. *The Journal of Gerontology, 61B*(6), 340–347.

Ahlborg, T., Dahlöf, L.-G., & Hallberg, L. R.-M. (2005). Quality of the intimate and sexual relationship in first-time parents six months after delivery. *The Journal of Sex Research, 42*(2), 167–175.

Aldwin, C. M., Sutton, K. J., Chiara, G., & Spiro, A. (1996). Age differences in stress, coping, and appraisal: Findings from the normative aging study. *The Journal of Gerontology, 51B*(4), 179–188.

Allen, J. P., Porter, M. R., & McFarland, F. C. (2006). Leaders and followers in adolescent close friendships: Susceptibility to peer influence as a predictor of risky behavior, friendship inability, and depression. *Development and Psychopathology, 18*, 155–172.

Allen, K. R., Blieszner, R., & Roberto, K. A. (2000). Families in the middle and later years: A review and critique of research in the 1990s. *Journal of Marriage and the Family, 62*(4), 911–926.

Amato, P. R., & Afifi, T. D. (2006). Feeling caught between parents: Adult children's relations with parents and subjective well-being. *Journal of Marriage and the Family, 68*(1), 222–236.

Andersen, B.-E. (1995). Does school stimulate young people's development? In B. Jonsson (Ed.), *Studies on youth and schooling in Sweden* (pp. 91–113). Stockholm: Stockhom Institute of Education Press.

Anonymous. (2004). Teenagers "apathetic and ignorant" about politics. *Education & Training, 46*(4/5), 217.

Arnett, J. J. (1999). Adolescent storm and stress, reconsidered. *American Psychologist, 54*(5), 317–326.

Arnett, J. J. (2001). Conceptions of the transition to adulthood: Perspectives from adolescence to midlife. *Journal of Adult Development, 8*, 133–143.

Arnett, J. J. (2004). *Emerging adulthood: The winding road from late teens through the twenties.* Oxford: Oxford University Press.

Arnett, J. J., Kloep, M., Hendry, L. B., & Tanner, J. L. (2011). *Debating emerging adulthood: Stage or process?* Oxford: Oxford University Press.

Ayman-Nolley, S., & Taira, L. L. (2000). Obsession with the dark side of adolescence: A decade of psychological studies. *Journal of Youth Studies, 3*(1), 35–48.

Bailey, L. L., & Hansson, R. O. (1995). Psychological obstacles to job or career change in late life. *The Journals of Gerontology, 50*, 280–289.

Baird, B. M., Lucas, R. E., & Donnellan, M. B. (2010). Life satisfaction across the lifespan: Findings from two nationally representative panel studies. *Social Indicators Research, 99*(2), 183–203.

Baltes, P. B. (1987). Theoretical propositions of life-span developmental psychology: On the dynamics between growth and decline. *Developmental Psychology, 23*, 611–626.

Baltes, P. B. (1997). On the incomplete architecture of human ontogenesis: Selection, optimization, and compensation as foundations of developmental theory. *American Psychologist, 52*, 366–381.

Baltes, P. B., & Goulet, L. R. (1970). Status and issues of a life-span developmental psychology. In L. R. Goulet & P. B. Baltes (Eds.), *Life-span developmental psychology: Research and therapy* (pp. 4–21). New York: Academic Press.

Baltes, P. B., Lindenberger, U., & Staudinger, U. M. (2006). Life-span theory in developmental psychology. In D. Damon & R. M. Lerner

(Eds.), *Handbook of child psychology: Theoretical models of human development* (6th ed., Vol. 1). New York: Wiley.

Baltes, P. B., Reese, H. W., & Lipsitt, L. P. (1980). Life-span developmental psychology. *Annual Review of Psychology, 31*, 65–110.

Baltes, P. B., Staudinger, U. M., & Lindensberger, U. (1999). Lifespan psychology: Theory and application to intellectual functioning. *Annual Review of Psychology, 50*, 471–507.

Bandura, A. (1972). The stormy decade: Fact or fiction? In D. Rogers (Ed.), *Issues in adolescent psychology* (2nd ed.). New York: Appleton Century Crofts.

Bank, B. J., & Hansford, S. L. (2000). Gender and friendship: Why are men's best same-sex friendships less intimate and supportive? *Personal Relationships, 7*(1), 63–78.

Barnes, H., Parry, J., & Lakey, J. (2002). *Forging a new future: The experiences and expectations of people leaving paid work*. Bristol: The Policy Press Joseph Rowntree Foundation.

Barry, M. (2001). *Young people's views and experiences of growing up*. Plymbridge: Save the Children.

Bates, J. S. (2009). Generative grandfathering: A conceptual framework for nurturing grandchildren. *Marriage and Family Review, 45*(4), 331–352.

Bauer, M., Nay, R., & McAuliffe, L. (2009). Catering to love, sex and intimacy in residential aged care: What information is provided to consumers? *Sexuality and Disability, 27*(1), 3–10.

Baumgartner, S. E., Valkenburg, P. M., & Peter, J. (2009). Online sexual solicitation and online risk taking: Age and gender differences in adolescence anf adulthood, *Annual meeting of the Association for Education in Journalism and Mass Communication.*

Baumrind, D. (1967). Child care practices anteceding three patterns of preschool behavior. *Genetic Psychology Monographs, 75*, 43–88.

Beck, K. H., Thombs, D. L., & Summons, T. G. (1993). The social context of drinking scales: Construct validation and relationships to indicants of abuse in an adolescent population. *Addictive Behaviors, 18*, 159–169.

Beckman, N., Waern, M., Gustafson, D., & Skoog, I. (2008). Secular trends in self-reported sexual activity and satisfaction in Swedish 70 year olds: Cross sectional survey of four populations, 1971–2001. *British Medical Journal, 337*, 279.

Bedford, V. H. (1998). Sibling relationship troubles and well-being in middle and old age. *Family Relations, 47*(4), 369–378.

Bell, A. P., & Weinberg, M. S. (1978). *Homosexualities: A study of diversity among men and women.* New York: Simon and Schuster.

Bennett, K. (2010). How to achieve resilience as an older widower: Turning points or gradual change? *Ageing and Society, 30*(3), 369–383.

Bergdahl, E., Allard, P., Alex, L., Lundman, B., & Gustafson, Y. (2007). Gender differences in depression among the very old. *International Psychogeriatrics, 19*(6), 1125–1141.

Berndt, T. J., & Zook, J. M. (1993). Effects of friendship on adolescent development. *Bulletin of the Hong Kong Psychological Society, 30–31*, 15–34.

Bessière, K., Kiesler, S., Kraut, R., & Boneva, B. (2008). Effects of Internet use and social resources on changes in depression. *Communication & Society, 11*(1), 47–70.

Binstock, R. H. (2010). From compassionate ageism to intergenerational conflict? *The Gerontologist, 50*(5), 574–585.

Birditt, K. S., Brown, E., Orbuch, T. L., & McIlvane, J. M. (2010). Marital conflict behaviors and implications for divorce over 16 years. *Journal of Marriage and the Family, 72*(5), 1188–1205.

Birditt, K. S., Fingerman, K. L., Lefkowitz, E. S., & Kamp Dush, C. M. (2008). Parents perceived as peers: Filial maturity in adulthood. *Journal of Adult Development, 15*, 1–12.

Bjørgen, I. A. (2001). *Læring, søken etter mening.* Trondheim: Tapir.

Blair, B. L., & Fletcher, A. C. (2011). "The only 13-year-old on planet earth without a cell phone": Meanings of cell phones in early adolescents' everyday lives. *Journal of Adolescent Research, 26*(2), 155–177.

Blais, J., Craig, W. M., Pepler, D., & Connolly, J. (2008). Adolescents online: The importance of Internet activity choices to salient relationships. *Journal of Youth and Adolescence, 37*, 522–536.

Blakemore, S. J., & Choudhury, S. (2006). Development of the adolescent brain: Implications for executive function and social cognition. *Journal of Child Psychology and Psychiatry, 47*, 296–312.

Blanchflower, D. G., & Oswald, A. J. (2008). Is well-being U-shaped over the life cycle? *Social Science and Medicine, 66*(8), 1733–1749.

Blandon, A. Y., Calkins, S. D., Grimm, K. J., Keane, S. P., & O'Brien, M. (2010). Testing a developmental cascade model of emotional and social competence and early peer acceptance. *Development and Psychopathology, 22*(4), 737–749.

Blinn-Pike, L., Worthy, S. H., Jonkman, J. N., & Smith, G. R. (2008). Emerging adult versus adult status among college students: Examination of explanatory variables. *Adolescence, 43*(171), 577–592.

Blos, P. (1962). *On adolescence: A psychoanalytic interpretation.* New York: The Free Press.

Blos, P. (1967). The second individuation process of adolescence. *Psychoanalytic Study of the Child, 22*, 162–168.

Bogaert, A. F. (2004). Asexuality: Prevalence and associated factors in a national probability sample. *Journal of Sex Research, 41*(3), 279–287.

Bohlin, G., Hagekull, K., & Andersson, K. (2005). Behavioral inhibition as a precursor of peer social competence in early school age; the interplay with attachment and nonparental care. *Merrill Palmer Quarterly, 51*(1), 1–9.

Boney, V. M. (2003). Alternative research perspectives for studying the effects of parental divorce. *Marriage and Family Review, 35*(1/2), 7–19.

Bongers, I. L., Koot, H. M., van der Ende, J., & Verhulst, F. C. (2008). Predicting young adult social functioning from developmental trajectories of externalizing behaviour. *Psychological Medicine, 7*, 989–1000.

Borell, K., & Karlsson, S. G. (2000). Ældre kjæresetfolk - hver for sig. *Gerontologi og samfund, 16*(4), 85–87.

Bosma, H. A., & Kunnen, S. (2001). Determinants and mechanisms in ego identity development: A review and synthesis. *Developmental Review, 21*, 39–66.

Boyle, P. A., Buchman, D. A., & Bennett, D. A. (2010). Purpose in life is associated with a reduced risk of incident disability among community-dwelling older persons. *The American Journal of Geriatric Psychiatry, 18*(12), 1093–1103.

Brandtstädter, J., & Rothermund, K. (2002). The life-course dynamics of goal pursuit and goal adjustment: A two-process framework. *Developmental Review, 22*(1), 117–150.

Branje, S. J., van Lieshout, C. F., van Aken, M. A., & Haselager, G. J. (2004). Perceived support in sibling relationships and adolescent adjustment. *Journal of Child Psychology and Psychiatry, 45*, 1385–1396

Brim, G. (1992). *How we measure success and failure throughout our lives.* New York: Basic Books.

Bronfenbrenner, U. (1970). *Two worlds of childhood.* New York: Russell Sage.

Bronfenbrenner, U. (1977). Toward an experimental ecology of human development. *American Psychologist, 32,* 513–530.

Bronfenbrenner, U. (1979). *The ecology of human development.* Cambridge, MA: Harvard University Press.

Bronfenbrenner, U., & Morris, P. (2006). The ecology of the developmental process. In W. Damon & R. M. Lerner (Eds.), *Handbook of child psychology: Theoretical modes of human development* (6th ed., Vol. 1). New York: Wiley.

Brooks-Gunn, J., & Petersen, A. C. (Eds.). (1983). *Girls at puberty.* New York: Springer.

Brown, B., Mory, M., & Kinney, D. (1994). Casting adolescent crowds in relational perspective: Caricature, channel and context. In R. Montemayor, G. Adams & T. Gullotta (Eds.), *Personal relationships during adolescence.* London: Sage.

Buchanan, C. M., Eccles, J. S., & Becker, J. B. (1992). Are adolescents the victims of raging hormones? Evidence for activational effects of hormones on moods and behavior at adolescence. *Psychological Bulletin, 111,* 62–107.

Buchanan, C. M., Eccles, J. S., Flanagan, C. A., Midgley, C., Feldlaufer, H., & Harold, R. D. (1990). Parents' and teachers' beliefs about adolescents: Effects of sex and experience. *Journal of Youth and Adolescence, 19,* 363–394.

Bucx, F., & van Wel, F. (2008). Parental bond and life course transitions from adolescence to young adulthood. *Family Therapy, 35*(2), 109–127.

Buhl, H. M. (2007). Well-being and the child-parent relationship at the transition from university to working life. *Journal of Adolescent Research, 22,* 550–571.

Bulcroft, R. A., & Bulcroft, K. A. (1991). The nature and functions of dating in later life. *Research on Aging, 13,* 244–260.

Bures, R. (2009). Moving the nest: The impact of coresidential children on mobility in later midlife. *Journal of Family Issues, 30*(6), 837.

Bures, R., Koropeckyi-Cox, T., & Loree, M. (2009). Childlessness, parenthood, and depressive symptoms among middle-aged and older adults. *Journal of Family Issues, 30*(5), 670–687.

Burt, I., Lewis, S. V., Beverly, M. G., & Patel, S. H. (2010). Does high educational attainment limit the availability of romantic partners? *Family Journal, 18*(4), 448–454.

Bynner, J. (2005). Rethinking the youth phase of the life course: The case for emerging adulthood? *Journal of Youth Studies, 8*, 367–384.

Bytheway, B. (1995). *Agism*. Buckingham: Open University Press.

Caldwell, L. L., Baldwin, C. K., Walls, T., & Smith, E. (2004). Preliminary effects of a leisure education program to promote healthy use of free time among middle school adolescents. *Journal of Leisure Research, 36*, 310–335.

Caldwell, L. L., Darling, N., Payne, M. A., & Dowdy, B. (1999). 'Why are you bored?' An examination of psychological and social control causes of boredom among adolescents. *Journal of Leisure Research, 31*, 103–121.

Carpenter, L. M., Nathanson, E. A., & Kim, Y. J. (2009). Physical women, emotional men: Gender and sexual satisfaction in midlife. *Archives of Sexual Behavior, 38*, 87–107.

Carr, D. (1997). The fulfilment of career dreams at midlife: Does it matter for women's mental health? *Journal of Health and Social Behavior, 38*(4), 331–345.

Cassidy, Jackson, M., & Brown, K. N. (2009). Sticks and stones can break my bones, but how can pixels hurt me? Students' experiences with cyber-bullying. *School Psychology International, 30*, 383–402.

Cassingham, B. J., & O'Neil, S. M. (1993). *And then I met this woman*. Freeland, WA: Soaring Eagle Publishing.

Cater, S., & Coleman, L. (2006). *Planned teenage pregnancy: Perspectives of young parents from disadvantaged backgrounds*. Bristol: Policy Press.

Centre for Disease Control and Prevention. (2010). *Data and statistics*. Retrieved 08 January 2011, from http://www.cdc.gov/DataStatistics/

Charlton, R. (2004). Ageing male syndrome, Andropause, androgen decline or mid-life crisis? *The Journal of Men's Health and Gender, 1*(1), 55–59.

Chiriboga, D. A. (1997). Crisis, challenge, and stability in the middle years. In M. E. Lachman & J. B. James (Eds.), *Multiple paths of midlife development* (pp. 293–322). Chicago: University of Chicago.

Chu, J. Y. (2004). A relational perspective on adolescent's boy's identity development. In N. Way & J. Y. Chu (Eds.), *Adolescent boys: Exploring diverse cultures of boyhood* (pp. 78–104). New York: New York University Press.

Chu, J. Y. (2005). Adolescent boy's friendships and peer group culture. *New Directions in Child Development, 107*, 7–22.

Cicirelli, V. (2004). Closeness, confiding, and contact among siblings in middle and late adulthood. *The Gerontologist, 44*(1), 541.

Cicirelli, V. (2009). Sibling death and death fear in relation to depressive symptomatology in older adults. *The Journals of Gerontology, 64B*(1), 24–33.

Clark, L. S. (1998). Dating on the net: Teens and the rise of 'pure' relationships. In S. Jones (Ed.), *Cybersociety 2.0: Revisiting computer-mediated communication and community* (pp. 159–183). Thousand Oaks: Sage.

Clemens, A. W., & Axelson, L. J. (1985). The not so empty nest: The return of the fledgling adult. *Family Relations, 34*, 259–264.

Cole, E., & Rothblum, E. (1990). Commentary on sexuality and the midlife woman. *Psychology of Women Quarterly, 14*, 509–512.

Coleman, J. C. (2010). *The nature of adolescence* (4th ed.). London: Routledge.

Coleman, J. C., & Brooks, F. (2009). *Key data on adolescence* (7th ed.). Brighton: Trust for the Study of Adolescence.

Coleman, J. C., & Hendry, L. B. (1999). *The nature of adolescence* (3th ed.). London: Routledge.

Collins, W. A., & Laursen, B. (2004). Changing relationships, changing youth: Interpersonal contexts of adolescent development. *The Journal of Early Adolescence, 24*(1), 55–62.

Collins, W. A., & Steinberg, L. (2006). Interpersonal contexts and the psychosocial tasks of adolescence. In W. Damon & R. M. Lerner (Eds.), *Handbook of child psychology* (6th ed., Vol. 3, Social, emotional and personality development, pp. 1003–1067). New York: Wiley.

Communities First Information Centre. (2010). *Providing more than just healthy eating for Cornelly residents at the food co operative* Retrieved 12 February 2011, from http://www.communities-first.org/eng/case_studies/cornelly_communities_first_partnership_bridgend/

Conley, C. S., & Rudolph, U. D. (2009). The emerging sex difference in adolescent depression: Interacting contributions of puberty and peer stress. *Development and Psychopathology, 21*, 593–620.

Conner, M., & Norman, P. (2005). *Predicting health behaviour* (2nd ed.). Buckingham: Open University Press.

Connidis, I. A., & Campbell, L. D. (1995). Closeness, confiding, and contact among siblings in middle and late adulthood. *Journal of Family Issues, 16*(6), 722–745.

Cooper, A., & Sportolari, L. (1997). Romance in cyberspace: Understanding online attraction. *Journal of Sex Education and Therapy, 22*(1), 7–14.

Cooper, H., & Davey, K. M. (2011). Teaching for life? Midlife narratives from female classroom teachers who considered leaving the profession. *British Journal of Guidance & Counselling. Cambridge:, 39*(1), 83–90.

Copeland, W., Shanahan, L., Miller, S., & Costello, E. J. (2010). Outcomes of pubertal timing in young women: A prospective population study. *American Journal of Psychiatry, 167*(10), 1210–1226.

Cornwell, B., Laumann, E., & Schumm, L. P. (2008). The social connectedness of older adults: A national profile. *American Sociological Review, 73*(2), 185–204.

Cornwell, B., Schumm, L. P., Laumann, E., & Graber, J. (2009). Sexuality: Measures of partnerships, practices, attitudes, and problems in the national social life, health, and aging study. *The Journal of Gerontology, 64B*, 156–166.

Cornwell, E. Y., & Waite, L. J. (2009). Measuring social isolation among older adults using multiple indicators from the NSHAP Study. *The Journal of Gerontology, 64B*, 138–146.

Côté, J. E. (2000). *Arrested adulthood: The changing nature of identity in the late modern world*. New York: NYU Press.

Côté, J. E., & Bynner, J. (2008). Changes in the transition to adulthood in the UK and Canada: The role of structure and agency in emerging adulthood. *Journal of Youth Studies, 11*, 251–268.

Coulthard, M., Farrell, M., Singleton, N., & Meltzer, H. (2002). *Tobacco, alcohol and drug use and mental health*. London: TSO

Cowie, H., & Hutson, N. (2005). Peer Support: A strategy to help bystanders tackle school bullying. *Pastoral Care in Education, 23*(2), 40–44.

Cox, M. J., Paley, B., Burchinal, M., & Payne, C. C. (1999). Marital perception and interactions across the transition to parenthood. *Journal of Marriage and Family, 61*, 611–625.

Crawford, M., & Unger, R. (2000). *Women and gender: A feminist psychology* (3rd ed.). Boston: McGraw Hill.

Crimmins, E. M., Hayward, M. D., & Saito, Y. (1996). Differentials in active life expectancy in the older population of the United States. *The Journals of Gerontology, 51B*, 111–120.

Crosnoe, R., & Elder, G. H. j. (2002). Successful adaptation in the later years: A life course approach to aging. *Social Psychology Quarterly, 65*(4), 309–329.

Csikszentmihalyi, M., & Larson, R. (1984). *Being adolescent: Conflict and growth in the teenage years.* New York: Basic Books.

De-Jong-Gierveld, J. (2004). Remarriage, unmarried cohabitation, living apart together: Partner relationships following bereavement or divorce. *Journal of Marriage and the Family, 66*(1), 236–244.

Defey, D., Storch, E., Cardozo, S., Diaz, O., & Fernández, G. (1996). The menopause: Women's psychology and health care. *Social Science Medicine, 42*(10), 1447–1456.

DeGoede, I. H. A., Branje, S. J., Delsing, M. J. M. H., & Meeus, W. H. J. (2009). Linkages over time between adolescent relationships with parents and friends. *Journal of Youth and Adolescence, 38*, 1304–1315.

Dehue, F., Bolman, C., & Vollink, T. (2008). Cyberbullying: Youngsters' experiences and parental perceptions. *CyberPsychology & Behavior, 11*, 217–223.

Del Castillo, J. M., Navarro, J. E. J.-B., Sanz, J. L. G., & Rodriguez, M. M. (2010). Being physically active in old age: Relationships with being active earlier in life, social status and agents of socialization. *Ageing and Society, 30*(7), 1097–1114.

DeLamater, J. D., & Sill, M. (2005). Sexual desire in later life. *The Journal of Sex Research, 42*(2), 138–150.

Demos, J., & Demos, V. (1969). Adolescence in historical perspective. *Journal of Marriage and the Family, 31*(4), 632–638.

Dennerstein, L., Dudley, E., & Guthrie, J. (2002). Empty nest or revolving door? A prospective study of women's quality of life in midlife during the phase of children leaving and re-entering the home. *Psychological Medicine, 32*(3), 545–551.

Dennison, C., & Coleman, J. C. (1998). Adolescent motherhood: Exprinces and relationships. In S. Clement (Ed.), *Psychological perspectives on pregnancy and childbirth*. Edinburgh: Churchill Livingstone.

Denton, F. T., & Spencer, B. G. (2009). What is retirement? A review and assessment of alternative concepts and measures. *Canadian Journal on Aging, 28*(1), 63–76.

Department for Children, Schools and Families. (2008). *Behavioral inhibition as a precursor of peer social competence in early school age: The interplay with attachment and nonparental care*: DCSF-RBX-09-14.

Department of Health, Social Services and Public Safety. (2004). *Home accident prevention*. Retrieved 01 February 2011, from http://www.dhsspsni.gov.uk.

Depp, C. A., & Jeste, D. V. (2006). Definitions and predictors of successful aging: A comprehensive review of larger quantitative studies. *The American Journal of Geriatric Psychiatry, 14*(1), 6–21.

Dhariwal, A., Connolly, J., Paciello, M., & Caprara, G. V. (2009). Adolescent peer relationships and emerging adult romantic styles: A longitudinal study of youth in an Italian community. *Journal of Adolescent Research, 24*, 579–600.

Diamond, L. M. (1998). Development and sexual orientation among adolescent and young adult women. *Developmental Psychology, 34*, 1085–1095.

Diamond, L. M. (2007). A dynamical systems approach to the development and expression of female same-sex sexuality. *Perspectives on psychological science, 2*(2), 142–161.

Dickson, F. C., Hughes, P. C., & Walker, K. L. (2009). An exploratory investigation into dating among later-life women. *Journal of Communication, 69*(1), 67–82.

Dillaway, H. E. (2005). Menopause is the 'good old': Women's thoughts about reproductive aging. *Gender and Society, 19*(3), 398–417.

Dittman-Kohli, F. (1990). The construction of meaning in old age: Possibilities and constraints. *Ageing and Society, 10*, 279–294.

Dix, T. (1991). The affective organization of parenting: Adaptive and maladaptive processes. *Psychological Bulletin, 110*, 3–25.

Doka, K. (2005). Ethics, end-of-life decisions and grief. *Mortality, 10*(3), 83–90.

Doka, K. (2007). *Living with grief: Before and after the death*. Washington: Hospice Foundation of America.

Douglass, C. B. (2005). *Barren States: The population implosion in Europe*. Oxford: Berg Publishers.

Douglass, C. B. (2007). From duty to desire: Emerging adulthood in Europe and its consequences. *Child Development Perspectives, 1*, 101–108.

Draper, B., & Anderson, D. (2010). The baby boomers are nearly here – but do we have sufficient workforce in old age psychiatry? *International Psychogeriatrics, 22*(6), 947–950.

Durbin, D., Darling, N., & Steinberg, L. (1993). Parenting style and peer group membership. *Journal of Research on Adolescence, 3*, 87–100.

Durlak, J. A., Weissberg, R. P., & Pachan, M. (2010). A meta-analysis of after-school programs that seek to promote personal and social skills in children and adolescents. *American Journal of Community Psychology, 45*(3–4), 294–309.

Dworkin, J. B., Larson, R., & Hansen, D. (2003). Adolescents' accounts of growth experiences in youth activities. *Journal of Youth and Adolescence, 32*(1), 17–27.

Easterlin, R. A. (2006). Life cycle happiness and its sources: Intersections of psychology, economics, and demography *Journal of Economic Psychology, 27*, 463–482.

Elder, G. H. Jr. (1972). *Children of the great depression: Social change in life experience*. Chicago: Chicago Press.

Elder, G. H. Jr. (1998a). *Children of the great depression: 25th anniversary edition*. Boulder CO: Westview Press.

Elder, G. H. Jr. (1998b). The life course as developmental theory. *Child Development, 69*(1), 1–12.

Elder, G. H. Jr., & Shanahan, M. J. (2006). The life course and human development. In D. Damon & R. M. Lerner (Eds.), *Handbook of child development: Theoretical modes of human development* (6th ed., Vol. 1). New York: Wiley.

Elder, G. H. Jr., Conger, R. D., Foster, E. M., & Ardelt, M. (1992). Families under economic pressure. *Journal of Family Issues, 13*, 5–37.

Elder, G. H. Jr., Van Nguyen, T., & Caspi, A. (1985). Linking family hardship to children's lives. *Child Development, 69*(1), 1–12.

Ellis, L. A., Marsh, H. W., & Craven, R. G. (2009). Addressing the challenges faced by early adolescence: A mixed method evaluation of the benefits of peer support. *American Journal of Community Psychology, 44*, 54–75.

Ellison, N. B., Steinfield, C., & Lampe, C. (2007). The benefits of Facebook 'friends': Social capital and college students' use of online social network sites. *Journal of Computer-Mediated Communication, 12*, 1143–1168.

Engels, R. C. M. E., & van den Eijnden, R. (2007). Substance use in adolescence. In J. C. Coleman, L. B. Hendry & M. Kloep. (Eds.), *Adolescence and health* (pp. 107–122). Chichester: Wiley.

Erikson, E. H. (1950). *Childhood and society*. New York: Norton.

Erikson, E. H. (1959). Identity and the life circle. *Psychological Issues, Monograph 1*. New York: International University Press.

Esturgó-Deu, M. E., & Sala-Roca, J. (2010). Disruptive behaviour of students in primary education and emotional intelligence. *Teaching and Teacher Education, 26*(24), 830–837.

Evandrou, M., & Glaser, K. (2004). Family, work and quality of life: Changing economic and social roles through the lifecourse. *Ageing and Society, 24*, 771–791.

Featherstone, M., & Hepworth, M. (1991). The mask of ageing and the post-modern life course. In M. Hepworth & B. Turner (Eds.), *The body, social process, and cultural theory* (pp. 371–389). London: Sage.

Fehr, B. (2004). Intimacy expectations in same-sex friendships: A prototype interaction-pattern model. *Journal of Personality and Social Psychology, 86*(2), 265–284.

Feinstein, L., & Hammond, C. (2004). The contribution of adult learning to health and social capital. *Oxford Review of Education, 30*(2), 199–221.

Ferguson, D. M., & Woodward, L. J. (2000). Teenage pregnancy and female educational achievement: A prospective study of a New Zealand Cohort. *Journal of Marriage and the Family, 62*(1), 147–161.

Field, D. (1999). Continuity and change in friendships in advanced old age: Findings from the Berkeley older generation study. *The International Journal of Aging and Human Development, 48*(4), 325–346.

Fingerman, K. L. (2001). *Aging mothers and their adult daughters*. New York: Springer.

Fingerman, K. L., & Pitzer, L. (2007). Socialisation in old age. In P. D. Hastings & J. E. Grusec (Eds.), *Handbook of socialisation* (pp. 232–255). New York: Guilford Press.

Fingerman, K. L., Hay, E. L., Kamp Dush, C. M., Cichy, K. E., & Hosterman, S. (2007). Parents' and offspring's perceptions of change and continuity when parents experience the transition to old age. *Advances in Life Course Research, 12*, 275–306.

Fischer, K. W., & Bidell, T. R. (1998). Dynamic development of psychological structures in action and thought. In W. Damon & R. M. Lerner (Eds.), *Handbook of child psychology* (5th ed., Vol. 1, pp. 467–561). New York: Wiley.

Fisher, S. (1995). The amusement arcade as a social space for adolescents. *Journal of Adolescence, 18*, 71–86.

Fiske, M., & Chiriboga, D. A. (1991). *Change and continuity in adult life*. San Francisco: Jossey Bass.

Flammer, A., Alsaker, F. D., & Noack, P. (1999). Time use by adolescents in an international perspective: The case of leisure activities. In F. D. Alsaker & A. Flammer (Eds.), *European and American adolescents in the 1990s* (pp. 33–60). New Jersey: Psychology Press.

Flanagan, C. A. (1990). Families and schools in hard times. *New Directions in Child Development, 46*, 7–26.

Flanagan, C., Schulenberg, J., & Fuligni, A. (1993). Residential setting and parent-adolescent relationships during the college years. *Journal of Youth and Adolescence, 22*, 171–189.

Fogel, J., Steven, M. A., Schnabel, F., Ditkoff, B. A., & Neugut, A. I. (2002). Use of the Internet by women with breast cancer. *Journal of Medical and Internet Research 4*(2), e9 http://www.jmir.org/2002/2/e9/.

Ford, D. H., & Lerner, R. M. (1992). *Developmental systems theory: An integrative approach*. New York: Sage.

Fraser, J., Maticka-Tyndale, E., & Smylie, L. (2004). Sexuality of Canadian women at midlife. *Canadian Journal of Human Sexuality, 13*(3–4), 171–187.

Frosh, S., Phoenix, A., & Pattman, R. (2002). *Young masculinities*. London: Palgrave.

Friedan, B. (1994). *The fountain of age*. New York: Touchstone.

Furlong, A., & Cartmel, F. (1997). *Young people and social change*. Buckingham: Open University Press.

Furman, W. (2001). Working models of friendships. *Journal of Social Personal Relationships, 18*, 583–602.

Galambos, N. L., Barker, E. T., & Krahn, H. J. (2006). Depression, self-esteem, and anger in emerging adulthood: Seven year trajectories. *Developmental Psychology, 42*(2), 350–363.

Galambos, N. L., Leadbeater, B. J., & Barker, E. T. (2004). Gender differences in and risk factors for depression in adolescence: A four-year longitudinal study. *International Journal of Behavioral Development, 28*, 16–25.

Giarrusso, R., Silverstein, M., & Bengtson, V. L. (1996). Family complexities and the grandparent role. *Generations, 22*(1), 17–23.

Giedd, J. N., Blumenthal, J., Jeffries, N. O., Castellanos, F. X., Liu, H., Zijdenbos, A., Paus, T., Evans, A.C., & Rapoport, J. L. (1999). Brain development during childhood and adolescence: A MRI study. *Nature Neuroscience, 2*(10), 861–863.

Glanville, J. L. (1999). Political socialization or selection? Adolescent extracurricular participation and political activity in early adulthood. *Social Science Quarterly, 80*(2), 279–291.

Goldbaum, S., Craig, W. M., Pepler, D., & Connolly, J. (2003). Developmental trajectories of victimization: Identifying risk and protective factors. *Journal of Applied Social Psychology, 19*, 139–156.

Goldscheider, F. K., & Goldscheider, C. (1999). Changes in returning home in 20th century America. *Social Forces, 78*, 695–720.

Golombok, S., & Fivush, R. (1994). *Gender development*. London: Routledge.

Goossens, L. (1995). Identity status development and students' perception of the university environment: A cohort-sequential study. In A. Oosterwegel & R. Wicklund (Eds.), *The self in European and North American culture: Developmental processes* (pp. 19–32). Dordrecht: Kluwer.

Gordon, H. R. (2008). Gendered paths to teenage political participation: Parental power, civic mobility, and youth activism. *Gender & Society, 22*(1), 31–55.

Gorin, S. H., & Lewis, B. (2004). The compression of morbidity: Implications for social work. *Health and Social Work, 29*, 249–255.

Gould, R. L. (1978). *Transformations: Growth and change in adult life*. New York: Simon and Schuster.

Graff, M. (2007). Rise of the cyber cheat. *The Psychologist, 20*(11), 678–679.

Granic, I. (2000). The self-organization of parent – child relations: Beyond bi-directional models In M. D. Lewis & I. Granic (Eds.), *Emotion, development and self-organization: Dynamic systems approaches to emotional development* (pp. 267–207). New York: Cambridge University Press.

Green, E. S. (2005). Adolescent perception of peer success, *Diss. submitted to the Wright Institute*. Ann Arbour: Microform Proquest.

Greenbaum, L. (2000). That's what it is. *The Lancet, 355*(9205), 745–747.

Greenfield, P. M., & Yan, Z. (2006). Children, adolescents, and the internet: A new field of inquiry in developmental psychology. *Developmental Psychology, 42*, 391–394.

Gresham, F. M., Cook, C. R., Crews, S. D., & Kern, L. (2004). Social skills training for children and youth with emotional and behavioral disorders: Validity considerations and future directions. *Behavioral Disorders, 30*(1), 32–47.

Gross, E. F. (2004). Adolescent Internet use: What we expect, what teens report. *Journal of Applied Developmental Psychology, 24*, 713–738.

Hahlweg, K., & Richter, D. (2010). Prevention of marital instability and distress: Results of an 11-year longitudinal follow-up stuy. *Behavior Research and Therapy, 48*(5), 377–383.

Hansen, L. B., & Jacob, L. B. (1992). Intergenerational support during the transition to parenthood: Issues for new parents and grandparents. *Families in society: The Journal of Contemporary Human Services, 73*(8), 471–479.

Harper, J. M., Schaalje, B. G., & Sandberg, J. G. (2000). Daily hassles, intimacy, and marital quality in later life marriages. *American Journal of Family Therapy, 28*(1), 1–19.

Hartrup, W. W., & Stevens, N. (1999). Friendships and adaptation across the lifespan. *Current Directions in Psychological Science, 8*, 76–79.

Hatch, S. L., Feinstein, L., Link, B. G., Wadsworth, M. E. J., & Richards, M. (2007). The continuing benefits of education: Adult education and midlife cognitive ability in the British 1946 birth cohort. *The Journals of Gerontology, 62B*(6), 404–415.

Havighurst, R. (1953). *Human development and education.* New York: Longman.

Hawk, S., Keijsers, L., Hale, W. W., & Meeus, W. H. J. (2009). Mind your own business! Longitudinal relations between perceived privacy invasion and adolescent-parent conflict. *Journal of Family Psychology, 23*, 511–520.

Hawking, S. W., & Mlodinow, L. (2010). *The grand design.* New York: Bantam.

Heinz, W. R., & Marshall, V. W. (2003). *Social dynamics of the life course.* New York: Aldine de Gruyter.

Helmes, E., & Gee, S. (2003). Attitudes of Australian therapists towards older clients: Educational and training imperatives. *Educational Gerontology, 29*, 657–670.

Hendry, L. B., & Kloep, M. (2002). *Lifespan development: Challenges, resources and risks.* London: Thomson Learning.

Hendry, L. B., & Kloep, M. (2006). Youth and leisure: A European perspective. In S. Jackson & L. Goossens (Eds.), *Handbook of adolescent development* (pp. 246–263). Hove: Psychology Press.

Hendry, L. B., & Kloep, M. (2010). How universal is emerging adulthood? *Journal of Youth Studies, 13*(2), 169–179.

Hendry, L. B., Glendinning, A., Reid, M., & Wood, S. (1998). *Lifestyles, health and health concerns of rural youth. A project report to the Department of Health.* Scottish Office: Edinburgh.

Hendry, L. B., Kloep, M., & Wood, S. (2002a). Young people talking about adolescent rural crowds and social settings. *Journal of Youth Studies, 5*(4), 357–374.

Hendry, L. B., Kloep, M., Glendinning, A., Ingebrigtsen, J. E., Espnes, G. A., & Woods, S. (2002b). Leisure transitions: A rural perspective. *Journal of Leisure Studies, 21*, 1–14.

Hendry, L. B., Mayer, P., & Kloep, M. (2007). Belonging or opposing? A grounded theory approach to young peoples' cultural identity in a majority/minority societal context. *Identity, 7*(3), 181–204.

Hendry, L. B., Shucksmith, J. S., Love, J., & Glendinning, A. (1993). *Young people's leisure and lifestyles.* London: Routledge.

Henkens, K., Sprengers, M., & Tazelaar, F. (1996). Unemployment and the older worker in the Netherlands: Re-entry into the labour force or resignation. *Ageing and Society, 16*, 561–578.

Hepworth, M. (1995). Change and crisis in mid-life. In B. Davey (Ed.), *Birth to old age: Health in transition* (pp. 143–154). Ballmore: Open University Press.

Herzog, A. R., House, J. S., & Morgan, J. N. (1991). Relation of work and retirement to health and well-being in older age. *Psychology and Aging, 6*, 201–211.

Hetherington, E. M. (2003). Intimate pathways: Changing patterns in close personal relationships across time. *Family Relations, 52*(4), 318–331.

Hines, A. R., & Paulson, S. E. (2006). Parents' and teachers' perceptions of adolescent storm and stress: Relations with parenting and teaching styles. *Adolescence, 41*, 597–614.

Hoff, A. (2007). Patterns of intergenerational support in grandparent-grandchild and parent-child relationships in Germany. *Ageing and Society, 27*(5), 643–666.

Hofman, M. A. (1997). Lifespan changes in the human hypothalamus. *Experimental Gerontology, 32*(4), 559–575.

Hollander, E., & Samons, D. M. (2003). Male menopause: An unexplored area of men's health. *Psychiatric Annals, 33*(8), 497–500.

Holmbeck, G. N. (1996). A model of family relational transformations during the transition to adolescence: Parent adolescent conflict and adaptation. In J. Graber, J. Brooks-Gunn & A. C. Pedersen (Eds.), *Transitions through adolescence: Interpersonal domains and context.* (pp. 167–199). Mahwah, NJ: Erlbaum.

Hooghe, M., & Wilkenfeld, B. (2008). The stability of political attitudes and behaviors across adolescence and early adulthood. A comparison of survey data on adolescents and young adults in eight countries. *Journal of Youth and Adolescence, 37*(2), 155–167.

House, J. S., Lepkowski, J. M., Kinney, A. M., Mero, R. P., Kessler, R. C., & Herzog, R. (1994). The social stratification of aging and health. *Journal of Health and Social Behavior, 35*, 213–234.

HSBC (Health Behaviour in School-aged Children, 2001/2002). *Survey of young people's health in context.* Copenhagen: WHO Regional Office for Europe.

Hsiu-Chen, Y., & Lempers, J. D. (2004). Perceived sibling relationships and adolescent development. *Journal of Youth and Adolescence, 33*(2), 133–147.

Huey, R. B., Salisbury, R., Wang, J.-L., & Mao, W. (2007). Effects of age and gender on success and death of mountaineers on Mount Everest. *Biology Letters, 22*(3), 498–500.

Hunter, J. P., & Csikszentmihalyi, M. (2003). The positive psychology of interested adolescents. *Journal of Youth and Adolescence, 32*, 27–35.

Iacovou, M. (2001). *Leaving home in the European Union.* Retrieved 02 February 2011, from http://www.iser.essex.ac.uk/pubs/workpaps

Ikkink, K. K., Tilburg, V. T., & Knipscher, M. P. C. K. (1999). Perceived instrumental exchanges in relationships betwen elderly parents and their adult children: Normative and structural explanations. *Journal of Marriage and the Family, 61*(4), 831–844.

Jackson, A. L., von Eye, A., Barbatsis, G., & Biocca, F. A. (2003). Internet attitudes and internet use: Some surprising findings from the HomeNetToo project. *International Journal of Human-Computer Studies, 59*, 355–382.

Jacobs, R. J., & Thomlison, B. (2009). Self-silencing and age as risk factors for sexually acquired HIV in midlife and older women. *Journal of Aging and Health, 21*(1), 102–128.

James, A. (2010). *School bullying. National society for the prevention of cruelty to children research briefing*. Retrieved 04 February 2011, from http://www.nspcc.org.uk/inform/research/briefings/school_bullying_wda73503.html

Jessor, R. (1987). Problem-behaviour theory, psychosocial devlopment, and adolescent problem drinking. *British Journal of Addiction, 82*, 331–342.

Johnson, S., Sudhinaraset, M., & Blum, R. W. (2010). Neuromaturation and adolescent risk taking: Why development is not determinism. *Journal of Adolescent Research, 25*(1), 4–23.

Joiner, Jr., T.E., Coyne, J.C., & Blalock, J. (1999). Overview and synthesis. In T.E. Joiner & J.C. Coyne (Eds.), *The interactional nature of depression* (pp. 3–19). Washington, D.C.: American Psychological Association.

Jones, J. B. (1997). Representations of menopause and their health care implications: A qualitative study. *American Journal of Preventative Medicine, 13*(1), 58–65.

Kahneman, D., Krueger, D., Schkade, D., Schwarz, N., & Stone, A. A. (2006). Would you be happier if you were richer? A focusing illusion. *CEPS Working Paper 125*(May).

Kain, J., & Jex, S. (2010). Karasek's (1979) job demands–control model: A summary of current issues and recommendations for future research. In P. Perrewé & D. Ganster (Eds.), *New developments in theoretical and conceptual approaches to job stress* (Vol. 8, Research in occupational stress and well-being, pp. 237–268). Bingley: Emerald Group Publishing Limited.

Kaiser, K. (1990). Cross-cultural perspectives on menopause. *Annals of the New York Academy of Sciences, 592*, 430–432.

Kaminski, J. W., Valle, L. A., Filene, J. H., & Boyle, C. L. (2008). A meta-analytic review of components associated with parent training program effectiveness. *Journal of Abnormal Child Psychology, 36*(4), 567–590.

Kaplan, M. S., Huguet, N., Orpana, H., & Feeny, D. (2008). Prevalence and factors associated with thriving in older adulthood: A 10-Year population-based study. *The Journal of Gerontology, 63A*(10), 1097–1105.

Karasek, R., & Theorell, T. (1990). *Healthy work: Stress, productivity, and the reconstruction of working life*. New York: Basic Books.

Kasen, S., Cohen, P., Chen, H., & Castille, D. (2000). Depression in adult women: Age changes and cohort effects. *American Journal of Public Health, 93*, 2061–2066.

Keating, D. P. (2004). Cognitive and brain development. In R. M. Lerner & L. Steinberg (Eds.), *Handbook of adolescent psychology* (pp. 45–84). New York: Wiley.

Kelly, J. B., & Emery, R. E. (2003). Children's adjustment after divorce: Risk and resilience perspectives. *Family Relations, 52*(4), 352–362.

Kenyon, D. B., & Koerner, S. S. (2009). Examining emerging adults' and parents' expectations about autonomy during the transition to college. *Journal of Adolescent Research, 24*, 293–320.

Kerr, M., Stattin, H., & Burk, W. J. (2010). A reinterpretation of parental monitoring in longitudinal perspective. *Journal of Research on Adolescence, 20*(1), 39–64.

Kim, J.-Y., McHale, S. M., Crouter, A. C., & Osgood, D. W. (2007). Longitudinal links between sibling relationships and adjustment from middle childhood through adolescence. *Developmental Psychology, 43*, 960–973.

Kim, O., & Kim, K. (2001). Body weight, self-esteem, and depression in Korean adolescents. *Adolescence, 36*, 315–322.

Kins, E. & Beyers, W. (2010). Failure to launch, failure to achieve criteria for adulthood? Poster presentation University of Ghent, Belgium.

Kins, E., Beyers, W., Soenens, B., & Vansteenkiste, M. (2009). Patterns of home-leaving and subjective well-being in emerging adulthood: The role of motivational processes and parental autonomy support. *Developmental Psychology, 45*, 1416–1429.

Kitzinger, C., & Wilkinson, S. (1995). Transitions from heterosexuality to lesbianism: The discursive production of lesbian identities. *Developmental Psychology, 31*, 95–104.

Klimes-Dougan, B., & Kopp, C. (1991). Children's conflict tactics with their mothers. *Merrill Palmer Quarterly, 45*, 226–242.

Kloep, M. (1998). *Att vara ung i Jämtland*. Österåsen: Uddeholt.

Kloep, M. (1999). Love is all you need? Focusing on adolescents' life concerns from an ecological point of view. *Journal of Adolescence, 22*, 49–63.

Kloep, M., & Hendry, L. B. (1999). Challenges, risks and coping in adolescence. In D. Messer & S. Millar (Eds.), *Exploring developmental psychology: From infancy to adolescence* (pp. 400–416). London: Arnold.

Kloep, M., & Hendry, L. B. (2003). Adult control and adolescent challenge? Dilemmas and paradoxes in young people's leisure. *World Leisure, 43*, 24–34.

Kloep, M., & Hendry, L. B. (2006). Transitions to retirement: Entry or exit? A Norwegian study. *Journal of Occupational and Organisational Psychology, 79*(4), 569–593.

Kloep, M., & Hendry, L. B. (2010). Letting go or holding on? Parents' perceptions of their relationships with their children during emerging adulthood. *British Journal of Developmental Psychology, 28*(4), 817–834.

Kloep, M., Güney, N., Çok, F., & Simsek, Ö. F. (2009). Motives for risk-taking in adolescence: A cross-cultural study. *Journal of Adolescence, 32*(1), 135–151.

Kloep, M., Hendry, L. B., Gardner, C., & Seage, C. H. (2010). Young people's views of their present and future selves in two deprived communities. *Journal of Community and Applied Social Psychology, 20*(6), 513–524.

Kloep, M., Hendry, L. B., Glendinning, A., Ingebrigtsen, J. E., & Espnes, G. A. (2001). Young people in 'drinking societies'? Norwegian, Scottish and Swedish adolescents' perceptions of alcohol use. *Health Education Research, 16*(3), 279–291.

Klumb, P. L., & Baltes, M. M. (1999). Time use of old and very old Berliners: Productive and consumptive activities as functions of resources. *The Journals of Gerontology, 54B*(5), 271–278.

Kohn, A. (2000). *The case against standardized testing*. Portsmouth: Heinemann.

Krantz, G., Berntsson, L., & Lundberg, U. (2005). Total workload, work stress and perceived symptoms in Swedish male and female white-collar employees. *European Journal of Public Health, 15*(2), 209–214.

Krappman, L. (1996). On the social embedding of learning processes in the classroom. In F. K. Oser, A. Dick & J. A. Patry (Eds.), *Effective and responsible teaching*. San Francisco: Jossey-Bass.

Kraut, R., Kiesler, S., Boneva, B., Cummings, J., Helgeson, J., & Crawford, A. (2002). Internet paradox revisited. *Journal of Social Issues, 58*(1), 49–74.

Kroger, J. (2000). *Identity development: Adolescence through adulthood.* Thousand Oaks: Sage.

Kroger, J. (2004). *Identity in adolescence: The balance between self and other* (3rd ed.). London: Routledge.

Kunnen, S. (2006). Are conflicts the motor in identity change? *Identity, 6,* 169–186.

Lachman, M. E. (2004). Development in midlife. *Annual Review of Psychology, 55,* 305–331.

Lachman, M. E., Lewkowicz, C., Marcus, A., & Peng, Y. (1994). Images of midlife development among young, middle-aged, and older adults. *Journal of Adult Development, 1*(4), 201–211.

Lang, F. R., & Carstensen, L. L. (1994). Close emotional relationships in late life: Further support for proactive aging in the social domain. *Psychology and Aging, 9*(2), 315–324.

Larson, E. B. (2010). Prospects for delaying the rising tide of worldwide, late-life dementias. *International Psychogeriatrics, 22*(8), 1197–1203.

Larson, R., & Ham, M. (1993). Stress and 'storm and stress' in early adolescence: The relationship of negative events with dysphoric affect. *Developmental Psychology, 29,* 130–140.

Laursen, B., Coy, K. C., & Collins, W. A. (1998). Reconsidering changes in parent-child conflict across adolescence: A meta-analysis. *Child Development, 69,* 817–832.

Lawson, H. M., & Leck, K. (2006). Dynamics of Internet dating. *Social Science Computer Review, 24*(2), 189–208.

Lee, J. (2009). Bodies at menarche: Stories of shame, concealment and sexual maturation. *Sex Roles, 60,* 615–627.

Lee, M. S., Jong-Hun, K., Park, M. S., Jaewon, Y., Young, H. K., Seung-Duk, K., & Sook-Haeng J. (2010). Factors influencing the severity of menopause symptoms in Korean post-menopausal women. *Journal of Korean Medical Science, 25*(5), 758–765.

Leiblum, S. R. (1990). Sexuality and the midlife woman. *Psychology of Women Quarterly, 14,* 495–508.

Lempers, J., Clark-Lempers, D., & Simons, R. L. (1989). Economic hardship, parenting, and distress in adolescence. *Child Development, 60,* 25–39.

Leonard, R., & Burns, A. (1999). Turning points in the lives of midlife and older women. *Australian Psychologist, 34*(2), 87–93.

Lerner, R. M., Fisher, C. B., & Weinberg, R. A. (2000). Toward a science for and of the people: Promoting civil society through the application of developmental science. *Child Development, 71*(1), 11–20.

Lerner, R. M., Lerner, J. V., Hess, L. E., Schwab, J., Jovanovic, J., Talwar, R., et al. (1991). Physical attractiveness and psychosocial functioning among early adolescents. *Journal of Early Adolescence, 11*, 300–320.

Levesque, L. M., & Caron, S. L. (2004). Dating preferences of women born between 1945 and 1960. *Journal of Family Issues, 25*(6), 833–846.

Levinson, D. J. (1978). *The season's of a man's life*. New York: Knopf.

Levinson, D. J. (1996). *The seasons of a woman's life*. New York: Knopf.

Lewinsohn, P. M., Duncan, E. M., Stanton, A. K., & Hautzinger, M. (1986). Age at first onset of non-bipolar depression. *Journal of Abnormal Psychology, 95*, 378–383.

Lewis, M. D. (2000). The promise of dynamic systems approaches for an integrated account of human development. *Child Development, 71*(1), 36–43.

Lichtwarck-Aschoff, A., Kunnen, S., & van Geert, P. (2010). Adolescent girls' perceptions of daily conflicts with their mothers: Within-conflict sequences and their relationship to autonomy. *Journal of Adolescent Research, 25*(4), 527–556.

Lieberman, M. A. (1992). Limitations of psychological stress model: Studies of widowhood. In M. L. Wykle, E. Kahara & J. Kowal (Eds.), *Stress and health among the elderly* (pp. 133–150). New York: Springer.

Liem, J. H., & Liem, G. R. (1990). Understanding the individual and family effects of unemployment. In J. Eckenrode & S. Gore (Eds.), *Stress between work and family* (pp. 175–204). New York: Plenum Press.

Lindau, S. T., Schumm, L. P., Laumann, E., Levinson, W., O'Muircheartaigh, C. A., & Waite, L. J. (2007). A study of sexuality and health among older adults in the United States. *New England Journal of Medicine 357*(8), 762–774.

Lindberg, S. M., Hyde, J. S., Petersen, J. L., & Linn, M. C. (2010). New trends in gender and mathematics performance: A meta analysis. *Psychological Bulletin, 136*(6), 1123–1135.

Ling, R. (2003). *New tech, new ties: How mobile communication is reshaping social cohesion*. Cambridge MA: MIT Press.

Lloyd, C. B., Behrman, J. R., Stromquist, N. P., & Cohen, B. (2006). *The changing transition to adulthood in developing countries: Selected studies*. Washington: The National Academy Press.

Lobb, E. A., Kristjanson, L. J., Aoun, S. M., Monterosso, L., Halkett, G. K. B., & Davies, A. (2010). Predictors of complicated grief: A systematic review of empirical studies. *Death Studies, 34*(8), 673–698.

Lock, M. (1998). Menopause: Lessons from anthropology. *Psychosomatic Medicine, 60*, 410–419.

Luhmann, M., & Eid, M. (2009). Does it really feel the same? Changes in life satisfaction following repeated life events. *Journal of Personality and Social Psychology, 97*(2), 363–381.

Lund, D. A., Caserta, M. S., & Dimond, M. F. (1993). The course of spousal bereavement in later life. In M. S. Stroebe, W. Strobe & R. O. Hansson (Eds.), *Handbook of bereavement: Theory, research and intervention* (pp. 240–254). Cambridge: Cambridge University Press.

Luyckx, K., Schwartz, D. S., Goossens, L., & Pollock, S. (2008). Employment, sense of coherence, and identity formation. *Journal of Adolescent Research, 23*(5), 566–591.

Maccoby, E. E. (1998). *The two sexes: Growing up apart, coming together.* New York: Simon & Schuster.

Maccoby, E. E., & Martin, J. A. (1983). Socialization in the context of the family: Parent–child interaction. In P. H. Mussen & E. M. Hetherington (Eds.), *Handbook of child psychology* (4th ed., Vol. 4). New York: Wiley.

Mäkinen, T., Kestilä, K. B., Borodulin, K., Martelin, T., Rahkonen, O., Leino-Arjas P., & Prättälä R. (2010). Occupational class differences in leisure-time physical inactivity - contribution of past and current physical workload and other working conditions. *Scandinavian Journal of Work, Environment and Health, 36*(1), 62–71.

Males, M. A. (2009). Does the adolescent brain make risk taking inevitable?: A skeptical appraisal. *Journal of Adolescent Research, 24*(2), 218–241.

Males, M. A. (2010). Is jumping off the roof always a bad idea? A rejoinder on risk taking and the adolescent brain. *Journal of Adolescent Research, 25*(1), 48–63.

Mancini, J. A., & Sandifer, D. (1995). Aging, family, and leisure. In R. Blieszner & V. Bedford (Eds.), *Handbook on aging and the family* (pp. 132–147). Westport: Greenwood.

Mansfield, P. K., Koch, P. B., & Voda, A. M. (1998). Qualities midlife women desire in their sexual relationships and their changing sexual response. *Psychology of Women Quarterly, 22*, 285–303.

Marcia, J. E. (1966). Development and validation of ego identity status. *Journal of Personality and Social Psychology, 3*, 551–558.

Marcia, J. E. (1980). Identity in adolescence. In J. Adelson (Ed.), *Handbook of adolescent psychology* (pp. 159–187). New York: Wiley.

Marcia, J. E. (1996). The importance of conflict for adolescent and lifespan development. In L. Verhofstadt-Denève, I. Kienhorst & C. Braet (Eds.), *Conflict and development in adolescence* (pp. 13–19). Leiden: DSWO Press.

Marcia, J. E., Waterman, A. S., Matteson, D. R., Archer, S. L., & Orlofsky, J. L. (1993). *Ego identity: A handbook for psychosocial research*. New York: Springer.

Martin, K. A. (1996). *Puberty, sexuality, and the self.* London: Routledge.

Martin, L. J. (2010). Anticipating infertility: Egg freezing, genetic preservation, and risk. *Gender and Society, 24*(4), 526–545.

Martini, S. T., Grusec, E. J., & Bernardini, C. S. (2001). Effects of interpersonal control, perspective taking and attributions on older mothers' and adult daughters' satisfaction with their helping relationship. *Journal of Family Psychology, 15*(4), 688–705.

Masten, A. S. (2007). Resilience in developing systems. *Development and Psychopathology, 19*, 921–930.

Maughan, R., Christiansen, E., Jenson, W. R., Olympia, D., & Clark, E. (2005). Behavioral parent training as a treatment for externalizing behaviors and disruptive behavior disorders: A meta-analysis. *School Psychology Review, 34*(3), 267–286.

Mayer, K. U., & Baltes, P. B. (1996). *Die Berliner Altersstudie*. Berlin: Akademie Verlag.

McDougall, P., & Hymel, S. (2007). Same-gender versus cross-gender friendship conception: Similar or different? *Merrill Palmer Quarterly, 53*(3), 347–380.

McMamish-Svensson, C., Samuelsson, G., Hagberg, G., & Dehlin, O. (1999). Social relationships and health as predictors of life satisfaction in advanced old age: Results from a Swedish longitudinal study. *International Journal of Aging and Human Development, 48*, 301–345.

McNelles, L., & Connolly, J. (1999). Intimacy between adolescent friends: Age and gender differences in shared affect and behavioral form. *Journal of Research on Adolescence, 9*, 143–159.

McQuide, S. (1998). Discontent at midlife: Issues and considerations in working toward women's well-being. *Families in Society, 79*(5), 532–542.

McVie, S. (2005). Patterns of deviance underlying the age-crime curve: The long term evidence. *British Society of Criminology E-Journal, 7.*

Meeus, W. H. J., Iedema, J., Helsen, M., & Vollebergh, W. (1999). Patterns of adolescent identity development: Review of literature and longitudinal analysis. *Developmental Review, 19*, 419–461.

Melchior, M., Caspi, A., Milne, B. J., Danese, A., Poulton, R., & Moffitt, T. E. (2007). Work stress precipitates depression and anxiety in young, working women and men. *Psychological Medicine, 37*(8), 1119–1130.

Meltzer, H., Bebbington, P., Brugha, T., Jenkins, R., McManus, S., & Stansfield, S. (2009). Job insecurity, socio-economic circumstances and depression. *Psychological Medicine, 39*, 1–7.

Merchant, G. (2001). Teenagers in cyberspace: An investigation of language use and language change in internet chatrooms. *Journal of Research in Reading, 24*, 293–306.

Merz, E.-M., & Huxhold, O. (2010). Wellbeing depends on social relationship characteristics: Comparing different types and providers of support to older adults. *Ageing and Society, 30*(5), 843–858.

Metzger, A. (2007). *Domain-specific judgments of civic and political engagement in late adolescence: Associations with adolescent activity involvement.* University of Rochester, Proquest ID 1404353761.

Metzger, A., Crean, H. F., & Forbes-Jones, E. (2009). Patterns of organized activity participation in urban, early adolescents: Associations with academic achievement, problem behaviors, and perceived adult support. *The Journal of Early Adolescence, 29*(3), 426–442.

Michell, L., & West, P. (1996). Peer pressure to smoke: The meaning depends on the method. *Health Education Research, 11*(1), 39–49.

Miles, L. M., Keitel, M., Jackson, M., Harris, F., & Licciardi, F. (2009). Predictors of distress in women being treated for infertility. *Journal of Reproductive and Infant Psychology, 27*(3), 238–257.

Millard, E. (1997). *Differentially literate: Boys, girls and the schooling of literacy.* London: Palmer Press.

Miller, P. H. (2001). *Theories of developmental psychology* (4 ed.). New York: Worth Publishers.

Mitchell, K. J., Finkelhor, D., & Wolak, J. (2001). Risk factors for and impact of online sexual solicitation of youth. *American Medical Association, 285*, 3011–3014.

Moffitt, T. E. (1993). 'Life-course persistent' and 'adolescent-limited' anti-social behaviour: A developmental taxonomy. *Psychological Review, 100*, 674–701.

Moloney, M. F., Strickland, O. L., DeRossett, S. E., Melby, M. K., & Dietrich, A. S. (2006). The experiences of midlife women with migraines. *Journal of Nursing Scholarship, 38*(3), 278–286.

Montross, L. P., Depp, C. A., Daly, J., Reichstadt, J., Golshan S., Moore D., Sitzer D., & Jeste D.V. (2006). Correlates of self-rated successful aging among community-dwelling older adults. *American Journal of Geriatric Psychiatry, 14*(1), 43–52.

Morrissey, K. M., & Werner-Wilson, R. J. (2005). The relationship between out-of-school activities and positive youth development: An investigation of the influences of communities and families. *Adolescence, 40*, 67–85.

Mortensen, G., & Relin, D. O. (2007). *Three cups of tea: One man's mission to promote peace – One school at a time.* New York: Penguin.

Mroczek, D. K., & Kolarz, C. M. (1998). The effects of age on positive and negative affect: A developmental perspective on happiness. *Journal of Personality and Social Psychology, 75*(5), 1333–1349.

Natale, L. (2010). *Factsheet – Youth crime in England and Wales*, retrieved 19 June 2011 from www.civitas.org.uk.

Nelson, H. D. (2008). Menopause. *The Lancet, 371*(9614), 760–770.

Nelson, L. J., & McNamara Barry, C. (2005). Distinguishing features of emerging adulthood: The self-classification as an adult. *Journal of Adolescent Research, 20*, 242–262.

Newcomb, A. F., & Bagwell, C. L. (1996). The developmental significance of children's friendship relations. In W. M. Bukowski, A. F. Newcomb & W. W. Hartrup (Eds.), *The company they keep: Friendship in childhood and adolescence* (pp. 289–321). New York: Cambridge University Press.

Newton, R. L., & Keith, P. M. (1997). Single women in later life. In J. M. Coyle (Ed.), *Handbook on women and aging* (pp. 385–399). Westport: Greenwood Press.

Nie, N. H., & Hillygus, D. S. (2002a). The impact of Internet use on sociability: Time-diary findings. *IT and Society, 1*(1), 1–29.

Nie, N. H., & Hillygus, D. S. (2002b). Where does Internet time come from? *IT and Society, 1*(1), 1–20.

Notman, M. T. (1990). Menopause and adult development. *Annals of the New York Academy of Sciences, 592*, 149–155.

OECD. (2009). *Society at a glance.* OECD Social Indicators: OECD Publishing.

Office for National Statistics. (2010). Retrieved 02 October 2010, from http://www.statistics.gov.uk.

Office of Statistics and Programming. (2007). *10 leading causes of death by age group, United States.* Retrieved 01 February 2011, from http://www.cdc.gov/injury/wisqars/pdf/Death_by_Age_2007-a.pdf.

Oldman, D. (1994). Adult-child relations as class-relations. In J. Qvortrup, M. Bardy, G. Sgritta & H. Winterberger (Eds.), *Childhood matters.* Avebury: Aldershot.

Oransky, M., & Marecek, J. (2009). 'I'm not going to be a girl': Masculinity and emotions in boys' friendships and peer groups. *Journal of Adolescent Research, 24*(2), 218–241.

Palmlund, I. (1997). The social construction of menopause as risk. *Journal of Psychosomatic Obstetrics and Gynecology, 18*, 87–94.

Pape, H. (1997). *Drinking, getting stoned or staying sober: A general population study of alcohol consumption, cannabis use, drinking related problems and sobriety among young men and women.* Unpublished Doctoral dissertation, NOVA, Oslo.

Pape, H., & Hammer, T. (1996). Sober adolescence: Predictor of psychosocial adjustment in young adulthood? *Scandinavian Journal of Psychology, 37*, 362–377.

Parent, A. S., Teilmann, G., Juul, A., Skakkebaek, N. E., Toppari, J., & Bourguignon, J. P. (2003). The timing of normal puberty and the age limits of sexual precocity: Variations around the world, secular trends, and changes after migration. *Endocrine Reviews, 24*, 668–693.

Payne, M. A. (2010). Teen brain science and the contemporary storying of psychological (im)maturity. In H. Blatterer & J. Glahn (Eds.), *Times of our lives: Making sense of growing up and growing old* (pp. 55–68). Oxford: Inter-Disciplinary Press.

Peake, M. D., & Thompson, S. (2003). Ageism in the management of lung cancer. *Age and Ageing, 32*, 171–177.

Philip, K., & Hendry, L. B. (1997). Young people and mentoring. *Journal of Adolescence, 19*, 189–201.

Phoenix, A. (1991). *Young mothers?* London: Polity Press.

Pickard, S. (1994). Life after a death: The experience of bereavement in South Wales. *Ageing and Society, 14*, 191–217.

Pillemer, K., & Lüscher, K. (2004). Ambivalence in parent-child relations in later life. *Comparative Perspectives in Family Research, 4*, 1–9.

Plomin, R., Asbury, K., & Dunn, J. (2001). Why are children in the same family so different? *Canadian Journal of Psychiatry, 46*, 225–233.

Pollack, W. (1998). *Real boys - rescuing our sons from the myths of boyhood.* London: Random House.

Pond, R., Stephens, C., & Alpass, F. (2010). How health affects retirement decisions: Three pathways taken by middle-older aged New Zealanders. *Ageing and Society, 30*(3), 527–546.

Porter, M., Penney, G. C., Russell, D., Russell, E., & Templeton, A. (1996). A population based survey of women's experience of the menopause. *British Journal of Obstetrics and Gynaecology, 103*, 1025–1028.

Prieto-Flores, M. E., Fernandez-Mayoralas, G., Rosenberg, M. W., & Rojo-Perez, F. (2010). Identifying connections between the subjective experience of health and quality of life in old age. *Qualitative Health Research, 20*(11), 1491–1499.

Pruchno, R. A., & Johnson, K. W. (1996). Research on grandparenting: Review of current studies and future needs. *Generations, 20*(1), 65–70.

Pruchno, R. A., Wilson-Genderson, M., Rose, M., & Cartwright, F. (2010). Successful aging: Early influences and contemporary characteristics. *The Gerontologist, 50*(6), 821–833.

Qu, K., & Ortolewa, P. (2008). Understanding stem cell differentiation through self-organisation theory. *Journal of Theoretical Biology, 250*(4), 606–620.

Qvortrup, J., & Christofferson, M. N. (1991). Childhood as a social phenomenon: National report Danmark. *Eurosocial Reports, 36*.

Ram, M., & Wong, R. (1994). Covariates of household extension in rural India: Change over time. *Journal of Marriage and the Family, 56*, 853–864.

Reichstadt, J., Sengupta, G., Depp, C. A., Palinkas, L. A., & Jeste, D. V. (2008). Older adults' perspective on successful aging: A process, not an outcome. *The Gerontologist, 48*, 117.

Reichstadt, J., Sengupta, G., Depp, C. A., Palinkas, L. A., & Jeste, D. V. (2010). Older adults' perspectives on successful aging: Qualitative interviews. *The American Journal of Geriatric Psychiatry, 18*(7), 567–576.

Rich, L. M., & Kim, S. (1999). Patterns of later life education among teenage mothers. *Gender and Society, 13*(6), 798–817.

Robins, R. W., Trzesniewski, K. H., Tracy, J. L., Gosling, D. S., & Potter, J. (2002). Global self-esteem across the life span. *Psychology and Aging, 17*, 423–434.

Robinson, G. (1996). Cross-cultural perspectives on menopause. *Journal of Nervous and Mental Diseases, 184*(8), 454–458.

Roe, S., & Ashe, J. (2008). *Young people and crime: findings from the 2006 Offending, Crime and Justice Survey*. Home Office Statistical Bulletin 09/08, London.

Rogol, A. D., Roemmich, J. N., & Clark, P. A. (2002). Growth at puberty. *Journal of Adolescent Health, 31*(6, Sup), 192–200.

Roker, D., Player, K., & Coleman, J. C. (1999). *Challenging the image: Young people as volunteers and campaigners*. Leicester: National Youth Agency.

Routasalo, P. E., Savikko, N., Tilvis, R. S., Strandberg, T. E., & Pitkälä, K. H. (2006). Social contacts and their relationship to loneliness among aged eople - A population-based study. *Gerontology, 52*(3), 181–187.

Rowe, J. W., & Kahn, R. L. (1998). *Successful aging*. New York: Pantheon Books.

Rubin, K. H., Coplan, R. J., & Bowker, J. C. (2009). Social withdrawal in childhood. *Annual Review of Psychology, 60*, 141–171.

Rudolph, K. D., Ladd, G., & Dinella, L. (2007). Gender differences in the interpersonal consequences of early-onset depressive symptoms. *Merrill Palmer Quarterly, 53*, 461–488.

Ruggles, S. (2010). Reconsidering the Northwest European family system. *Population Development Review, 35*(2), 249–273.

Rutter, M., Tizard, J., Yule, W., Graham, P., & Whitmore, K. (1976). Research report: Isle of Wight studies. *Psychological Medicine, 6*, 313–332.

Ryan, J., Reid, R., & Epstein, M. (2004). Peer mediated intervention studies on academic achievement for students with EBD. *Remedial and Special Education, 25*(6), 330–341.

Ryff, C., & Seltzer, M. (1996). The unchartered years of midlife parenting. In C. Ryff & M. Seltzer (Eds.), *The parental experience in midlife*. Chicago: University of Chicago Press.

Sakraida, T. J. (2008). Stress and coping of midlife women in divorce transition. *Western Journal of Nursing Research, 30*(7), 869–887.

Salmivalli, C., Karhunen, J., & Lagerspetz, K. M. J. (1996). How do the victims respond to bullying? *Aggressive Behavior, 22*(2), 99–109.

Sassler, S. (2010). Partnering across the life course: Sex, relationships, and mate selection. *Journal of Marriage and the Family, 72*(3), 557–576.

Saucier, M. G. (2004). Midlife and beyond: Issues for aging women. *Journal of Counselling and Development, 82*(4), 420–426.

Savin-Williams, R., & Berndt, R. (1990). Friendship and peer relations. In S. Feldman & G. Elliot (Eds.), *At the threshold: The developing adolescent*. Cambridge: Harvard University Press.

Sawchuk, D. (2009). The raging grannies: Defying stereotypes and embracing aging through activism. *Journal of Women and Aging, 21*(3), 171–185.

Schäfer, M. (2004). Lonely in the crowd: Recollections of bullying. *British Journal of Developmental Psychology, 22*, 379–394.

Scheidt, P. C., Harel, Y., Trumble, A. C., Jones, D. H., Overpeck, M. D., & Bijur, P. E. (1995). The epidemiology of nonfatal injuries among US children and youth. *American Journal of Public Health, 85*(7), 932–938.

Scheithauer, H., Hayer, T., Petermann, F., & Jugert, G. (2006). Physical, verbal and relational forms of bullying among German students: Age trends, gender differences, and correlates. *Aggressive Behavior, 32*, 261–275.

Scherger, S., Nazroo, J., & Higgs, P. (2011). Leisure activities and retirement: Do structures of inequality change in old age? *Ageing and Society, 31*(1), 146–173.

Schmidt, L. (2006). Psychosocial burden of infertility and assisted reproduction. *The Lancet, 367*(9508), 379–381.

Schmitt, K. L., Dayanim, S., & Matthias, S. (2008). Personal homepage construction as an expression of social development. *Developmental Psychology, 44*(2), 496–506.

Schnaiberg, A., & Goldenberg, S. (1989). From empty nest to crowded nest: the dynamics of incompletely-launched young adults. *Social Problems, 36*, 251–269.

Scholte, R. H. J., Engels, R. C. M. E., de Kemp, R. A. T., Harakeh, Z., & Overbeek, G. (2007). Differential parental treatment, sibling relationship and delinquency in adolescence. *Journal of Youth and Adolescence, 36*, 661–671.

Schouten, A. P., Valkenburg, P. M., & Peter, J. (2009). An experimental test of processes underlying self-disclosure in computer-mediated communication. *Cyberpsychology, 3*(2), http://www.cyberpsychology. eu/view.php?cisloclanku=2009111601&article=2009111603.

Schürer, K. (2003). Leaving home in England and Wales. In F. v. Poppel, M. Oris & J. Leo (Eds.), *The road to independence* (pp. 33–84). Bern: Peter Lang.

Schwartz, D., Dodge, K. A., Pettit, G. S., & Bates, J. E. (2000). Friendship as a moderating factor in the pathway between early harsh home environment and later victimisation in the peer group. *Developmental Psychology, 36,* 646–662.

Seidel, D., Richardson, K., Crilly, N., & Matthews, F. E. (2010). Design for independent living: Activity demands and capabilities of older people. *Ageing and Society, 30*(7), 1239–1246.

Seiffge-Krenke, I. (2006). Leaving home or still in the nest? Parent-child relationships and psychological health as predictors of different leaving home patterns. *Developmental Psychology, 42,* 864–876.

Seligman, M. E. P. (2008). Positive health. *Applied Psychology: An International Review, 57,* 3–18.

Seligman, M. E. P., & Csikszentmihalyi, M. (2000). Positive psychology: An introduction. *American Psychologist, 7,* 5–14.

Senior, K. (2001). The double-edged sword of postmenopausal hormone therapy. *The Lancet, 357*(9249), 46.

Sercombe, H. (2010). The gift and the trap: Working the 'teen brain' into our concept of youth. *Journal of Adolescent Research, 25*(1), 31–47.

Shanahan, L., McHale, S. M., Crouter, A. C., & Osgood, D. W. (2008). Linkages between parents' differential treatment, youth depressive symptoms and sibling relationships. *Journal of Marriage and the Family, 70*(2), 480–494.

Shapiro, A. (2004). Revisiting the generation gap. *Journal of Aging and Human Development, 58,* 127–146.

Sharp, E. H., Caldwell, L. L., Graham, J. W., & Ridenour, T. A. (2006). Individual motivation and parental influence on adolescents' experiences of interest in free time: A longitudinal examination. *Journal of Youth and Adolescence, 35*(3), 340–372.

Shek, D. T. L. (1996). Midlife crisis in Chinese men and women. *The Journal of Psychology, 130*(1), 109.

Shucksmith, J. S., & Hendry, L. B. (1998). *Health issues and adolescents: Growing up and speaking out.* London: Routledge.

Shucksmith, J. S., Hendry, L. B., & Glendinning, A. (1995). Models of parenting: Implications for adolescent well-being within different types of family contexts. *Journal of Adolescence, 18,* 253–270.

Silverstein, S. B. (1984). Igbo kinship and modern entrepreneurial organization: The transportation and spare parts business. *Studies in Third World Societies, 28,* 191–209.

Singer, D., & Hunter, M. (1999). The experience of premature menopause: A thematic discourse analysis. *Journal of Reproductive and Infant Psychology, 17*(1), 63–81.

Singleton, N., & Lewis, G. (2003). *Better or worse: A longitudinal study of the mental health of adults living in private households in Great Britain.* London: TSO.

Skinner, M. L., Elder, G. H. jr., & Conger, R. D. (1992). Linking economic hardship to adolescent aggression. *Journal of Youth and Adolescence, 21,* 259–276.

Slomkowski, C., Rende, R., Conger, K. J., Simons, R. L., & Conger, R. D. (2001). Sisters, brothers and delinquency: Evaluating social influence during early and middle adolescence. *Child Development, 72,* 271–283.

Smetana, J. G., & Gaines, C. C. (1999). Adolescent-parent conflict in middle class African-American families. *Child Development, 70,* 1447–1463.

Smith, D. J. (2004a). Factors influencing midlife workers' attitude toward aging and retirement anticipation *The Gerontologist, 44*(1), 541.

Smith, P. K. (2004b). Bullying: Recent developments. *Child and Adolescent Mental Health, 9,* 98–103.

Smith, D. J., & Baltes, P. B. (1999). Lifespan perspectives on development. In H. D. Bornstein & M. E. Lamb (Eds.), *Developmental Psychology* (pp. 47–72). Hillsdale: Lawrence Erlbaum Associates.

Smollar, J., & Youniss, J. (1989). Transformation in adolescent perceptions of their parents. *International Journal of Behavioral Development, 12*(1), 71–84.

Snell, P. (2010). Emerging adult civic and political disengagement: A longitudinal analysis of lack of involvement with politics. *Journal of Adolescent Research, 25*(2), 258–287.

Solomontos-Kountouri, O., & Hurry, J. (2008). Political, religious and occupational identities in context: Placing identity status paradigm in context. *Journal of Adolescence, 31*(2), 241–258.

Somary, K., & Stricker, G. (1998). Becoming a grandparent: A longitudinal study of expectations and early experiences as a function of sex and lineage. *The Gerontologist, 38*(1), 53–62.

Sowell, E. R., Peterson, B. S., Thompson, P. M., Welcome, S. E., Henkenius, A. L., & Toga, A. W. (2003). Mapping cortical change across the human life span. *Nature Neuroscience, 6*(3), 309–315.

Spencer, R. (2007). 'I just feel safe with him': Close and enduring male youth mentoring relationships. *Psychology of Men and Masculinity, 8*(3), 185–198.

Sperry, L., Carlson, J., & Peluso, P. (2005). *Marital therapy.* Denver, CO: Love.

Spitze, G., & Gallant, M. P. (2004). Older adults' strategies for handling ambivalence in relations with their adult children. *Research on Aging, 26*, 387–412.

Stafström, M., Östergren, P.-O., Larsson, S., Lindgren, B., & Lundborg, P. (2006). A community action programme for reducing harmful drinking behaviour among adolescents: The Trelleborg Project. *Addiction, 101*(6), 813–823.

Stanley, S. M., Markaman, H. J., & Whitton, S. W. (2002). Communication, conflict, and commitment: Insights on the foundations of relationship success from a national survey. *Family Process, 41*(4), 659–675.

Stassen Berger, K. (2007). *The developing person through the life span.* New York: Worth Pub.

Stattin, H., & Kerr, M. (2000). Parental monitoring: A reinterpretation. *Child Development, 71*(4), 1072–1085.

Steinberg, L. (2001). We know some things: Parent-adolescent relationships in retrospect and prospect. *Journal of Research on Adolescence, 11*(1), 1–19.

Steinberg, L. (2007). Risk taking in adolescence: New perspectives from brain and behavioral science. *Current Directions in Psychological Science, 16*(2), 55–59.

Steinberg, L. (2008). A social neuroscience perspective on adolescent risk-taking. *Developmental Review, 28*, 78–106.

Steinberg, L., & Silverberg, S. (1986). The vicissitudes of autonomy in early adolescence. *Child Development, 57*, 841–851.

Stephen, J., Fraser, E., & Marcia, J. E. (1992). Moratorium-achievement (Mama) cycles in lifespan identity development: Value orientations and reasoning system correlates. *Journal of Adolescence, 15*, 283–300.

Stevens, N. (1995). Gender and adaptation to widowhood in later life. *Ageing and Society, 15*, 37–58.

Stewart, I. R., & Vaitilingam, R. (2004). *Seven ages of man and women: A look at life in Britain in the second Elizabethan era*. Swindon: ESRC.

Strawbridge, W. J., Wallhagen, M. I., & Cohen, R. D. (2002). Successful aging and well-being: Self-rated compared with Rowe and Kahn. *The Gerontologist, 42*(6), 725–726.

Stuart-Hamilton, I. (2006). *The psychology of ageing: An introduction.* (4th ed.). London: Jessica Kingsley.

Subrahmanyam, K., & Lin, G. (2007). Adolescents on the net: Internet use and well-being. *Adolescence, 42*(168), 659–677.

Subrahmanyam, K., Smahel, D., & Greenfield, P. M. (2006). Connecting developmental processes to the Internet: Identity presentation and sexual exploration in online teen chatrooms. *Developmental Psychology, 42*, 1–12.

Sutton, J., Smith, P. K., & Swettenham, J. (1999). Bullying and 'theory of mind': A critique of the 'social skills deficit' view of anti-social behaviour. *Social Development, 8*(1), 117–134.

Svenson, E. (2005). *The woman's experience of menopause: Its effect on her sense of self and her marital/partnered relationship.*: Dissertation. Massachusetts School of Professional Psychology. UMI Microform 3170161.

Tanner, J. L. (2006). Recentering during emerging adulthood. In J. J. Arnett & J. L. Tanner (Eds.), *Emerging adults in America: Coming of age in the 21st century* (pp. 193–217). Washington: American Psychological Association.

Tapper, K., & Boulton, M. J. (2005). Observed victim and peer responses to physical, verbal, indirect and relational aggression amongst primary school children. *Aggressive Behavior, 31*, 238–253.

Taylor, R., & Gozna, L. (2011). *Deception: A young person's life skill.* Hove: Psychology Press.

Terhell, E. L., Broese van Groenau, M. I., & van Tilburg, T. (2004). Network dynamics in the long-term period after divorce. *Journal of Social and Personal Relationships, 21*(6), 719–738.

Thelen, E., & Smith, L. B. (1998). *A dynamic systems approach to the development of cognition and action* (3 ed.). Cambridge: MIT Press.

Thelen, E., & Smith, L. B. (2006). Dynamic system theories. In D. Damon & R. M. Lerner (Eds.), *Handbook of child psychology: Theoretical models of human development* (5 ed., Vol. 1). New York: Wiley.

Thomas, J., & Dauburan, K. (2001). The relationship between friendship quality and self-esteem in adolescent girls and boys. *Sex Roles, 45*, 53–65.

Thurlow, C. (2001). The usual suspects? A comparative investigation and social-type labelling among young British teenagers. *Journal of Youth Studies, 4*(3), 319–334.

Tikoo, M. (1996). An explanatory study of differences in developmental concerns of middle-aged men and women in India. *Psycholgical Reports, 78*(3), 883–887.

Times Higher Education (2010) Love HE: Bin there, done that.19th August, p. 24.

Tremblay, R., & Nagin, D. (2004). Physical aggression during early childhood: Trajectories and predictors. *Pediatrics, 114*, 43–50.

Trudel, G., Turgeon, L., & Piche, L. (2000). Marital and sexual aspects of old age. *Sexual and Relationship Therapy, 15*(4), 381–406.

Turow, J. (1999). The Internet and the family: The view from parents, the view from the press. *Annenberg Public Policy Center Reports, Philadelphia University*(27).

Twenge, J. M. (2006). *Generation me: Why today's young Americans are more confident, assertive, entitled - and more miserable than ever before.* New York: Free Press.

Tynes, B. M. (2007). Internet safety gone wild? Sacrificing the educational and psychosocial benefits of online social environments. *Journal of Adolescent Research, 22*(6), 575–584.

Underwood, H., & Findlay, B. (2004). Internet relationships and their impact on primary relationships. *Behaviour Change, 21*(2), 127–140.

Underwood, M. K. (2007). Girlfriends and boyfriends diverging in middle childhood and coming together in romantic relationships. *Merrill Palmer Quarterly, 53*(3), 520–526.

Ungar, M. T. (2000). The myth of peer pressure. *Adolescence, 35*, 167–180.

Vaillancourt, T., Hymel, S., & McDougall, P. (2003). Bullying is power: Implications for school-based intervention strategies. *Journal of Applied School Psychology, 19*, 157–176.

Vainionpaa, K. J., & Topo, P. (2005). The making of an ageing disease: The representation of the male menopause in Finnish medical literature. *Ageing and Society, 25*(6), 841–862.

Valkenburg, P. M., & Peter, J. (2007a). Adolescents' online communication and their well-being: Testing the stimulation versus the displacement hypothesis. *Journal of Computer-Mediated Communication, 12*(4), 1169–1182.

Valkenburg, P. M., & Peter, J. (2007b). Who visits online dating sites? Exploring some characteristics of online daters. *CyberPsychology and Behavior, 10*, 849–852.

Valkenburg, P. M., & Peter, J. (2009). Social consequences of the Internet for adolescents: A decade of research. *Current Directions in Psychological Science, 18*(1), 1–5.

Van der Maas, H., & Molenaar, P. (1992). Stagewise cognitive development: An application of catastrophe theory. *Psychological Review, 99*, 395–417.

van Solinge, H., & Henkens, K. (2010). Living longer, working longer? The impact of subjective life expectancy on retirement intentions and behaviour. *European Journal of Public Health, 20*(1), 47–51.

Vanderwerker, L. C., & Prigerson, H. G. (2004). Social support and technological connectedness as protective factors in bereavement. *Journal of Loss and Trauma, 9*(1), 45–57.

Vaupel, J. W. (2010). Biodemography of human ageing. *Nature, 464*(7288), 536–543.

Vernberg, E. M. (1990). Experiences with peers following relocation during early adolescence. *Journal of Orthopsychiatry, 60*(3), 466–472.

Victor, C. R., Scambler, S. J., Bowling, A., & Bond, J. (2005). The prevalence of, and risk factors for, loneliness in later life: A survey of older people in Great Britain. *Ageing and Society, 25*(3), 357–376.

Victor, C. R., Scambler, S. J., Shah, S., & Cook, D. G., Harris T., Rink E., & de Wilde S. (2002). Has loneliness amongst older people increased? An investigation into variations between cohorts. *Ageing and Society, 22*(5), 585–598.

Vogt Yuan, A. (2007). Gender differences in the relationship of puberty with adolescents' depressive symptoms: Do body perceptions matter? *Sex Roles, 57*, 69–80.

von Bertalanffy, K. L. (1951). General system theory – A new approach to unity of science. *Human Biology, 23*, 303–361.

Wagner, M. K. (2001). Behavioral characteristics related to substance abuse and risk-taking, sensation-seeking, anxiety sensitivity, and self-reinforcement. *Addictive Behaviors, 26*, 115–120.

Waterman, A. S. (1982). Identity development from adolescence to adulthood: An extension of theory and a review of research. *Developmental Psychology, 18*, 342–358.

Waterman, A. S. (1999). Identity, the identity statuses, and identity status development: A contemporary statement. *Developmental Review, 19*, 591–621.

Watson, W. K., & Bell, N. J. (2005). Narratives of development experience of risk: Adult women's perspectives on relationships and safer sex. *British Journal of Health Psychology, 10*, 311–127.

Way, N. (2004). *Adolescent boys: Exploring diverse cultures of boyhood.* New York: New York University Press.

Way, N. (2011). *Deep secrets: Boys' friendships and the crisis of connection.* Cambridge: Harvard University Press.

Way, N., Gingold, R., Rotenberg, M., & Kuriakose, G. (2005). Close friendships among urban ethnic-minority adolescents. *New Directions in Child Development, 107*, 41–59.

Webber, R., & Butler, T. (2007). Classifying pupils by where they live: How well does this predict variations in their GCSE results? *Urban Studies, 44*(7), 1229–1253.

Weisskirch, R. S. (2008). Parenting by cell phone: Parental monitoring of adolescents and family relations. *Journal of Youth and Adolescence, 38*, 1123–1139.

Wentzel, K. R., & Erdley, C. (1993). Strategies for making friends: Relations to social behaviour and peer acceptance in early adolescence. *Developmental Psychology, 29*, 819–826.

Whitbeck, L., Hoyt, R. D., & Huck, M. S. (1994). Early family relationships, intergenerational solidarity, and support provided to parents by their adult children. *The Journals of Gerontology, 49B*, 85–94.

White, N. R. (2002). "Not under my roof!" Young people's experience of home. *Youth and Society, 34*, 214–231.

White, M. H., & Dorman, S. M. (2000). Online support for caregivers: Analysis of an Internet Alzheimer mailgroup. *Computers in Nursing, 18*, 168–176.

Whitehead, J. M. (2003). Masculinity, motivation and academic success: A paradox. *Teacher Development, 7*(2), 287–309.

Whiteman, S. D., McHale, S. M., & Crouter, A. C. (2007). Longitudinal changes in marital relationships: The role of offsprings' pubertal development. *Journal of Marriage and the Family, 69*(4), 1005–1020.

Wichstrøm, L. (1999). The emergence of gender difference in depressed mood during adolescence: The role of intensified gender socialization. *Developmental Psychology, 35*(1), 232–245.

Wickrama, K., Surjadi, F., Lorenz, F., & Elder, G., Jr. (2008). The influence of work control trajectories on men's mental and physical health during the middle years: Mediational role of personal control. *The Journals of Gerontology, 63B*(3), S135.

Wilbur, J., Miller, A., & Montgomery, A. (1995). The influence of demographic characteristics, menopausal status, and symptoms on women's attitudes toward menopause. *Women and Health, 23*(3), 19–39.

Williams, A., & Nussbaum, J. F. (2001). *Intergenerational communication across the life span.* Mahwah: Erlbaum.

Williams, A., & Thurlow, C. (2005). *Talking adolescence: Language and communication in the teenage years.* New York: Peter Lang.

Williams, B. R., Baker, P. S., Allman, R. M., & Roseman, J. M. (2006). The feminization of bereavement among community-dwelling older adults. *Journal of Women and Aging, 18*(3), 3–17.

Williams, S., & Williams, L. (2005). Space invaders: The negotiation of teenage boundaries through the mobile phone. *The Sociological Review, 53*, 314–331.

Winston, J., & Barnes, J. (2007). Anticipation of retirement among baby boomers. *Journal of Women and Aging, 19*(3/4), 137–159.

Witherington, D. C., & Margett, T. E. (2010). The dynamic interplay of theory and method through time. *Human Development, 53*, 160–165.

Wolf, A. D., Freedman, V., & Soldo, J. B. (1997). The division of family labour: Care for elderly parents. *The Journals of Gerontology, 52B*, 102–109.

Wolke, D., & Samara, M. (2004). Bullied by siblings: Association with peer victimisation and behaviour problems in Israeli lower secondary school children. *Journal of Child Psychology and Psychiatry, 45*(5), 1015–1029.

World Health Organisation. (1946). *Preamble to the Constitution of the World Health Organization as adopted by the International Health Conference, New York, 19–22 June, 1946.* Official Records of the World Health Organization, no. 2, p. 100.

Wortman, C. B., Silver, R. C., & Kessler, R. C. (1993). The meaning of loss and adjustment to bereavement. In M. S. Stroebe, W. Strobe & R. O. Hansson (Eds.), *Handbook of bereavement: Theory, research and intervention* (pp. 349–365). Cambridge: Cambridge University Press.

Yang, Y. (2008). Social inequalities in happiness in the United States, 1972 to 2004: An age-period-cohort analysis. *American Sociological Review, 73*(2), 204–227.

Yeh, C. J., Ching, A. M., & Okubo, Y. L., S. S. (2007). Development of a mentoring program for chinese immigrant adolescents' cultural adjustment. *Adolescence, 42*, 733–748.

Youniss, J., & Yates, M. (1997). *Community service and social responsibility in youth.* Chicago: Chicago University Press.

Zhang, Z. (2006). Marital history and the burden of cardiovascular disease in midlife. *The Gerontologist, 46*(2), 266–271.

Ziebland, S., Robertson, J., Jay, J., & Neil, A. (2002). Body image and weight change in middle age: A qualitative study. *International Journal of Obesity, 26*, 1083–1091.

Zinnecker, J. (1990). Vom Strassenkind zum verhäuslichten Kind. In I. Behnke (Ed.), *Stadtgesellschaft und Kindheit im Prozess der Zivilisation* (pp. 142–162). Opladen: Leske und Budrich.

Index

Reading guide

This table identifies where in the book you'll find relevant information for those of you studying or teaching A-level. You should also, of course, refer to the Index and the Glossary, but navigating a book for a particular set of items can be awkward and we found this table a useful tool when editing the book and so include it here for your convenience.

TOPIC	PAGE(S)
Lifespan theory: Erikson's 'eight ages of man'	5–8, 13
Lifespan theory: Levinson's 'seasons of a mans life'	10–11, 13
Lifespan theory: Gould's 'Evolution of adult consciousness'	8–9, 13
Adolescent identity: Blos' psychoanalytic theory	88–89
Adolescent identity: Erikson's theory of psychosocial development	5–8, 42
Adolescent identity: Marcia's theory	42–44
Conflict: Storm and Stress	45
Conflict: Alternative views	42–57
Middle adulthood: Marriage	104–109
Middle adulthood: Parenthood	109–112
Middle adulthood: Divorce	107–109
Late adulthood: Retirement	137–140
Late adulthood: Adjustment to old age	140–143
Late adulthood: Bereavement	132–137